Embracing Vulnerability

This book brings together legal scholars engaging with vulnerability theory to explore the implications and challenges for law of understanding vulnerability as generative and a source of connection and development.

The book is structured into five sections that cover fields of law where there is already significant recourse to the concept of vulnerability. These sections include a main chapter by a legal theorist who has previously examined the creative potential of vulnerability and responses from scholars working in the same field. This is designed to draw out some of the central debates concerning how vulnerability is conceptualised in law.

Several contributors highlight the need to refocus on some of these more positive aspects of vulnerability to counter the way law is being used to enable persons to escape the stigma associated with vulnerability by concealing that condition. They seek to explore how law might embrace vulnerability, rather than conceal it. The book also includes contributions that seek to bring vulnerability into a non-binary relationship with other core legal concepts, such as autonomy and dignity. Rather than discarding these legal concepts in favour of vulnerability, these contributions highlight how vulnerability can be entwined with relational autonomy and embodied dignity.

This book is essential reading for both students studying legal theory and practitioners interested in vulnerability.

Dr Daniel Bedford, Senior Lecturer in Law, University of Portsmouth.

Jonathan Herring, DW Wolfe-Clarendon Fellow in Law at Exeter College, Oxford University and Professor of Law at the Law Faculty, Oxford University.

Embracing Vulnerability

The Challenges and Implications for Law

Edited by
Daniel Bedford and
Jonathan Herring

Routledge
Taylor & Francis Group

LONDON AND NEW YORK

First published 2020
by Routledge
2 Park Square, Milton Park, Abingdon, Oxon OX14 4RN

and by Routledge
605 Third Avenue, New York, NY 10017

Routledge is an imprint of the Taylor & Francis Group, an informa business

First issued in paperback 2021

British Library Cataloguing-in-Publication Data
A catalogue record for this book is available from the British Library

Library of Congress Cataloging-in-Publication Data
Names: Bedford, Daniel (Law teacher) editor. |
Herring, Jonathan, editor.
Title: Embracing vulnerability : the challenges and implications for law / edited by Daniel Bedford and Jonathan Herring.
Description: Abingdon, Oxon ; New York, NY : Routledge, 2020. |
Includes bibliographical references and index.
Identifiers: LCCN 2019057017 | ISBN 9781138476929 (hardback) |
ISBN 9781351105705 (ebook)
Subjects: LCSH: Social legislation. | Domestic relations—Social aspects. |
Vulnerability (Personality trait)—Social aspects.
Classification: LCC K1700 .E45 2020 | DDC 344.01—dc23
LC record available at https://lccn.loc.gov/2019057017

ISBN 13: 978-1-138-47692-9 (hbk)
ISBN 13: 978-1-351-10570-5 (ebk)
ISBN 13: 978-1-03-223831-9 (pbk)

DOI: 10.4324/9781351105705

Typeset in Galliard
by codeMantra

Contents

Table of cases

UK Cases

International

Table of legislation and legislative instruments

UK Statutes

UK Statutory Instruments

National Instruments

International Instruments

Contributors

Dr Daniel Bedford is Senior Lecturer in Law at the University of Portsmouth.
His research focuses on the meaning and function of the concept of human dignity in shaping human rights, particularly within the field of social care. He draws on different theoretical perspectives, including the phenomenology of embodied subjectivity, ethics of care, capabilities approach and vulnerability theory, to evaluate the current uses of human dignity.

Jo Bridgeman is Professor of Healthcare Law and Feminist Ethics at the Sussex Law School, University of Sussex where she teaches on modules in Perspectives on Healthcare Law, Tort, Gender Equality, and Feminism, Law and Society. Her research adopts a critical feminist perspective informed by and developing the feminist ethics of care in considseration of parental, professional and state responsibilities to children. She has published widely on the medical treatment of children, including: the care of children with complex needs; parental responsibility for children undergoing treatment for cancer; withholding/withdrawal of life-sustaining treatment from a child; and issues arising from the Bristol Royal Infirmary Inquiry. She is currently working on a book concerning public responsibilities for, and professional duties to, seriously ill children.

Nicole Busby is Professor of Human Rights, Equality and Justice at the University of Glasgow.
Her research is socio-legal and interdisciplinary, and it utilises a range of empirical and doctrinal methods. She is particularly interested in how individuals and groups seek to use and shape law and policy frameworks through lived experience. She has conducted research on law's potential to improve the experiences of rural communities, carers, those in precarious work, and litigants in person and is currently exploring the interface between the UK's social security system and gender equality laws.

Dr Beverley Clough is Associate Professor in Law and Social Justice at the University of Leeds.
She has written widely on issues around disability and mental capacity law. She holds an ISRF Early Career Fellowship for a project entitled 'The Spaces

of Mental Capacity Law'. Her main research interests are in mental capacity law, disability rights and theory, human rights law, medical law and ethics, care theory, capabilities theory and the concept of vulnerability.

Alison Diduck is Professor of Law at the University College London.

She teaches and researches in the areas of family law and feminist legal theory. She has authored and edited a number of books and many articles on the regulation of family living, all from a feminist perspective.

Anna Grear is Professor of Law and Theory at the University of Cardiff.

Her work, broadly speaking, engages with law's imagination and construction of the world, offering a sustained critical engagement with law's underlying philosophical and political assumptions. She has a longstanding theoretical interest in human rights, materiality and vulnerability.

Rosie Harding is Professor of Law and Society at the University of Birmingham and Chair of the Socio-Legal Studies Association.

She was awarded a Philip Leverhulme Prize for Law in 2017 and was a 2016/2017 British Academy Mid-Career Fellow. Her research focuses on the place of law in everyday life, with a focus on the regulation and legal recognition of intimate and caring relationships, particularly as these topics intersect with age, disability, gender, sexuality, human rights, discrimination and equality. She is the author of *Duties to Care* (2017, Cambridge University Press) and *Regulating Sexuality* (2011, Routledge Social Justice, winner of the 2011 SLSA-Hart Book Prize and the 2011 SLSA-Hart Early Career Prize), and the editor of *Revaluing Care in Theory, Law and Politics: Cycles and Connections* (2017, Routledge Social Justice), *Ageing and Sexualities: Interdisciplinary Perspectives* (2016, Ashgate), *Law and Sexuality* (2016, Routledge Critical Concepts) and the book series *Law, Society, Policy* (Bristol University Press).

Jonathan Herring is DW Wolfe-Clarendon Fellow in Law at Exeter College, Oxford University and Professor of Law at the Law Faculty, Oxford University.

He has written on family law, medical law, criminal law and legal issues surrounding care and vulnerability. His books include: *Law and The Relational Self* (CUP, 2019); *Vulnerability, Childhood and the Law* (Springer, 2018); *Vulnerable Adults and the Law* (2016); *Caring and the Law* (2014); *Older People in Law and Society* (OUP, 2009); *European Human Rights and Family Law* (Hart, 2010; With Shazia Choudhry); *Medical Law and Ethics* (OUP 2020); *Criminal Law* (Oxford University Press 2020); *Family Law* (Pearson, 2018); and *The Woman Who Tickled Too Much* (Pearson, 2009).

Fiona de Londras is Professor of Global Legal Studies at the School of Law, University of Birmingham.

Her research concerns constitutionalism, human rights and transnationalism. She is particularly interested in the role and function of rights in contentious policy fields, enquiring about whether – and if so how – rights shape the making of law and policy in complex contexts of, for example, counterterrorism, the European Court of Human Rights, and abortion law in Ireland. She undertakes this through her academic scholarship, public engagement and political advisory work. Together with her BLS colleague Máiréad Enright, she has been particularly involved in the ongoing process of abortion law reform in Ireland.

Dr Mary Neal is Senior Lecturer in Law at the University of Strathclyde.

Her main research interests are in healthcare law, bioethics and legal theory, and her current research focuses on conscientious objection in healthcare, beginning- and end-of-life issues, theories of property, and meta-disciplinary concepts such as dignity, sanctity and love.

Dr Lisa Rodgers is Lecturer in Law at the University of Leicester and Course Director of the LLM in Employment Law by distance learning. Her research interests lie in the conjunction between employment law and theories of law. She has an ongoing interest in the possibilities of the application of vulnerability theory in the employment law field, publishing a book entitled *Labour Law Vulnerability and the Regulation of Precarious Work* (Edward Elgar) in 2016.

Abbreviations

CRPD	Committee on the Rights of Person with Disabilities
ECR	European Court Reports
ECtHR	European Court of Human Rights
EHRR	European Human Rights Reports
ER	English Reports
EU	European Union
EWCA	England and Wales Court of Appeal
EWCOP	England and Wales Court of Protection
EWHC	The Equality and Human Rights Commission
FLR	Family Law Review
GDP	Gross Domestic Product
HCLE	Healthcare Law and Ethics
ICESCR	International Covenant on Economic, Social and Cultural Rights
ICR	Industrial Cases Reports
IMF	International Monetary Fund
NHS	National Health Service
OED	Oxford English Dictionary
UDHR	Universal Declaration of Human Rights
UKHL	UK House of Lords
UKSC	UK Strength Council
UN	United Nations
UNECE	United Nations Economic Commission for Europe
WLR	Weekly Law Reports

Introduction

Vulnerability refigured

Daniel Bedford

The binaries of law: vulnerability as deficiency

Vulnerability is often portrayed as a threat to well-being; it is something to be resisted or avoided, not embraced. This is particularly the case within Western liberal society, where vulnerability is seen as an unfavourable condition, equated with incapacity. In these societies, vulnerability has come to identify categories of persons who are unable to safeguard their own needs and interests. Vulnerable persons are thus understood to lack the independent means to protect their interests[1] or are seen as ill-equipped to resist extraneous influences or irrational impulses that threaten their well-being. Due to this relative passivity, such persons are rendered particularly susceptible to agents who have the power to harm their interests or deny their needs (see Goodin 1986). As they cannot provide for those interests or needs, these vulnerable persons require special protection (ibid., 109).

Cast in this light, vulnerability has been positioned as the opposite, or 'other', of the ideal of individual autonomy. Hence, the autonomous agent is often characterised as someone who can sustain themselves and pursue their interests without having to depend on other people,[2] unless via contractual relations based on mutual advantage. They are also usually presented as able to

---

1 A good example of this sort of definition can be seen in a resolution adopted by the European Parliament on the protection of vulnerable adults. The parliament in its resolution defined a 'vulnerable adult' as 'a person who has reached the age of 18 years and who, by reason of an impairment or insufficiency of his or her personal faculties, is not in a position to protect his or her interests (personal affairs and/or personal property, whether temporarily or permanently)', European Parliament, Resolution of 1 June 2017 with recommendations to the Commission on the protection of vulnerable adults, File 2015/2085(INL). Guideline 13 of the CIOMS *International Ethical Guidelines for Biomedical Research Involving Human Subjects* also describes 'vulnerable groups' as being 'incapable of protecting their own interests'.

2 As Lorraine Code (1991, 78) has summarised, autonomy has come to be associated with an "Autonomous man [who] is – and should be – self-sufficient, independent, and self-reliant, a self-realizing individual who directs his effort towards maximizing his personal gains. His independence is under constant threat from other (equally self-serving) individuals: hence he devises rules to protect himself from intrusion. Talk of rights, rational self-interest, expedience, and efficiency permeates his moral, social, and political discourse.'

free themselves from social influences or irrational impulses in order to determine what those interests are, or, at least, carve out their life plan in a struggle against those forces (see on this MacKenzie and Stoljar 2000, 17; Atkins 2006; Tappolet 2016, 189). In this respect, as Margrit Shildrick (2009, 20) suggests, an individual is likely to be considered more autonomous to the extent that they are 'independent, closed and secure in [their]…own integrity, and invulnerable to extraneous influence'. This puts the emphasis on seeing those influences as an obstacle or threat to autonomy and as something to be guarded against or mastered by the subject through patterns of self-protection, self-assertion or self-expansion (Bakan 1966). This can lead to the domination of another, as the individual seeks to remain 'in control' by 'keeping influent others under control' (Keller 1986, 200).

Closely related to autonomy in the liberal pantheon is respect for human dignity. As with autonomy, this concept has been defined in opposition to vulnerability. Some accounts of human dignity in the Kantian tradition, for instance, encourage us to value ourselves as capable of employing reason to discipline our material bodies, including our passions, sentiments and emotions that find their origin in our bodies (see Harris 1997; Card 1998). Because these features of our embodiment render us vulnerable to pressures that might impede our rational activity, they cannot also be sources of human dignity. Those features are thus resigned to the realm of nature, and below the public domain of reason. The latter is, as Martha Nussbaum (2001, xxii) puts it, 'imagined as relatively impervious to changes in the former'.

Moreover, human dignity has come to identify the particular features of ourselves that are non-animal, which elevate us above nature (see Riley 2010; Sensen 2011; Rosen 2012). Dignity thus signifies how we are distinct from other animals, whereas our vulnerable corporeality is what we share with other animals. The result is a dualistic depreciation of the body and the construction of a set of 'others' who lack full human subjectivity because they are unable to transcend their embodiment (see Oliver 2011; Anker 2012; Neal 2016). Indeed, those who are imagined to be 'captive' to their animal bodies may be perceived as debased by that condition (Anker 2012, 18, 48). This includes, in particular, those who lack the capacity for self-containment and are thus unable to independently manage or control the dirt and decay of their unbounded bodies (see Lawton 1998; Shildrick 2002). But it also extends to carers of those bodies who engaged in degrading work through their interaction with dirt and decay that pollutes their own bodily boundaries (see Lawton 1998; Ashforth and Kreiner 1999; Wolkowitz 2002; Hughes et al. 2005; Isaksen 2005; Akroyd 2007; Twigg et al. 2011; Howarth 2014;). As Bill Hughes et al. (2005, 267) have put it, 'those who care, who enter [the] world of waste, place themselves in a domain of peripheral value outside the masculinist boundaries that define proper productivity and, therefore, have no claim upon the values of success, dignity or respect.'

Across various fields of law, these binaries shape and structure legal relations and institutions. Thus, those who are recognised as vulnerable are often situated on the margins of law, as figures that need to be subject to a special protective regime.

In contrast, those who resemble dignified autonomous agents occupy a central place in the mainstream. As is recognised by various contributors, this latter figure forms the foundation for constructing legal rights as tools that an individual can rely on to reinforce their boundaries and assert independence. Jonathan Herring (p. 68) thus suggests, in this collection, that legal rights have primarily been designed to 'protect the individual from unwanted intrusions and to protect the liberty to pursue one's goal for one's life'. By doing this, rights constrain the power and sphere of the state, but they also require the state to police the boundaries of the individual. This is consistent with the focus of treating autonomy as a matter of resisting or overcoming external pressures that primarily represent an obstacle or threat to self-governance. Moreover, as Jo Bridgeman claims in her contribution, this vision of rights encourages us to think in terms of a clash of conflicting interests, rather than seeing how interests can become intermingled in relationships defined by vulnerability. For Anna Grear, we also need to recognise the intertwining of the human and nonhuman living beings and systems in a co-constitutive relationship. She highlights how the current individualised vision of human rights has facilitated the oppression of the nonhuman, through treating the individual as separate from the environment and free to exercise control over commodified natural resources. Fiona de Londras does not deny these arguments but suggests that the continued focus on rights is unlikely to provide a sufficient basis for addressing these issues.

In addition, rights may function to prohibit treatment that would divest the liberal subject of their distinctly human qualities and reduce them to the status of vulnerable bodies. Critical human rights scholars, for instance, have highlighted the role that human rights norms play in preventing the indignity of being rendered vulnerable (Bergoffen 2013). Rather than affirming the dignity of the already vulnerable body of the human being, those rights seek to prevent the dehumanising descent into vulnerable embodiment (Oliver 2011). Anna Grear similarly claims that those who are imagined to be too fully embodied in human rights law often exist on the margins of the truly human community. This leads, she argues, to a paradox whereby the marginal subject is recognised as 'inherently vulnerable' due to the fact that they lack the 'unique vulnerability' to injury to rational agency that distinguishes the quasi-disembodied, relatively 'invulnerable' subject. To put things another way, the marginal subject lacks the capacity for autonomy due to their agency-impairing vulnerability, whereas the paradigm subject is vulnerable to having their autonomy impaired. This binary is occasionally reflected in the practice of human rights. For example, the European Court of Human Rights (ECtHR) has been criticised for occasionally adopting an approach to vulnerability that treats certain groups as incapable of autonomy and independence, in contrast to the 'normal' subject of human rights law (Peroni and Timmer 2013; Ippolito 2015; Timmer 2016). Another example is found in the Hague Convention on the International Protection of Adults, aimed at protecting 'vulnerable adults', which applies to all those 'who, by reason of an impairment or insufficiency of their personal faculties, are not in a position to protect their interests'. Fiona De Londras also highlights, in her response to Grear, how human rights have provided a limited mechanism for addressing the material needs of the embodied subject.

On the margins of the law, therefore, are those whose vulnerability is over-emphasised as a mark of difference. Due to this vulnerability, these subjects are typically exposed to a special protective regime that is designed to remedy an undesirable affliction and establish the security that they are denied so long as their vulnerability remains (Shildrick 2002, 77; Bedford 2018). Such measures often attract criticism for the way in which they recognise the vulnerable as passive objects of concern in need of 'saving' (Wiesemann 2016), whose subjective perspective is all too easily ignored (Dunn et al 2008). Resulting in 'paternalistic' and disrespectful interventions, which can actually reinforce the experience of vulnerability as weakness, incapacity, passivity and powerlessness (see Luna 2009; MacKenzie et al. 2014; Bagnoli 2016, 15–16; Straehle 2016, 2).

Escaping vulnerability as the destiny of progress

One of the ways in which law has been developed in response to the stigma associated with vulnerability has been to redraw the boundaries between the mainstream and margins. Across the different chapters in this collection, there is a notable concern with the manner in which vulnerability is being further marginalised, as more and more people are brought into the mainstream by reimagining them as autonomous rights-bearing individuals. This redrawing of boundaries leaves intact the binaries that structure legal relations and institutions but enables some groups, who can now pass as part of the mainstream, to discard the stigma once associated with being part of a vulnerable population. In turn, that stigma is then projected on to an even narrower class of persons who become the objects of paternalism or discrimination. The concern of several contributors is that these developments are being presented as progress, but only by concealing vulnerability in a manner that actually compounds disadvantage and entrenches inequality. Law is thus enabling more people to hide from the reality of their embodied vulnerability, but only by ignoring lived realities. Moreover, these contributors are further concerned with the way in which the ideal of the autonomous citizen has been co-opted by neoliberal political agendas based on market choice and consumer freedom. As is noted throughout, this agenda has supported the individualisation of responsibility and concomitant retreat of the state.

In her contribution on labour law, Lisa Rodgers (p. 130) highlights how certain labour protections have been seen as 'overly protective and an unnecessary restraint on employee and employer autonomy'. She goes on to recognise that the application of employment protections is associated with weakness and implies that the person is a marginal subject who is not able to assert their autonomy in a contractual arrangement. In turn, this 'negative' construction has provided support for recent deregulation, through the expansion of liberal approaches. Rodgers discusses, for instance, the recent emphasis on economic efficiency during recent times of austerity, which assumes that society as a whole will

benefit from affording the greatest freedom to parties in the employment contract to manage their affairs. As she notes, however, these liberal assumptions
only hide the realities of subordination and domination in the employment
relationship and reinforce the inequalities and disadvantages present in those
relationships.

The vision of the autonomous market citizen is also beginning to expand its
influence over areas of law where it has previously been less significant. Alison
Diduck, for instance, discusses how family law has been told to 'get in step'
with the 'libertarian instinct' of the common law by shifting away from the unenlightened focus on 'paternalism and protection'. She critically reflects on the
suggestion that progress is inevitably achieved when legal relations in the family
are restructured based on contract, such as through prenuptial agreements. This
narrative, she argues, portrays individualistic autonomy and independence as the
markers of progress, which should displace family law's focus on the oppositional
(and 'pathetic') notions of relational vulnerability and interdependence. However, Diduck demonstrates how ostensible progress is achieved not by escaping
these aspects of the human condition, but only by ignoring them, with the effect
of benefiting some family members to the disadvantage of others.

Jonathan Herring expresses similar concerns regarding the notion of progress
when he addresses the national and international policy frameworks that have
come to emphasise 'successful ageing'. He notes how 'success in ageing' has
come to be defined in terms of the ability of a person to remain independent
and self-sufficient into old age. Rosie Harding in her response also suggests
these frameworks involve neoliberal governmentality and the personalisation
of responsibility (see Newman et al. 2008; Moulaert and Biggs 2013; Lloyd
et al. 2014). In these frameworks, the individual is required to exercise self-
management and responsible decision-making throughout the life course, with
the view to avoiding dependence in later life. Indeed, we are instructed to see
our level of productivity in old age as the outcome of our choices and to structure our lives to avoid the possibility of becoming a burden on society (Moulaert
and Biggs 2013, 32) The United Nations Economic Commission for Europe
(UNECE, 2012) provides a useful example:

> Active ageing requires investments at the individual level. Everyone has a
> personal responsibility for their active ageing. Even the perceptions of age-
> ing that people adopt when they are younger impacts on the quality of their
> ageing processes. At the same time, governments and societies can strategi-
> cally invest in conducive frameworks that set the right incentives and enable
> all members of society to live actively throughout their life-course. As a
> result people may be less dependent and contribute more to society. This
> can also help generate considerable cost savings for both individuals and
> public budgets.

Society thus has the responsibility to create conducive frameworks and incen-
tives to enable and encourage responsible choices, but it is ultimately up to the

individual to look after themselves (Holstein and Minkler 2003; Cardona 2008; Boudiny 2013; Lloyd et al. 2014; Kesby 2017). The corollary of this is that those who do not 'age well' can be blamed for their 'proverbially out of control body' (Holstein and Minkler 2003, 792) and even their 'vulnerable situation' (Boudiny 2013, 1084). This fails to account, as Martinson (2006, 62) argues, for the 'structural inequities that affect people's life course experiences and their likelihood of fitting into these glorified ways of being old'.

Herring recognises that no individual possesses such control over the ageing process that they can escape vulnerability and dependency altogether. Moreover, old age often reveals what was true all along – that we were never the independent, in-control and self-sufficient subjects that we believed we were. Thus, Herring refers to liberal subjectivity as little more than a mask that conceals our vulnerability and dependency over the life course. Those who are 'successful in ageing' can sustain the façade into old age, whereas those who fail are unable to do so. Here, vulnerability is projected onto all those who have 'failed at ageing'. For this façade to be maintained, there must be a binary category of 'failed agers' who carry the stigma of vulnerability in order to reinforce the illusion (Holstein and Minkler 2003, 792). The result is a more selective form of ageism, with the 'vulnerable elderly' the new objects of fear (Kesby 2017). This has material implications for both groups, as the former struggle to keep up the façade in order to avoid becoming a burden, resulting in the potential deprivation of necessary support, whereas the latter can be held responsible for the burden they have become. Moreover, as Harding notes, this means that positive attention is directed only at those who age successfully. Those who fail at ageing are instead treated as the objects of care – with care elided with paternalistic treatment (Boudiny 2013).

In these instances, 'progress' is not achieved by the actual elimination of vulnerability and dependency from human experience. These aspects of the human experience are only concealed behind the mask of liberal subjectivity, which is little more than a comforting illusion that seduces us into believing that we can escape our vulnerable condition. Mary Neal and Beverley Clough address this point in their discussion on healthcare law. Neal discusses the image of the autonomous patient as a rhetorical device for the countering of paternalistic power, which requires the ignoring of vulnerability within the realities of the healthcare encounter. Beverley Clough builds on this to highlight how progress has been equated with replacing the image of the vulnerable patient, trusting in their doctors, with that of the autonomous consumer in the healthcare marketplace. Rather than a 'passive recipient' of care, this consumer is treated as informed and proactive in exercising choice among the competing healthcare products and services on the market and assumes responsibility for the risks involved with those choices. However, as Clough notes, vulnerability never actually disappears from patients' lives, but is simply hidden from view, which can paradoxically lead to healthcare encounters that exacerbate the negative experience of vulnerability. Moreover, she notes how this framing of the patient is more than merely rhetorical, as it results in personal responsibility for the consequences to their health that flow from their choices.

In the context of social care more generally, there has been an even more significant shift towards a neoliberal market-based model. Progress has been associated, in this context, with achieving independence through treating the former recipient of care as an 'employer' and 'manager' of a personal assistant, and 'risk-taker' and 'entrepreneur' in the innovative way they shape the market (Hughes et al. 2005; Scourfield, 2007, 112). This shift is evident, for instance, in the extension of direct payments that entitle service users to employ 'personal assistants' under the Care Act 2014. In their new role, the 'employer' is in a position to exert control over the personal assistance that they receive. They can, for instance, set the terms of employment and better ensure that their interests take priority in the contractual relationship (Leece 2010). One of the appeals of this shift is that it enables the former 'person in receipt of care' to believe that they have 'escaped from the chains of many everyday forms of dependency' (Hughes et al. 2005, 270), as they are now in the same position as the autonomous market citizen to gain contractual assistance. No longer are they passive objects of care, but are instead in control of how the other person will influence them. In this way, the stigma previously attached to being a vulnerable person in need of care is discarded by those who can now 'pass' as part of the mainstream. We see, for instance, in the disability movement the suggestion that emancipation has been achieved through the transformation of care (unequal and controlling) into contract (choice and control) and the turning of carers into personal assistants (Wood 1991; Beresford 2008).

In order for this transformation to occur, however, personal assistance relationships need to be stripped of their emotional and personal significance. For these are aspects of an interpersonal relationship that imply that the well-being of the individual is dependent upon the specific emotional connection that has formed (Watson et al. 2004; Shakespeare 2013, 175). These relationships are not capable of being exchanged without this being detrimental to the well-being of the parties; they have, in other words, become a vulnerable component of their well-being.[3] In contrast, in a commercial arrangement, emphasis is placed on the relationship as an interchangeable commodity that is available from a range of suppliers in the market place. In these circumstances, exchanging the provider of practical support is a mere matter of exchanging the instruments by which to achieve independence.

The formal transformation of care into contract does not mean, in practice, that the experience of vulnerability and dependency has been removed from the lives of those who are drawn into the mainstream. Studies have highlighted how different relational dynamics can emerge, which continue to be characterised by varying patterns of vulnerability.[4] Some relationships are characterised, for

---

3 These relationships 'offer rewards of deep trust and shared emotional confidence. But they leave both parties vulnerable, for example if they end because of the departure of one party, or if they break down' (Shakespeare et al. 2017, 16). See also Ungerson (1999, 597).

4 As Marian Bares (2011) has noted, the devaluing of care within social care policy does not mean the practice of care has been abandoned. The formal contractual nature of the relationship may only disguise the actual practice.

instance, by reciprocal care in which the well-being of one party is vulnerable to, and is an aspect of, the well-being of the other party (Shakespeare 2013, Shakespeare et al. 2017). Other relationships emphasise the vulnerability of the employee to exploitation and poor employment conditions (Shakespeare 2006; Ahlström and Wadensten 2010, 184; Ahlström and Wadensten 2012; Christensen 2012). In line with the contractual framing of the personal assistant as a 'mechanical tool' of independence, there have arisen relationships in which the personal assistant has been reduced to the status of a servant, with little agency of their own (Twigg 2002; 2006; Christensen 2012; Shakespeare 2013; Shakespeare et al 2017). Still other relationships are characterised by the employer struggling to cope with the burdens associated with that role, at the same time as feeling under pressure to continue in that role in order to exercise 'choice and control' that they would otherwise be denied (Owens et al 2017). Focusing on the relationship as a commercial exchange between independent actors can obscure and conceal these different dynamics.

The risk that those in the mainstream will have their vulnerability ignored stands in stark contrast to those on the margins. The marginal subject is at risk of having choice and control denied to them because they are deemed vulnerable. In the personal assistance model, for instance, exercising control is equated with the ability to purchase and manage a subordinate. However, not all are able or willing to assume the mantle of the autonomous market citizen. For this group, care remains the appropriate response and continues to be associated with 'paternalism and protection' (Barnes 2011; Owens et al. 2017). Because of this, little positive attention needs to be paid to the feelings and preferences of these recipients of care. As Caroline Barnes (2011, 166) summarises, 'care continues to be relegated to policies that focus exclusively on those considered to be vulnerable and in need of particular support.'

Martha Fineman (2003) has argued that we must revalue care as central to human life rather than continuing to marginalise it. This includes creating the conditions in which the burdens of care are shared more equally among society (Fineman 2010; 2017). However, in order to achieve this, our own need for care must be recognised. This is problematic, as it requires us to confront our shared vulnerability and value our dependence on others who nurture us. Moreover, promoting the equal sharing of care requires more people to render themselves vulnerable through caring for others – as (genuine) caring involves a form of 'receptivity' that means being 'truly open to the other, vulnerable to what she or he is feeling' (see Noddings, 2010, 9; see also Noddings 1984). This is not achievable, however, so long as vulnerability remains something to be avoided. Indeed, as Hamrouni (2017) argues, contempt for vulnerability has led to the exploitation of carers. In particular, 'body work' has been assigned to some categories of persons in order to enable others to avoid having to confront what might remind them of their own human vulnerability (ibid., 75). By also imagining that they are self-reliant, those who fall into the liberal mainstream can deny their indebtedness to the institutional and social support that has nurtured them (Fineman 2004).

Thus, the exploitation of care is linked to the desire to maintain the illusion of liberal subjectivity. The 'vulnerable other' is a threat to that illusion. As Margrit Shildrick (2002, 81) argues, when we are confronted with the acute vulnerability of another, it threatens to 'stir recognition within, a sense of our openness and vulnerability that western discourse insists on covering over'. As she goes on to say, '[t]he unified embodied self is not faced with an unknown other, but rather with its own being stripped of the "armour of an alienating identity"' (ibid., 80). Therefore, if we are to create a more caring society, as Fineman desires, we must 'unmask the subterfuge' of the illusion, that is the liberal subject, and 'radically reverse the independence standard' (Hamrouni 2017, 72). In order to do so, however, we must 'rethink…human vulnerability' (ibid.). Indeed, Fineman (2012, 96) has suggested that we need to consider how vulnerability 'can be embraced, not ignored' in the (re)structuring of legal institutions.

Purpose of the collection

This collection takes up the challenge of considering how law might embrace vulnerability rather than conceal it or treat it as a deficiency. It brings together leading legal scholars who are working on vulnerability theory to consider how vulnerability can be a source of multiple forms of well-being and can be a condition that makes possible connection and human development. As indicated in studies in ethics and feminist philosophy recently, understanding these more positive dimensions of vulnerability is important to appreciating the full normative implications of that concept, beyond the duty to minimise or eradicate it. Indeed, as Straehle argues (2016, 9), 'pathologizing all vulnerability' may 'represent a failure of justice'. This failure can be seen, for instance, in the discarding of care as too closely associated with vulnerability as a contemptible condition.

Careful consideration needs to be given to the obligations that might arise with respect to human vulnerability. In particular, there is a need to evaluate the diverse ways in which vulnerability can be lived in different relational and social contexts. Sometimes the particular experience of vulnerability may contribute to, rather than undermine, the well-being of the individual (Carse 2006; Staehle 2016). The response here may be to support and respect vulnerability, so that it remains the basis of flourishing and connection: ensuring that vulnerability does not become pathogenic, rather than eradicating or reducing it on the assumption that it is *always* pathogenic (Bedford 2018). At the same time, as several contributors note, we must avoid romanticising all experiences of vulnerability. Some relational and social contexts will produce pathogenic vulnerability, which should be resisted rather than embraced (see on pathogenic vulnerability, Mackenzie et al. 2014; MacKenzie 2016). Decoupling vulnerability from the purely negative does not mean treating it as an unequivocal good. What is called for is a more nuanced understanding of the relationship between vulnerability and well-being, which moves beyond the negative/positive binary. In some contributions, this binary is rejected in favour of describing vulnerability as a value-neutral fact about the human condition (Harding, this volume). However, other contributors note that, in order for vulnerability to produce normative results, it must be combined with evaluative premises about human beings that can guide our decision-making (Neal, this volume). Thus, we need to evaluate the ways in which particular experiences of vulnerability can undermine or contribute to well-being as a morally important interest in order to determine the obligations it generates (see MacKenzie 2016; Ten Have 2016, 107).

In their efforts to transcend the binary framework cultivated by liberalism, several contributors also seek to understand how key legal concepts, like autonomy and dignity, are constituted by particular experiences of vulnerability. Not only does this move vulnerability beyond incapacity, it also involves a fundamental reworking of the individualistic understandings of autonomy and dignity that assume an independent and self-reliant liberal subject. Conceptions of relational autonomy and embodied dignity, in particular, are drawn on and developed in this collection to refigure the connection to vulnerability. Contributors to this volume do not seek, therefore, to discard autonomy or dignity entirely by focusing exclusively on vulnerability. Nor do they simply add vulnerability as another concept to be considered alongside autonomy and dignity. The approach adopted is one that centres on how our vulnerability is entwined with autonomy and dignity (on such approaches, see Anderson 2014, 134; MacKenzie 2016).

The following sections of this introduction account for the development in the understanding of the concept of vulnerability. It outlines the shift in emphasis towards vulnerability as a condition of susceptibility to change in our well-being. It then considers how this conception is brought into a more constructive relationship with the principles of autonomy and dignity in the contributions to this collection.

Vulnerability as susceptibility to change

Drawing vulnerability out of the margins has been the goal of vulnerability theorists. Fineman, in particular, has sought to argue that vulnerability is a universal and constant aspect of the human condition that arises from our embodied and embedded existence. This goes some way to dissociate vulnerability from negative notions of victimhood, deprivation or pathology that afflict only certain stigmatised populations. This dissociation also has the potential to disrupt the binaries of liberalism and challenge the notion that independence and self-reliance are desirable and achievable states for human beings. However, in her earlier work, Fineman (2008, 9) aligns vulnerability closely with the 'ever-present possibility of harm, injury, and misfortune from mildly adverse to catastrophically devastating events, whether accidental, intentional, or otherwise'. It was also associated with being 'susceptible to destructive external forces and internal disintegration' (ibid., 12). Such an understanding is consistent with envisioning vulnerability as a regrettable fact about the human condition that we would transcend, if only we could. As noted earlier, it is the desire for transcendence that drives the construction of the liberal subject as an illusion that enables us to avoid confronting our vulnerable condition. It is not, therefore, just the construction of the liberal subject that establishes the marginal view of vulnerability. It also arises out of our desire to hide from the anxiety that vulnerability arouses in us (Bergoffen 2013; Gilson 2013).

It is interesting, in this light, to note how Fineman has sought to move beyond the idea of vulnerability as the potential for suffering. She has argued (Fineman 2012, 96) that vulnerability is 'generative and [has] positive aspects' and that there are 'positive possibilities inherent' in that condition (ibid., 71). This refocusing on the positive possibilities appears designed to counter the continued ignorance of vulnerability, by considering how it can be embraced. Fineman has thus set out these possibilities in response to the negative perceptions of vulnerability that have led to its marginalisation in the process of law reform.[5] Fineman develops two strategies for connecting these possibilities to vulnerability. First, she recognises that vulnerability is a background condition that compels the creation of social institutions and relational networks that enhance opportunities and development. Vulnerability is understood to instigate us into community with one another and is what encourages cooperation (see Fineman 2012, 126; 2014, 104). Moreover, positive forms of connection and engagement are thought to emerge from our striving to fulfil our emotional needs, which we may not otherwise have if we were invulnerable subjects. Fineman (2012, 126) gives as an example the creation of adult activity centres and specialised transportation for older adults as programs that we establish in order to enable human contact, which is a need that arises from our vulnerable condition. In responding to these needs, we are creating the conditions for the well-being of a certain sort of being – one that is vulnerable, and in need of friendship. It can be added to this that vulnerability forms part of the building blocks for, and is a constituent feature of, the formation of genuine community. Love and care, for instance, require that we make ourselves vulnerable in the person of another. To put it another way, our need for love and care arises from our vulnerability, but these also require us to be vulnerable. On this view, vulnerability is not a limitation but a condition of potentiality that makes these relational goods possible (on vulnerability as potentiality, see Gilson 2013; Ten Have 2016). These goods are potentialities inherent only in a vulnerable life and would thus be lost in a life defined by self-protective detachment (Card 1998; Nussbaum 2001; Carse 2006).

In her more recent work, Fineman (2017) develops a second strategy for connecting some of these more positive possibilities to vulnerability. This strategy makes these connections by focusing on the concept of change. This would appear to represent an evolution, or refinement, of her account of vulnerability;

---

5 She warns, as in the contexts discussed earlier, that the 'denial of human vulnerability and the possibility of dependency will not eliminate the experience of either in individual lives' (Fineman 2012, 90).

one that is able to counter the continued ignorance of that shared condition. She states that (2017; 2019, 82, emphasis added)

> As embodied beings, we are universally and individually constantly *susceptible to change in our well-being. Change can be positive or negative* – we become ill and are injured or decline, but we also grow in abilities and develop new skills and relationships. The term 'vulnerable', used to connote the continuous *susceptibility to change* in both our bodily and social well-being that all human beings experience, makes it clear that there is no position of invulnerability – no conclusive way to prevent or avoid change.

This decouples vulnerability from susceptibility to injury, harm or misfortune and attaches it to the idea of a universal susceptibility to change in our well-being. These negative possibilities do not therefore define vulnerability but point to a more general condition of exposure to change. These possibilities are, in other words, just *one* of the particular ways in which we can undergo change. This is in line with other recent scholarship, which has shifted emphasis onto vulnerability as enabling personal development and growth. Henk Ten Have (2016), for instance, has described vulnerability as the condition of continual exposure to change and transformation. Erin Gilson (2013) has also referred to it as a fundamental openness to alterations that we are unable to predict or control. Whereas Margrit Shildrick (2002) refers to embodied vulnerability as openness to alterity, which is the condition of becoming with others. Becoming acknowledges that we are not static beings but that we constantly undergo changes through our dynamic interactions with the world.

Common to these accounts is the focus on the ways in which we are susceptible to change as embodied social entities. Rather than privileging the function of the body as a protective boundary against the world, these accounts emphasise how the body represents an opening to the world (Shildrick 2002). The body is less a boundary than it is a permeable interface. From this perspective, the body is open to other bodies in the world that join with it to compose and recompose it. It is impossible therefore to be, or to exist as a human body, without this openness. It is what constitutes our bodies: if the human body is not open to being affected by what is outside itself in the world, then it cannot exist, grow or mature (Gatens 1996, 110; Gilson 2013). The material form of the body means that it is in a fluid exchange with the world. What is outer becomes inner and what is inner becomes outer (Keller 1986, 234; Herring and Chau 2007). Moreover, the sensory form of the body means that it is 'sensationally open to the world' (Bernstein 2015, 84). The skin, for instance, is sensitive and responsive to the touch of another, in a way that can transform what the body feels. Empathetic touch, for instance, has the capacity to draw us out of periods of despair and re-establish a sense of connection to others (Carse 2006).

The example of touch highlights how the openness of the body need not signify passive objectivity. Instead, as Judith Butler (2009, 34) argues, openness can be what 'animates responsiveness' in the form of a 'wide range of affects:

pleasure, rage, suffering, hope, to name a few'. The 'body is vulnerable,' she declares, in the way that it 'suffers, enjoys and responds to the exteriority of the world' (Ibid.). Indeed, she goes as far as to state that '[a]ll responsiveness to what happens is a function and effect of vulnerability' including 'all the various ways in which we are moved, entered, touched, or ways that ideas and others make an impression on us' (Butler in Lloyd 2015, 214). From this perspective, vulnerability is associated with the way in which the world can move us and inspire change in our embodied-affective disposition. This denies an approach to vulnerability that would equate it with the condition of being passively determined and includes as part of its possibilities all the ways in which we respond to an impinging world (Butler 2009, 34). Being susceptible to change can mean, on this view, being moved to action by that which calls for our response; vulnerability is a form of 'dynamic receptivity' (Gilson 2013, 133).

The necessary openness of the body means that it is invariably connected to the world and a set of relations within it. Our fleshy selves, on this view, are composed and shaped by the relations that surround them (Lloyd 2015, 212). However, it is a defining feature of vulnerability that we do not control all the ways in which the body will be affected by these relationships to alterity.[6] Since we not do control all the ways the world will impinge on the body, we are unable to control all the changes we may undergo. An element of uncertainty thus defines our interactions with the world and others. It is this uncertainty that gives vulnerability a more ambiguous quality, taking us beyond the binary understanding that would seek to define it exclusively as positive/negative or activity/passivity. As Henk Ten Have (2016, 114) puts it:

> [V]ulnerability is ambiguous; it may lead to care and compassion but also to abuse and violence, it may produce transformation or devastation, healing or suffering.

Judith Butler (2009, 61) also captures this ambiguous quality when she describes unwilled exposure to others as not only the promise of desire and intimacy but also the threat of cruelty and subjugation. Thus, while a universal condition, in the sense that we are inescapably open to the world, on an individual level we can experience that openness differently. This is because we are not just open to the world but are also open to particular social, political and environmental forces within that world (Ten Have 2016). Those forces leave us more or less susceptible to particular ways of being affected (Gilson 2013). It is possible, for instance, that we will become subject to forces that turn the inevitable world-relation into captivity to a largely hostile world from which we feel alienated. Instead of this

---

6 Judith Butler (Butler in Berbec 2017, 70) states that because of the human body 'I am open to a world that acts on me in ways that cannot be fully predicted or controlled in advance, and something about my openness is not, strictly speaking, under my control. That opening toward the world is not something that I can exactly will away.' She also refers to the fact that 'I am impressionable, given over to the Other in ways that I cannot fully predict or control' (Butler 2004, 46).

relation being experienced as open responsiveness to the world, and to the rich range of affects it can awaken in us, it is limited to the experience of passivity to a world that makes us suffer. This suffering can turn inwards, in a way that disrupts the integrity of the embodied subject (Gadow 1980). This arises when the embodied subject feels that part of itself, the vulnerable body, is that which attacks the self. The self–body relation is thus disrupted and the self comes to feel betrayed by the hostile body (Scarry 1985, 47–48; Bernstein 2015). It is not just that their body is made to suffer; it is turned into the source of suffering.[7]

One context where it possible to gain a clearer insight into the different experiences of vulnerability is in regards to intimacy and abuse of intimacy. Debra Bergoffen (2013) has explained how intimacy is one of the positive forms that vulnerability can take, in which we experience the sensual pleasures of tactile contact and the bonds of trust that sustain it. She highlights how abuse of intimacy can transform corporeal openness from the basis of experiencing those sensual pleasures and bonds of trust, into a tool that destroys those pleasures and trust in those bonds (ibid., 31–32). Her understanding of abuse is not primarily explainable in terms of whether the boundaries of the subject are breached. Her focus is on how the abuse turns corporeal openness against the victim and how that openness is made into an instrument of their destruction (ibid., 1–2). This not only entails the infliction of harm on the body; it also devastates the promise of vulnerability. Thus, the abuse destroys any confidence in the subject that corporeal openness can be the basis of sensual engagement with the world or be the basis for the creation of bonds of affection. In other words, the abuse alienates us from the positive possibilities of vulnerability.

Different power dynamics enable these relational patterns. Intimacy is sustained, for instance, by relations of reciprocity and dynamic receptivity. Luce Irigaray (2001; see also Irigaray, Shildrick 2002, 103–120), for instance, has explored how in intimacy we gift to each other a touch that enlivens us to the pleasures of our corporeal openness, at the same time as we open up to the feelings, pleasures and sensations of another. It can be difficult in this context to differentiate the touch sensation into touching (active) and being touched (passive). Instead, in the intermingling of the flesh, we form a sensory circuit (Cohoon 2011). In that circuit there is a flowing of affective sensations between those who touch – a sense that affection flows from me as it flows back to me: a flowing together between openings that meet (Irigaray 2001, 25). In fact, in the caress, it is such that each person is receptive in the giving and active in the receiving. This is because it is not possible for the touching to constitute a gifting between us if we are not receptive to each other. For we are unable to attend to the other, to their feelings, sensations, and pleasures, which is the gift of the caress, without being receptive. The result is a 'touching between us' that is 'neither passive

---

7 As Sophie Oliver (2011, 91) summarises, 'The persecuted body becomes persecutory, alien, other. The body, once a source of pleasure, becomes the source of torment, something to be feared, avoided, fled from, and the [victim]…is left in a paradoxical predicament, both detached from and consumed by his body.'

nor active' (ibid.) and 'always untouched by mastery' (Irigaray 2005, 186). For Shildrick (2002, 199), this represents a mode of corporeal interrelating in which each subject is being shaped and reshaped in and through their relation to the other. The self and other are thus envisaged as mutable entities that are dynamically formed in a reciprocal corporeal relationship.

In contrast to reciprocal relations that are untouched by mastery, abuse of intimacy is made possible by the mastery of one over another. In these dynamics, a hierarchical relationship exists in which an active subject seeks to appropriate or possess the sensual powers of another (Bergoffen 2013). They aim to appropriate those powers in order to use them to express their meaning of the world (ibid.) and in order to support the assertion of their self (Lorraine 2018, 38). This means that the masterful subject is never passive to the affective powers of another, as they control those powers. They are not moved, touched or otherwise affected in ways that they do not control. This leaves the victim unable to invoke their affective powers and shape the interaction. Here a 'relation of mastery' is enabled by one person being invulnerable to the power of another and another who is forced to live their vulnerability as involuntary passivity.

It is not the absence or presence of vulnerability that separates intimacy from abuse of intimacy. Both depend on vulnerability. However, the different power dynamics of these relationships mean that vulnerability is experienced in distinct ways. But it is not just the immediate relational nexus that structures those experiences. That nexus is often situated in a wider network of political, social and economic conditions. Law is also important in shaping those relational dynamics and those wider social conditions that support those dynamics. This is acknowledged within vulnerability theory, although the focus is often on how law makes a contribution to perpetuating or ameliorating misfortune. But, once it is understood that vulnerability is not just about misfortune, then consideration can also be given to how law can support the social conditions in which vulnerability is experienced as the basis of reciprocal corporeal connection and collaborative creative activity. Caring, for instance, can be envisaged as an intercorporeal relationship that is creatively formed through the mutual receptiveness and open responsiveness of each participant to the needs and interests of the other. Importantly, as Herring (2013, 22) argues, such relationships can be 'multi-directional' as each participant can be 'open to learn from and grow with each other'. There is reciprocal openness to change.

The attempt at eliminating vulnerability by transforming care into contract may be undermining these dynamics. It may be encouraging, as noted earlier, the treatment of a personal assistant as a servant who is expected to carry out mechanical tasks under the direction of the superior. It is nonetheless clear that relationships defined by mutuality, reciprocity and interdependency have emerged despite the contractual framing. However, formally envisaging the relationship as purely contractual may misrepresent what is involved and mean the law is inadequately responsive to the needs of the parties. Presuming the obligations of the parties are based on the terms of the contract settled at the start, for instance, may fail to appreciate the fluid dynamic of the relationship. It may not account for how the demands of caring are unpredictable and change over time or how the receptive and responsive qualities of an individual mean the parties are vulnerable to those changing demands (Bubeck 2003). These qualities associated with vulnerability cannot be removed without undermining the care, but they require a more flexible 'open-ended' response (Marin 2013).

Beyond the binaries of law: autonomy, dignity and vulnerability

A common misperception of vulnerability theory is that it requires us to cast aside the legal values of autonomy and dignity because of their incompatibility with vulnerability. If autonomy and dignity have contributed to positioning vulnerability on the margins, then we must abandon them in order to bring vulnerability into the mainstream, or so the argument goes. In particular, Fineman has been misinterpreted as having rejected the concept of autonomy in its entirety (Hirschmann 2014; MacKenzie et al 2014). This does not account for the way in which Fineman leaves open the possibility of reconciling autonomy with vulnerability. This is possible, she suggests, when autonomy is understood as an 'aspiration' rather than an 'inherent characteristic' that must be 'cultivated by a society that pays attention to the needs of its members, the operation of institutions, and the implications of human fragility and vulnerability' (Fineman 2010, 260). Fineman thus gestures towards a constructivist account of autonomy, which is achievable only when an individual has assets or resources that give them resilience and enable them to take advantage of opportunities for action. Rather than abandoning autonomy, this represents an attempt to embed autonomy within the fact of human vulnerability. It does so by indicating that autonomy is possible only in the context of a society that is responsive to vulnerability.

The aim of vulnerability theory is not, on this view, to replace autonomy or dignity with the concept of vulnerability. It might be better understood as seeking to reconstruct the relationship between autonomy and dignity with vulnerability in a non-binary way. It has already been seen that well-being has been affirmatively reconciled with vulnerability as change. It is also possible for this reconciliation to be achieved with respect to autonomy and dignity. Rather than conceiving of these concepts as the antagonists of vulnerability, they can be understood as sharing a similarly ambiguous relationship with vulnerability. For instance, it is possible to understand exposure to others as the basis for developing autonomy in addition to being a threat to it (Bagnoli 2016, 21). This has the potential to transform our understanding of the role of the state in protecting autonomy. No longer is its role confined to reinforcing boundaries around the subject so that the individual is secured in their ability to determine their own interests without interference. It should recognise that the autonomy of an individual is vulnerable to changes that can enhance as well as diminish their autonomy competences and should shape the social conditions that structure the changes to which the individual is exposed. Contributors develop these themes by focusing on accounts of relational autonomy.

(Relational) autonomy and vulnerability

Integral to relational accounts is the recognition that autonomy is a fluid capacity and fragile achievement that emerges in social conditions without which it cannot develop (Anderson and Honneth 2005, 137). These social conditions shape both the process of identity formation[8] and agents' abilities for critical reflection.[9] Autonomy is, in this way, rendered vulnerable to social conditioning; it is not a static human characteristic but is susceptible to changes in the relational network in which the individual is situated.[10] Because an individual does not possess complete control over these relational networks, they also lack complete control over whether they will develop the relevant autonomy competences. Indeed, the formation of autonomy is a partially 'receptive, passive process' – as the development of the relevant competences are dependent on social influences that the individual inherits (Kong 2017, 85). Furthermore, it is not possible to secure autonomy by escaping dependence on these influences. In fact, disengaging from relationships can deprive the person of the forms of support needed to sustain the relevant competences (ibid., 67). This can also be, as Camillia Kong (2017, 86) argues, 'an important indicator of underdeveloped self-understanding and autonomy competencies'. In direct contrast, then, to most legal accounts, relational accounts conceive of separation and independence as threats to the development of mature autonomy.

There are several ways in which to examine how relational autonomy incorporates relational vulnerability. In this collection, there is particular focus on the importance of intersubjective recognition and trusting relationships. Alison Diduck addresses the former when she discusses the importance of intersubjective recognition with respect to various family identities. Her account draws on a conception of relational autonomy that incorporates self-authorisation as a requirement (MacKenzie 2014). In order to satisfy this requirement, there is a need to sustain certain affective attitudes towards the self, such as self-trust, self-respect, and self-esteem. This includes having an affective appreciation of one's worth and competency as a person and recognising that one's decisions carry significance. As Mackenzie (2008, 525) has noted elsewhere, when we lack these self-referring attitudes, we also lack the motivational structure needed for

---

8 Catriona MacKenzie (2008, 527) has argued that the 'sense of who we are is intrinsically bound up with, and vulnerable to, our relationships with others in all the different spheres of our lives.'

9 According to MacKenzie (2014, 59), '[i]f persons are socially constituted, then external conditions, including our social relations with others, shape the process of practical identity formation – the *self* of self-governance – and the development of the skills and competences for *governing* the self. On the one hand, this is not necessarily problematic from a relational perspective – it points to the facts of developmental and ongoing dependency and to the extensive interpersonal, social, and institutional scaffolding necessary for self-governance.'

10 'Vulnerability plays an ineluctable role within the relationships that enable autonomy and afford its expression – one's autonomy is vulnerable to disruptions in one's relationship to others' (Anderson 2014, 136).

autonomy: 'if one does not think of one's life and one's activities as worthwhile it is difficult to determine what to do and how to act.'

Diduck draws on the work of Anderson and Honneth (2005) to argue that the attitudes of others constitute and condition our self-referring attitudes. In other words, our attitudes towards self are susceptible to changes in the attitudes of others (Anderson 2014, 140). An internal appreciation of our worth, for instance, depends on the external messages we receive from significant others about ourselves. If we receive messages that we are valued and matter to others, we are likely to think our life worthwhile, whereas denigrating messages will have the opposite effect. Of particular importance is the recognition and approval conferred by intimate relationships, societal structures and solidaritistic communities that surround us. In many respects, these social influences on our sense of self are not within our control. Often we simply inherit these influences.

Diduck discusses several examples where recognition is important to constituting autonomy. One notable example relates to sociocultural attitudes towards caretaking. It was noted earlier how care has been recognised as a 'social sphere in which all participants are blighted because they live wasted lives' (Hughes et al. 2005, 267), which contrasts with the productive activities of the autonomous market citizen. Diduck's approach highlights how the low value placed on caretaking not only creates material disadvantage but can also undermine the autonomy by undermining relations to self. Other areas where intersubjective recognition impacts on our sense of self are touched on in other contributions to this collection. These contributions examine the importance of social attitudes at the beginning and the end of the life course. Focusing on the former, Jo Bridgeman discusses complex relational networks in which social attitudes, from difference sources, impinge on a child's sense of self. She gives as an example the case *In the Matter of M* [2017] EWCA Civ 2164. In that case, it was accepted that the welfare of five children might by negatively affected if they were to have direct contact with their father who was transgender, due to the hostile (and intransigent) attitudes of the religious community in which they were enmeshed. At the same time, their development was vulnerable to loss of contact with their father. This is all set within the context of an understanding of child welfare that is judged by the standards of the reasonable person, who is receptive to change and will thus have regard to evolving social attitudes. Bridgeman highlights how the judicial response to this case sought to encourage a change of attitude in the community, in order to enable the contact. She also notes how the case focuses on the role of professional assistance in enabling the children to adapt to the changes in their father and in sensitising them to the outlook of the community. For Bridgeman, this represents an appropriate collective response to the vulnerability of children to changes in the attitudes of others. Moreover, it is this less individualistic form of response that Bridgeman suggests we should begin to adopt when addressing the vulnerability of adults.

At the other end of the life course, Jonathan Herring reflects on how older adult's attitudes to self are vulnerable to social attitudes towards ageing. He criticises social norms that treat old age as undesirable in contrast to youth.

In particular, he focuses on norms that accord value to the individual based on standards (e.g. productivity, beauty and vigour) defined from a youthful perspective. Several examples are discussed where these norms may have been internalised. One example is resort to cosmetic surgery in order to counter or delay the effects of the ageing process. This example alerts us to the societal practices that reinforce the belief that self-worth is contingent on physical appearance and that the ageing body is unattractive. Another example is recourse to suicide in order to put an end to the humiliation of being a 'worthless old person'. Herring intimates that we need to counter these damaging attitudes by not only conferring recognition on the neglected contributions that older people make to society but also to the value of their 'simply being'.

The emphasis on intersubjective recognition entails an important recalibration of the focus of state institutions and legal systems. Protecting autonomy requires far more than upholding rights that guard an individual from outside influence or enable contractual agreement. First, it requires the state to adopt measures that demonstrate proper regard for individual and group differences and to guard against policies that express attitudes of denigration or humiliation (Anderson and Honneth 2005, 131; MacKenzie 2014, 37). Second, it requires collective support and recognition of relationships that sustain appropriate self-regarding attitudes. Third, there may be ways in which the law can require changes in social attitudes that influence the development of others, as evidenced in the example of *In the Matter of M*, discussed previously.

Finally, in order to promote autonomy, there may be a need to challenge unjustifiable self-conceptions that are the result of the individual internalising oppressive social norms. Catriona Mackenzie (2008, 528) has argued, for instance, that the obligation to promote autonomy may require us to find ways to counter a sense of personal worthlessness that arise from oppressive socialisation and to promote self-respect. This imposes much more demanding requirements on, for example, healthcare professionals in the area of informed consent or supported decision-making, than would usually be recognised in relation to classical liberal notions of autonomy (ibid.; Stoljar 2011). Importantly, these obligations are not concerned with rendering the person invulnerable to the attitudes of others. Rather, they involve identifying the ways in which an individual can change their practical identity, which draws upon alternative sources of self-esteem within their social network (MacKenzie 2008, 526). Engaging in an open dialogue about their practical identity, in this way, inevitably involves the acceptance of vulnerability and building of trust. It also demands sympathy and sensitivity on the part of those who are engaging with the individual (ibid.). As some of the nursing literature highlights, these character attributes require a carer to embrace, rather than repudiate, their vulnerability (Stenbock-Hult and Sarvimaki 2011). This is because sympathy and sensitivity entail emotional exposure and the possibility that our feelings will be impacted by others. Emphasising these attributes shifts the emphasis onto vulnerability as a resource for developing the competences and social conditions that enable autonomy to develop. However, this very same vulnerability leaves those in the relational network exposed to emotional hurt and exhaustion. This cannot be eradicated without undermining the conditions for supporting autonomy, but those embedded in the network can be provided with the necessary resilience to cope with these challenges.

The second way in which vulnerability is realigned with autonomy in this collection is through the focus on trusting relationships. Mary Neal, for instance, discusses how vulnerability is consistent with autonomous agency when a patient actively embraces trusting relationships in their interactions with medical professions. Trust is understood by Neal to be contingent on embracing vulnerability – as it involves the acceptance of the uncertainty that comes with believing that another person will further our interests. For Neal, drawing on Wieseman (2016) and O'Neill (2002), the appropriate response to this sort of vulnerability is not always to minimise it, by eliminating the need for trust, but to create and sustain a culture wherein trust is reciprocated and respected.

This is a challenge to the perception that progress should always be equated with reducing the need for trust in medical professionals, which is precisely the direction of travel that is seen in relation to informed consent. It was earlier noted that Beverley Clough, in her contribution, observes how progress in this area is measured in terms of whether the empowered autonomous consumer has supplanted the vulnerable patient trusting in their doctors. For Neal this is a problematic distinction, as trust is consistent with being both an autonomous agent *and* vulnerable subject. It is also problematic in the way that autonomy is associated with the individualisation of responsibility. For if the autonomy of a patient is respected when trust is responded to appropriately, then respecting autonomy means attending to the social conditions in which trusting relationships can flourish. In particular, it requires us to attend to the practices needed in order to honour trust and the infrastructure required to support those practices (Wieseman 2016, 167). As with intersubjective recognition, then, there is an acceptance that autonomy requires social support because it is coupled to vulnerability. It means that a responsive state is one that not only provides resources for resilience but is also one that actively fosters relational contexts that support autonomy.

(Embodied) dignity and vulnerability

Other contributions in this collection focus on reconciling human dignity with vulnerability. These contributions reject the idea that the vulnerable features of the human being should be seen as a threat to human dignity and that a life in dignity is one that transcends uncontrollable materiality. Instead, contributors argue that human dignity should be understood as *positively embracing* those features of ourselves. In particular, there is an emphasis on how the human being should be valued as embodied, relational and emotional subjects. Lisa Rodgers, in her contribution on labour law, draws on the work of Martha Nussbaum (2009, 278) who has argued that 'need and capacity, rationality and animality, are thoroughly interwoven, and the dignity of the human being is the dignity of a needy enmattered being.' For Rodgers, this allows for a fuller appreciation of the ways in which the human condition can be compromised by labour market forces. Moreover, it directs us to the way human need provides us with the impetus to form interpersonal relationships in networks of solidarity, such as trade unions. These relationships, and the institutions that support them, would be neither necessary nor possible in an invulnerable life. However, they are, for Nussbaum (2011, 39), central to what we value about human existence. For Rodgers, this helps us to understand more fully the positive contribution of trade unions, beyond their role in responding to threats to autonomy. Rodger contrasts this account with classical narratives of labour law that understand the dignity of workers only in terms of their autonomy, independence and rationality. Her concern is that these reductive narratives have the potential to reinforce the perception that employment protections are associated with negative dependence and are unnecessary for core labour market participants. She suggests that the lack of success of these narratives in countering the downgrading of labour protections may be linked to their attachment to thin conceptions of the human person in accounts of human dignity.

The way in which vulnerability is entwined with our agential capacities is also something that Mary Neal discusses in her contribution. Neal refers to her account of human dignity, developed elsewhere (2012, 198), which combines the fragile/material/finite and the transcendent/sublime/immortal. Her account requires that we maintain an appropriate balance between these different aspects of human existence and that we fail to maintain such a balance when we pursue the transcendent at the expense of the material and vice versa. Another way of thinking is that we must aspire to find meaning and purpose in life without ignoring or having others ignore our basic needs and frailties. An area of healthcare where this account has potential implications is in regards to decisions about the care and treatment of people who may lack capacity. Mary Donnelly (2016), for example, has suggested elsewhere that Neal's account reveals why the 'will and preferences' paradigm that has been developed by the UN Committee on the Rights of Person with Disabilities (CRPD) is not in fact required by human dignity and may be inconsistent with it in some situations. One such situation is a 'person living in conditions of extreme self-neglect who rejects all offers of assistance and refuses all attempts at communication' (ibid., 325). Here, the lack of care for material needs and daily living tasks would indicate a potential lack of balance between the different aspects of human existence. However, it is important to note that responding to these material needs requires sensitivity to the feelings and unique personality of the subject, if we are to respect their dignity (Bedford 2019; see also Clark Miller 2013, 61).

Anna Grear, in her contribution, turns to Neal's account of dignity as an alternative to the rationalist anthropocentrism that dominates human rights theory and practice. Grear works with the idea, developed by Neal, that dignity is a 'particular sort of ethical responsiveness to vulnerability that values us because of, rather than in spite of, our universal vulnerability'. For both scholars, universal vulnerability is here associated with not only the openness of the body, which is the source of pain and suffering, but also multiple forms of well-being

(Neal 2012, 187; Grear 2010, 129). Unlike Neal, however, Grear wants to extend the recognition of dignity (as a form of ethical responsiveness to vulnerability) to nonhumans. For Grear, there is no good reason why the universal vulnerability of nonhumans should not be basis for nonhuman dignity. Neal, in contrast, seems to maintain the position that human beings are unique and elevated above other creatures in nature. She suggests that dignity is attached to human beings as 'transcendent animals rather than brute beasts' (Neal 2014, 42) who are 'possibly unique' in combining the 'material/finite/mortal, and the transcendent/infinite/sublime' (ibid.; 2012, 198). Human vulnerability is thus a basis for human dignity, but it is not the sole basis.

Neal herself claims she is arguing for a particular form of intertwining of vulnerability with other morally salient characteristics of the human being in her account of human dignity. It is possible that Grear is offering an argument that dignity should be ascribed to the nonhuman on the basis that there is a similar intertwining in such creatures, making them similarly worthy of respect. Grear, for instance, refers to the intelligences, agencies and socialities of nonhumans that might provide the basis of ethical regard in her discussion on dignity. However, it is not always clear what entities possess the relevant intelligence or agency to ground nonhuman dignity. There is reference, for instance, to the distribution of intelligence and vulnerability across not only animal, bird and fish populations but also trees and other living systems. She also gives an expanded meaning to agency that includes non-sentient entities. A related issue is whether there are different types of nonhuman dignity and, indeed, whether nonhuman dignity is distinct from human dignity (see Nussbaum 2008). Whatever the answer to these questions, it is evident that Grear wants us to recognise the rights and vulnerability of nonhuman entities and living systems within the examination of the human rights of the human animal. She advocates for an understanding of human rights as a form of particular attention to the vulnerable situation of the human animal, which forms part of a wider framework of concern for the vulnerability of bodies of all kinds.

Structure of the collection

The collection is structured into five sections that cover areas of law where there is already significant recourse to the concept of vulnerable and, for which, a less negative construction of vulnerability may have the greatest implications. Each section includes a main chapter by a legal theorist who has previously questioned the assumption that vulnerability is exclusively associated with suffering and has challenged reductively negative (and binary) accounts of the meaning and implications of vulnerability. In this collection, these theorists engage in closer examination of the implications for law of understanding vulnerability as 'generative' and as a source of 'opportunities for innovation and growth, as well as creativity and fulfillment' (Fineman 2012, 96). Each main chapter is then followed by shorter responses from a scholar working in the same field. Some of these responses build on the foundations laid in the main chapter, with further consideration given to the creative and generative potential of vulnerability in the legal regulation of other aspects of the relevant field. Other responses involve a more critical engagement with how vulnerability is being refigured or highlight alternative vulnerability perspectives on the issues raised. These 'dialogues' are intended to draw out the central debates surrounding the changing meaning of vulnerability in law.

Bibliography

Ahlström G and Wadensten B, 'Encounters in close care relations from the perspective of personal assistants working with persons with severe disability' (2010) 18(2) *Health & Social Care in the Community* 180.

Ahlström G and Wadensten B, 'Enjoying work or burdened by it? How personal assistants experience and handle stress at work' (2012) 11(2) *Journal of Social Work in Disability & Rehabilitation* 112.

Akroyd S, 'Dirt, work and dignity' in Bolton S (ed), *Dignity at Work* (Butterworth-Heinemann 2007).

Anderson J and Honneth A, 'Autonomy, vulnerability, recognition, and justice' in J Christman and J Anderson (eds), *Autonomy and the Challenges to Liberalism: New Essays* (Cambridge University Press 2005).

Anderson J, 'Autonomy and vulnerability entwined' in C Mackenzie, W Rodgers, and S Dodds (eds), *Vulnerability: New Essays in Ethics and Feminist Philosophy* (Oxford University Press 2014).

Anker E, *Fictions of Dignity: Embodying Human Rights in World Literature* (Cornell 2012).

Ashforth B and Kreiner G, '"How can you do it?": dirty work and the challenge of constructing a positive identity' (1999) 24(3) *The Academy of Management Review* 413.

Atkins K, 'Autonomy and autonomy competencies: a practical and relational approach' (2006) 7 *Nursing Philosophy* 205.

Bagnoli C, 'Vulnerability and the incompleteness of practical reason' in C Straehle (ed), *Vulnerability, Autonomy and Applied Ethics* (Routledge 2016).

Bakan D, *The Duality of Human Existence: Isolation and Communion in Western Man* (Beacon Press 1966).

Barnes M, 'Abandoning care? A critical perspective on personalisation from an ethic of care' (2011) 5(2) *Ethics and Social Welfare* 153.

Bedford D, 'Embracing vulnerability: our route to flourishing in old age?' in B Clough and J Herring (eds), *Ageing, Gender and Family Law* (Routledge 2018).

Bedford D, 'Human dignity in Great Britain and Northern Ireland' in Becchi P and Mathis K (eds), *Handbook of Human Dignity in Europe* (Springer 2019).

Berbec S, 'We are wordless without one another: an interview with Judith Butler in The Other Journal, *Identity* (Wipf and Stock 2017).

Beresford P, 'What future for care?' https://www.jrf.org.uk/report/what-future-care (access 13th June 2019).

Bergoffen D, *Contesting the Politics of Genocidal Rape: Affirming the Dignity of the Vulnerable Body* (Routledge 2013).

Bernstein JM, *Torture and Dignity: An Essay on Moral Injury* (University of Chicago Press 2015).

Boudiny K, '"Active Ageing": from empty rhetoric to effective policy tool' (2013) 33(6) *Ageing Society* 1077.

Bubeck D, 'Justice and the labour of care' in F E Kittay and E K Feder (eds), *The Subject of Care: Feminist Perspectives on Dependency* (Rowman and Littlefield 2003).

Butler J, *Frames of War* (Verso 2009).

Butler J, *Precarious Life: The Powers of Mourning and Violence* (Verso 2004).

Card C, 'Stoicism, evil, and the possibility of morality' (1998) 29(4) *Metaphilosophy* 245.

Cardona B. '"Healthy ageing" policies and anti-ageing ideologies and practices: on the exercise of responsibility' (2008) 11(4) *Medicine, Health Care, and Philosophy* 475.

Carse, A, 'Vulnerability, agency, and human flourishing' in, C Taylor and R Dell'Oro (eds), *Health and Human Flourishing: Religion, Medicine, and Moral Anthropology* (Georgetown University Press 2006).

Christensen K, 'Towards sustainable hybrid relationships in cash-for-care systems' (2012) 27(3) *Disability & Society* 399.

Clark Miller S, *The Ethics of Need: Agency, Dignity, and Obligation* (Routledge 2013).

Code L, *What Can She Know?: Feminist Theory and the Construction of Knowledge* (Cornell 1991).

Cohoon C, 'Coming together: the six modes of Irigarayan Eros' (2011) 26(3) *Hypatia* 478.

Donnelly M, 'Best interests in the mental capacity act: time to say goodbye? (2016) 24(3) *Medical Law Review* 318.

Dunn M, Clare I, and Holland A. 'To empower or to protect? Constructing the 'vulnerable adult' in English law and public policy' (2008) 28 *Legal Studies* 234.

Fineman MA, *The Autonomy Myth: A Theory of Dependency* (The New Press 2003).

Fineman MA, 'The vulnerable subject: anchoring equality in the human condition' (2008) 20(1) *Yale Journal of Law & Feminism* 1.

Fineman MA, 'The vulnerable subject and the responsive state' (2010) 60 *Emory Law Journal* 251.

Fineman MA, '"Elderly" as vulnerable: rethinking the nature of individual and social responsibility' (2012) 20(1) *The Elder Law Journal* 101.

Fineman MA, 'Vulnerability, resilience, and LGBT youth' (2014) 23 *Temple Political & Civil Rights Law Review* 307.

Fineman MA, 'Vulnerability and inevitable inequality' (2017) 4(3) *Oslo Law Journal* 133.

Fineman MA, 'The limits of equality: vulnerability and inevitable inequality' in R West and C Bowman (eds), *Research Handbook on Feminist Jurisprudence* (Edward Elgar 2019).

Gadow S, 'Body and self: a dialectic' (1980) 5(3) *The Journal of Medicine and Philosophy* 172.

Gatens M, *Imaginary Bodies: Ethics, Power and Corporeality* (Routledge 1996).

Gilson E, *The Ethics of Vulnerability: A Feminist Analysis of Social Life and Practice* (Routledge 2013).

Goodin RE, *Protecting the Vulnerable: A Reanalysis of Our Social Responsibilities* (Chicago Press 1986).

Grear A, *Redirecting Human Rights: Facing the Challenges of Corporate Humanity* (Springer 2010).

Hamrouni N, 'Ordinary vulnerability, institutional androgyny, and gender justice' in C Straehle (ed), *Vulnerability, Autonomy and Applied Ethics* (Routledge 2016).

Harris G, *Human Dignity and Vulnerability: Strength and Quality of Character* (University of California Press 1997).

Herring J and Chau P-L, 'My body, your body, our bodies' (2007) 15(1) *Medical Law Review* 34.

Hirschmann N, 'Autonomy? Or freedom? A return to psychoanalytic theory' in A Veltman and M Piper (eds), *Autonomy, Oppression, and Gender* (Oxford University Press 2014).

Holstein M and Minkler M, 'Self, society and the "New Gerontology"' (2003) 43(6) *Gerontologist* 787.

Howarth C, Encountering the ageing body in modernity: fear, vulnerability and "contamination" (2014) 18(3) *Journal for Cultural Research* 233.

Hughes B, McKie L, Hopkins D, and Watson N, 'Love's labours lost? Feminism, the disabled people's movement and an ethic of care' (2005) 39(2) *Sociology* 259.

Ippolito F, '(De)constructing children's vulnerability under European law' in F Ippolito and SI Sánchez (eds), *Protecting Vulnerable Groups: The European Human Rights Framework* (Bloomsbury 2015).

Irigaray L, *To be Two* (Routledge 2001).

Irigaray L, *An Ethics of Sexual Difference* (A & C Black 2005).

Isaksen L, 'Gender and care: the role of cultural ideas of dirt and disgust' in D Morgan, B Brandth and E Kvande (eds) *Gender Bodies and Work* (Ashgate 2005).

Keller C, *From a Broken Web: Separation, Sexism, and Self* (Beacon Press 1986).

Kesby A, 'Narratives of aging and the human rights of older persons' (2017) 18(4) *Human Rights Review* 371.

Kong C, *Mental Capacity in Relationship: Decision-Making, Dialogue, and Autonomy* (Cambridge University Press 2017).

Lawton J, 'Contemporary hospice care: the sequestration of the unbounded body and 'dirty dying'' (1998) 20(2) *Sociology of Health and Illness* 121.

Leece J, 'Paying the piper and calling the tune: Power and the direct payment relationship' (2010) 40(1) *British Journal of Social Work* 188.

Lloyd L, Tanner D, Milne A, Ray M, Richards S, Sullivan MP, Beech C, Phillips J, 'Look after yourself: active ageing, individual responsibility and the decline of social work with older people in the UK' (2014) 17(3) *European Journal of Social Work* 322.

Lloyd M, 'The ethics and politics of vulnerable bodies' in M Lloyd (ed), *Butler and Ethics* (Edinburgh University Press 2015).

Lorraine T, *Irigaray and Deleuze: Experiments in Visceral Philosophy* (Cornell University Press 2018).

Luna F, 'Elucidating the concept of vulnerability: layers not labels' (2009) 2(1) *International Journal of Feminist Approaches to Bioethics* 121.

MacKenzie C and Stoljar N, 'Introduction: Autonomy Refigured' in C MacKenzie and N Stoljar (eds), *Relational Autonomy: Feminist Perspectives on Autonomy, Agency, and the Social Self* (Oxford University Press 2000).

MacKenzie C, 'Relational autonomy, normative authority and perfectionism' (2008) 39(4) *Journal of Social Philosophy* 512.

MacKenzie C, Rogers W, and Dodds S (eds), 'Introduction' in C Mackenzie, W Rodgers, and S Dodds (eds), *Vulnerability: New Essays in Ethics and Feminist Philosophy* (Oxford University Press 2014).

MacKenzie C, 'Responding to the agency dilemma' in Oshana M (ed), *Personal Autonomy and Social Oppression: Philosophical Perspectives* (Routledge 2014).

MacKenzie C, 'Three dimensions of autonomy: a relational analysis' in A Veltman and M Piper (eds), *Autonomy, Oppression, and Gender* (Oxford University Press 2014).

MacKenzie C, 'Vulnerability, needs and moral obligation' in C Straehle (ed), *Vulnerability, Autonomy and Applied Ethics* (Routledge 2016).

Martinson M, 'Opportunities or obligations? Civic engagement and older adults' (2006) 46(3) *Generations* 318.

Moulaert T and Biggs S, 'International and European policy on work and retirement: Reinventing critical perspectives on active ageing and mature subjectivity' (2013) 66(1) *Human Relations* 23.

Neal M, 'Not gods but animals: human dignity and vulnerable subjecthood' (2012) 23 *Liverpool Law Review* 177.

Neal M, 'Respect for human dignity as 'substantive basic norm'' (2014) 10 *International Journal of Law in Context* 26.

Neal M, 'Discovering dignity: unpacking the emotional content of 'killing narratives'' in H Conway and J Stennard (eds), *Emotional Dynamics of Law and Legal Discourse* (Bloomsbury 2016).

Nedelsky J, *Law's Relations. A Relational Theory of Self, Autonomy, and Law* (Oxford University Press 2011).

Newman J, Glendinning C, and Hughes M, 'Beyond modernisation? Social care and the transformation of welfare governance' (2008) 37(4) *Journal of Social Policy* 531.

Noddings N, *Caring, a Feminine Approach to Ethics & Moral Education* (University of California Press 1984).

Noddings N, 'Complexity in caring and empathy' (2010) 6(2) *Abstracta* 6.

Nussbaum M, *The Fragility of Goodness: Luck and Ethics in Greek Tragedy and Philosophy* (Cambridge University Press 2001).

Nussbaum M, 'Human dignity and political entitlements' in President's Council on Bioethics, *Human Dignity and Bioethics: Essays Commissioned by the President's Council on Bioethics* (President's Council on Bioethics 2008).

Nussbaum M, *Frontiers of Justice: Disability, Nationality, Species Membership* (Harvard University Press 2009).

Nussbaum M, *Creating Capabilities: The Human Development Approach* (Harvard University Press 2011).

Oliver S, 'Dehumanization: perceiving the body as (in)human' in Kaufmann K, Kuch C, Webster E (eds), *Humiliation, Degradation, Dehumanization: Human Dignity Violated* (Springer 2011).

Owens J, Mladenov T and Cribb A, 'What justice, what autonomy? The ethical constraints upon personalisation' (2017) 11(1) *Ethics and Social Welfare* 3.

Peroni L and Timmer A, 'Vulnerable groups: The promise of an emerging concept in European Human Rights Convention law' (2013) 11(4) *International Journal of Constitutional Law* 1056.

Riley S, 'Dignity as the absence of the bestial: a genealogy' (2010) 14(2) *Journal for Cultural Research* 143.

Rosen M, *Dignity: Its History and Meaning* (Harvard University Press 2012).

Scarry E, *The Body in Pain: The Making and Unmaking of the World* (Oxford University Press 1985).

Scourfield P, 'Social care and the modern citizen: client, consumer, service user, manager and entrepreneur' (2007) 37(1) *The British Journal of Social Work* 107.

Sensen O, *Kant on Human Dignity* (Walter de Gruyter 2011).

Shakespeare T, *Disability Rights and Wrongs* (Routledge 2006).

Shakespeare T, *Disability Rights and Wrongs Revisited* (2nd ed Routledge 2013).

Shakespeare T, Porter T, and Stockli A, 'Personal Assistance Relationships: Power, Ethics and Emotions' (2017) Report on ESRC Project ES/L007894/1 <https://www.skillsforcare.org.uk/Employing-your-own-care-and-support/Resources/Information-for-local-authorities-NHS-and-support/Reports-and-research/Personal-assistance-relationships-study-June-2017/Personal-assistance-relationships-research-report.pdf> (access 9th August 2019).

Shildrick M, *Embodying the Monster: Encounters with the Vulnerable Self* (Sage 2002).

Shildrick M, *Dangerous Discourses of Disability, Subjectivity and Sexuality* (Springer 2009).

Staehle C, Vulnerability, autonomy and self-respect' in C Straehle (ed), *Vulnerability, Autonomy and Applied Ethics* (Routledge 2016).

Stenbock-Hult B, Sarvimaki A, 'The meaning of vulnerability to nurses caring for older people' (2011) 18(1) *Nursing Ethics* 31.

Stoljar N, 'Informed consent and relational conceptions of autonomy' (2011) 36 *Journal of Medicine and Philosophy* 375.

Straehle C, 'Introduction' in C Straehle (ed), *Vulnerability, Autonomy and Applied Ethics* (Routledge 2016).

Tappolet C, *Emotions, Values, and Agency* (Oxford University Press 2016).

Ten Have H, *Vulnerability: Challenging Bioethics* (Routledge 2016).

Timmer A, 'A quiet revolution: vulnerability in the European Court of Human Rights' in MA Fineman and A Grear (eds), *Vulnerability: Reflections on a New Ethical Foundation for Law and Politics* (Routledge 2016).

Twigg J, *Bathing--the Body and Community Care* (Psychology Press 2002).

Twigg J, *The Body in Health and Social Care* (Macmillan 2006).

Twigg J, Wolkowitz C, Cohen RL, and Nettleton S, 'Conceptualising body work in health and social care' (2011) 33(2) *Sociology of Health & Illness* 171.

Ungerson C, 'Personal assistants and disabled people: An examination of a hybrid form of work and care' (1999) 13(4) *Work, Employment and Society* 583.

Watson N, McKie L, Hughes B, Hopkins D, and Gregory S, '(Inter) dependence, needs and care: the potential for disability and feminist theorists to develop an emancipatory model' (2004) 38(2) *Sociology* 331.

Wiesemann C, 'On the interrelationship of vulnerability and trust' in C Straehle (ed), *Vulnerability, Autonomy and Applied Ethics* (Routledge 2016).

Wolkowitz C, 'The social relations of body work' (2002) 16(3) *Work, Employment and Society* 497.

Wood, R, 'Care of disabled people' in G Dalley (ed), *Disability and Social Policy* (Policy Studies Institute 1991).

Part 1
Family and child law

Part I

Family and child law

Family law's instincts and the relational subject

Alison Diduck

Introduction

There have been many critiques of family law's adoption of norms and principles derived from liberal, market-based positive law. Eekelaar (2006, 2016), for example, suggested in 2006 that the values that ought to inform family law, or personal law, as he would call it, are friendship, truth, respect, responsibility and rights and, in 2016, thought kindness ought to be the primary value in family law. Barlow (2016) argues that family law's discourse ought to be solidarity rather than individuality. In common with others, these scholars criticise family law's recent turn to autonomy as a guiding principle. Feminist critiques in particular highlight the inappropriateness of promoting autonomy in intimate relationships (Herring 2014) not least because its supposed gender-neutral content and gender-blind application tend to disadvantage women (e.g. Herring 2014; Barlow 2016; Diduck 2016). Fineman (2011) goes further and takes the view that the legal subject in all areas ought to be understood as vulnerable rather than autonomous. Others suggest that there is something to be said for autonomy, but that the problem lies in the way it has been conceived and applied (e.g. Mackenzie and Stoljar 2000). They develop the notion of relational autonomy which, although crucial to all areas of law, has particular resonance in family living (e.g. Herring 2014). All of these critiques have in common their rejection of the norms and assumptions which underlie the liberal common law and the legal principles it has engendered.

This chapter offers a reflection on the received canon of the common law and family law's place within it, or indeed, outside it. I aim to provide another challenge to the idea that the problematic principles of the liberal law of the market can be extended justly to family law. Much of my focus will be on the principle of autonomy and its liberal 'other' – vulnerability, and my point of departure is Lord Sumption's speech entitled 'Family law at a distance' delivered to the Royal College of Surgeons in June 2016 wherein he defines for us family law's and the common law's 'instincts'. After suggesting the two are opposed, he makes a case for their melding or at least meeting. He criticises what he sees as family law's unenlightened specialisation or insularity and, to do so, relies upon

a number of assumptions about both the common law and family law. His plea
to loosen the boundaries that he sees family law as creating between itself and
other areas of law relies at the same time upon a whiggish view of legal history,
an ahistorical view of the 'nature' of law and its subjects, and a particular understanding of autonomy that is set in opposition to relationality and vulnerability.
But his is not a particularly controversial perspective; it is the orthodox, liberal
one that has become simply obvious. My comments are not intended therefore
to be a challenge to his Lordship, but rather to that orthodox or standard view.
My aim is not only to contest it; feminist and other critical scholars have been
doing that for a generation. My aim is to challenge its seeming obviousness or
apparent reasonableness as an argument for the continued reach of autonomy in
family law, with its concomitant pursuit of contractualisation and privatisation.
My reflections are feminist; first of all because they challenge the dichotomy
assumed to be inherent in the standard view of autonomy and vulnerability.
Second, they challenge the view's faith in law's coherence, and, thirdly, they
offer a critical rather than liberal view of legal history and where we may be in
that history right now. My reflections also acknowledge the material realities
of gendered family living and family identities rather than neutralising them or
abstracting them away.

As a reminder, here are Lord Sumption's words (pp. 2–3):

> There is, however, a more fundamental reason for deprecating an ex-
> cessively specialised approach. Law is, or at least should be, a coherent
> system. ... The practice of law, whether by judges or advocates, involves
> applying a range of common techniques and common instincts to a variety
> of legal problems. The common techniques are the objective construction
> of legislation and other written instruments, a respect for the body of de-
> cided case-law, and a sensitivity to changing attitudes in the world outside
> the law. The common instincts are those of the common law, which are
> essentially libertarian. They are founded on respect for the autonomy of
> the individual.

He goes on (p. 3):

> Family law is in some respects special. Historically, it was not part of the
> common law, but belonged to the jurisdiction of the ecclesiastical courts.
> Traditionally, its instincts have been very different from those of the com-
> mon law. They were paternalist and protective ... They were an assertion
> of the power of the state in an area of human affairs where the principle of
> autonomy has usually counted for much less.

He then agrees that '[m]odern family law has moved a long way from its origins'
(p. 3). Its instincts he says, 'are not immutable, and the last few years has seen a
convergence between family law and the instincts of the common law.' He uses

Prest v Petrodel Resources Ltd and Others [2013] UKSC 34[1] as one illustration, but says that

> in some ways the most striking pointer to the direction of travel is to be found in the cases about nuptial agreements ... In *Radmacher* the majority of the Supreme Court overtly justified the weight that they attached to them by reference to the principle of autonomy, rejecting the protective approach which had characterised the law administered by family courts for more than a century and a half. 'It would be paternalistic and patronising', they said, 'to override their agreement simply on the basis that the court knows best'.

Here we have his Lordship clarifying for us the 'instincts' of the common law and those of family law. He goes on to make a plea for increased 'cross-fertilisation between different areas of law' and gently chastises family lawyers for seeming to rebuff this enlightened direction of travel: 'The family bar, I think, remains one of the more insular areas of practice. This deprives it of perceptions which would enrich it, as it has enriched other areas of law' (p. 6).

I will break down my reflections into three areas, although they are inter-linked. The first is his Lordship's characterisation of the instincts of the common law and of family law; the second is the lens of evolution, or progress, through which he sees developments in family law over the years, and the third is his normative plea for coherence over all areas of law which ought to be advanced by extending to family law the common law's multipurpose common techniques and legal principles, including principles of autonomy and liberty.

Law's instincts

Lord Sumption's choice of words here is interesting. 'Instinct' is defined in the OED as 'a natural or intuitive way of acting or thinking'. Its synonyms are natural, inherent, unlearned. While this is a surprisingly ahistorical view for a historian like his Lordship to adopt, it comports well with a lawyer's view of the law which identifies human nature and human rationality as the sources of its norms of liberty and autonomy. As many have said, however, and here I will illustrate with Joanne Conaghan's (2013, p. 216) words, there is ample reason to suppose that this framework of modern law 'emerges as the product of a confluence of historical contingencies yielding a particular historically specific instantiation of reason with deep roots in Enlightenment values and aspirations'. Indeed, 'there is a direct correlation between the emergence of liberal, political philosophical ideas premised on values of individual autonomy, freedom of choice and limited state intervention, and the shared human capacity to reason' which has 'clear and significant implications for law' (ibid.). Law has

---

1 And see discussion below p 47.

come to be reason, and reason is defined by what it is not: emotion, esteem, desire, tradition, corporeality.

Further, not only is this enlightenment idea of reason a historical political construction, so is the conception of the autonomous individual who possesses it. The unconnected agent whose 'actions are willed into being' arose at a particular time in history, but has now come to be seen as simply obvious, as natural and instinctual (Anderson and Honneth 2005, p. 128). And finally, liberty – as it has come to be understood in the predominant view – is a negative liberty, the freedom to be left alone. Positive conceptions of liberty, which invoke principles intended to assist individuals to achieve the 'goods' or facilities necessary for well-being or our individually or collectively defined 'good life', are deemed an interference with the autonomy of the individual deemed capable of achieving them on their own. If these principles are applied at all, they are usually restricted to those characterised as 'vulnerable', often with the aim of helping them to achieve autonomy (Diduck 2014, 2016).

My concern with this idea of the common law's 'instincts' is, therefore, both with its supposed content and with its claim to naturalness. There may be much to be said for enlightenment values, but their source in human nature or instinct is not one.

There are as we know, other conceptions of law's subject and its autonomy and liberty which take issue with the standard liberal version. These confirm the value of autonomy, but appeal for law to recognise and value as a part of autonomy an individual's connectedness, relations with others and social location. Rather than seeing the legal subject as an abstract 'everyone and no-one' whose autonomy is expressed by a series of freely made rational choices, these views are firmly rooted in the material world in which abstract individuals become real, embodied individuals who relate to their world with reason but also with emotion, respect, self-reflection and a relationally constructed self that is neither universal nor abstract. '[T]hey point to the need to think of autonomy as a characteristic of agents who are emotional, embodied, desiring, creative, and feeling, as well as rational creatures' (Mackenzie and Stoljar 2000, p. 21).

Relationality is an important part of what the standard view misses in its unquestioned acceptance of enlightenment subjectivity. Again, here I am not saying much that is new; many have written about the importance to justice and to autonomy of our everyday connections and relationships. They share the assumption that 'persons are socially embedded and that agents' identities are formed within the context of social relationships and shaped by a complex of intersecting social determinants, such as race, class, gender, and ethnicity' (Mackenzie and Stoljar 2000, p. 4). As Herring (2010, p. 267) says, 'a relational life is inevitable,' and Nedlesky (2011) argues that relatedness and interdependence are preconditions for autonomy. The autonomous self, as we experience it, emerges from these relationships.

Relational autonomy is therefore the 'label that has been given to alternative conceptions of what it means to be a free, self-governing agent who is also socially constituted and who possibly defines her self and her basic value commitments in terms of inter-personal relations and mutual dependencies' (Christman 2004, p. 143). Relational views of the autonomous person, then, 'underscore the social embeddedness of selves while not forsaking the basic value commitments of (for the most part, liberal) justice. The[y] ... underscore the social components of our self-concepts as well as emphasize the role that background social dynamics and power structures play in the enjoyment and development of autonomy' (ibid.).

These ideas do not reject autonomy outright. Autonomy is an important and fundamental concern for all citizens and all legal subjects, and for women, children and other disenfranchised groups it has particular significance (Diduck 2014). These ideas do, however, challenge the particular understanding of autonomy in the standard view that has come to be understood as instinctual.

Relational autonomy and situational vulnerability

freedom / dependence / the right of self – government ✱

The standard view does not recognise 'the social conditions necessary for the possibility of autonomy, including the need for education, adequate food and shelter, real opportunities for participating in one's (minority) culture and in intimate living and loving, not to mention physical accommodations such as lifts, drive-throughs, wheelchair ramps, accessible vehicles, and so on' (Anderson and Honneth 2005, p. 129). It does not acknowledge our everyday situational realities. A more compassionate and honest way to view humans would, on the other hand, see that our connections and particular social conditions are vital to the development and expression of our autonomy. And more fundamentally, these same connections, conditions and dependencies, which actually constitute our autonomy, also at the same time constitute our vulnerability, our *need* for shelter, education, food, intimate living and the like. Our situational realities, in other words, constitute us as simultaneously autonomous and vulnerable.

And so seeing autonomy differently allows us to see vulnerability differently. Our connectedness with others and our locations within social structures mean that we are always vulnerable, both in the social dynamics and power structures that affect the constitution and enjoyment of our autonomy and in the personal relationships and dependencies we experience. Vulnerability then, like autonomy, is constituted by human relationality; at this conceptual level, it is not a flaw or a weakness that must be remedied, it simply is. Vulnerability is inherent in human relationality and, in this way, is also an essential element of autonomy.

Acknowledging that all are simultaneously autonomous and vulnerable as a result of situations sometimes of our own choosing and sometimes not within our control is realistic. How we experience our autonomy/vulnerability may change over time, place and situation, but in business transactions as much as in families it means that the choices we make are both constrained and enabled by our autonomy/vulnerability. 'Our decisions are not just "ours," they usually affect those we are in relationship with and their decisions will affect others' (Herring 2010, p. 267).

This acknowledgement goes some way towards disrupting a dichotomous view of autonomy/vulnerability; the view that one is either vulnerable or autonomous and cannot at the same time be both (Diduck 2014). It may also tell us something about the common law's supposed 'instincts' which accept the dichotomy and gives those instincts meaning and influence. It may reveal that that dichotomous view of autonomy and vulnerability is in fact a political construction or choice which intentionally or unintentionally supports a legal framework designed for the universal autonomous contractor who, unlike the vulnerable subject, is deemed both politically and legally responsible for their choices and whose liberty requires freedom from state or legal intervention, or 'paternalism' (Diduck 2014). And even if as we know, the common law's 'instincts' are not consistently enacted or reproduced (consider undue influence, unjust enrichment or doctrines of 'good faith' which are simply separated out from contract law's will theory as exceptional [Herring 2014]), they are held up in law's imagination to provide the mutual support neoliberal politics and law offer to each other. In this imagination, the subject's life choices are autonomously and freely made and therefore become their sole responsibility; as Fineman (2011) says, the 'messy' parts of being human are seen as individual rather than social problems.

These challenges to the standard view may also tell us something about family law's so-called instincts, which, according to the standard view, remain both outside the reach of the common law and a 'paternalistic assertion of the power of the state'. Historically, they may have indeed expressed a concern for a certain paternalistic morality and the sacredness of the marital union concern. It seems to me, however, that these concerns, similar to contemporary ones for the welfare of children and for the needs generated by the constitution of family identities and the performance of family roles, actually acknowledge an individual's situational vulnerability. In this way, they do seem removed from the common law's preoccupation almost exclusively with autonomy. But this othering of family law's instincts does not arise for any 'natural' reasons; as I shall discuss in what follows, they are displaced from the common law as a consequence of the same political, structural and historical contingency that created their other, and their displacement in this way supports the political foundations of the common law. Indeed, each side of this, like all dichotomies, needs the other to give it meaning. While autonomy in the common law is linked to independence, liberty and freedom, its 'other' – vulnerability – will always be linked to connection, dependence and care; in other words, to family living. And in this discourse, where dependence and vulnerability are pathetic, conditions always to be eliminated or mitigated, we see the argument for their elimination from family law.

But we can label family law's 'instincts' in contrast to those of 'real' law pejoratively, as pathetic and patronising, or we can say that like those other legal principles that are seen as 'exceptional' they actually reflect a more realistic and humane instinct that accepts a non-oppositional view of autonomy/vulnerability. First of all, they acknowledge that the autonomy of family members is exercised by agents with the capacity for self-determination, but whose autonomy is also characterised by their situational relatedness or vulnerability (*Miller v Miller; McFarlane v McFarlane* [2006] UKHL 34, per Baroness Hale [138]):

> Even dual career families are difficult to manage with completely equal opportunity for both. Compromises often have to be made by one so that the other can get ahead. All couples throughout their lives together have to make choices about who will do what, sometimes forced upon them by circumstances such as redundancy or low pay, sometimes freely made in the interests of them both.

Another example is in the context of parenthood, where we see a degree of autonomy exercised by increasing numbers of women who choose to raise a child on their own. These 'autonomous mothers' (Boyd et al. 2015, pp. 14–15) may be able to achieve a degree of autonomy over their lives and decisions and 'forge a space for their self-defined families', but they, like all parents, invariably rely upon numerous different support networks, from friends and family to social and public supports. Motherhood, particularly autonomous motherhood, is a 'relationship within larger social and economic structures' that both 'enable and constrain' the simultaneous autonomy and vulnerability of mothers and their children (ibid., 20). Reece (2013) notes also the ways in which parents are often advised to make their own independent and personal parenting decisions, while at the same time being influenced by external factors. Parents are encouraged, for example, to 'reclaim the first-person perspective, which means that for the parent, any judgement about what to do in a particular situation is inseparable from the fact that the decision concerns his or her own child' while at the same time other advice 'stress[es] the inter-subjective nature of the enterprise, be it with one's own child or other parents (ibid., 51).

But there may be more, and it is suggested by Reece's observations. I have written before about the importance of recognition for claims to justice in family law drawing upon Nancy Fraser's links between recognition and redistribution (Diduck 2009). The cultural or recognitional value we place on individuals, groups, actions and so on is as crucial a part of justice as is redistribution of economic resources and has similar concrete material consequences. Here there may be another aspect of recognition to consider.

Relational autonomy and recognitional vulnerability

Anderson and Honneth (2005, p. 130) offer a way of understanding autonomy that adds an internal focus that they call recognitional. They claim that one's ability to lead one's own life, to be autonomous, is dependent on one's being supported by relations of recognition. The central idea, they say, is that

> the competencies that comprise autonomy require that one be able to sustain certain attitudes toward oneself (in particular, self-trust, self-respect, and self-esteem) and that these self-conceptions are dependent, in turn, on

the sustaining attitudes of others. One's relationship to oneself, then, is not a matter of a solitary ego reflecting on itself, but is the result of an ongoing *intersubjective* process, in which one's attitude toward oneself emerges in one's encounter with an other's attitude toward oneself.

To them, self-trust, self-respect and self-esteem are fundamental parts of what make us human and the intersubjective process of developing them is necessary for a fully developed autonomy. On this view, 'others' attitudes towards us can profoundly affect our autonomous agency by supporting or undermining our sense of self' (Anderson 2014, p. 140). Where they undermine that sense of self they constitute threats to autonomy and justice demands they be mitigated.

Anderson (ibid., 139) later develops the idea that these relations of recognition which are partly constitutive of autonomy also make us vulnerable to the attitudes of others and means that there is a sense in which 'autonomy and vulnerability are entwined' and not oppositional. As he states, 'the more clear it becomes that autonomy depends on intersubjective conditions, the less clear it becomes how there can be a straightforward opposition between autonomy and vulnerability.'

To accept that autonomy and vulnerability are 'entwined' in Anderson's words, or simultaneous, does not, of course, absolve society or law from the responsibility to mitigate some harmful experiences of vulnerability. But it may mean that there are good reasons to acknowledge that the inevitable vulnerability that is entwined with recognitional autonomy can be seen in some situations as a morally, socially and politically valuable feature of human life. First of all, '[r]ealising autonomy as an ideal of personal agency *requires* certain forms of vulnerability' (ibid., 135, my emphasis). Secondly and importantly, the social relations of mutual recognition on which the conditions of self-realisation turn 'include intimate relationships (e.g., marriages, families, close friendships), societal structures in which equal standing is secured by the rule of law, and solidaristic communities within which individuals can secure a basic sense of belonging and worth' (ibid., 142). Engaging with and not withdrawing from these relations of recognition is an important part of the human experience that a relational understanding of autonomy/vulnerability accepts. Indeed, this vulnerability is 'part and parcel of what makes those practices particularly valuable, rewarding, and autonomy enhancing' (ibid., 136).

Straehle (2017, p. 34) also argues that there is a type of self-constituting vulnerability, linked to autonomy, that falls outside the 'vulnerability as harm to autonomy' model. She proposes that the vulnerability that comes with love not only provides emotional and psychological gains but also 'helps us to constitute ourselves as agents in the world'.

On these views, family law's so-called exceptional instincts may reflect therefore not only the connectedness and *situational* autonomy that simultaneously incorporate inevitable situational vulnerability but also a *recognitional* autonomy that itself also incorporates vulnerability. Despite family law's recent moves to de-gender and abstract its subjects – for example, we see consistently that family members see themselves in these relational ways – family members rarely understand themselves to be either abstract and autonomous subjects or completely vulnerable subjects. They come to law as mothers (e.g. Kaganas and Day Sclater 2004), fathers (e.g. Collier 2001a, 2001b), husbands and wives (e.g. Diduck 2011), civil partners (e.g. Auchmuty 2016) and cohabitants (e.g. Barlow and Smithson 2010) who make choices about their family lives, but who are located within their situational and relational, cultural and structural conditions that both enable and constrain those choices. More than that, however, their very selves – their subjectivities as mothers, fathers and so on – are also formed within those relations.

The complex autonomous/vulnerable family law subject on this view is shaped by one's self-respect, self-trust and self-esteem as they are developed, sustained or impaired by cultural/institutional recognition and the recognition of others. Self-respect, for example, can be impaired or empowered by potentially a number of factors, including subordination, marginalisation and exclusion or inclusion and institutional respect (Anderson and Honneth 2005, p. 132). Self-esteem, determining the worth of one's self and one's activities, is framed within 'a whole constellation of evaluatively loaded ways of talking' (ibid., 136). Self-trust, so necessary for autonomy, but also developed through relationships of vulnerability, is born of and facilitated or impaired by the love and openness of connection with others (ibid., 135).

These claims implicate both intimacy and the social and institutional roles cast for and the value conferred upon becoming a particular family law subject, such as homemaker or breadwinner (Diduck 2009), father (Collier 2001), lesbian co-parent (Diduck 2007) or autonomous mother (Boyd et al. 2015). Living these family identities not only has material consequences; the recognitional value placed upon them also profoundly affects relation-to-self and therefore one's autonomy/vulnerability. When homemaking or care, for example, are devalued, we see the effect on property and financial settlements on divorce (Diduck 2009). When same-sex families are devalued, we see non-recognition legally of parental status (Diduck 2007). What we may not see, however, but which may be equally important, is that the subjecthood, the complex autonomy/vulnerability of a full-time middle-class mother is affected by recognitional factors, as is that of the 'good' father (Collier and Sheldon 2008), the lone mother (Barlow and Duncan 2000; Boyd et al. 2015) or the lesbian co-parent (Diduck 2007). Their very selves are formed in part by institutional recognition and the recognition of others, including other aspects defined by Anderson and Honneth, such as social and cultural marginalisation, exclusion, evaluatively loaded ways of talking and strength of openness of connection with others. In other words, intersubjective recognition, including the vulnerability that comes with love relationships and institutional cultural/recognitional patterns of valuation, affects not only one's choices made as a parent, or partner, but may also affect the constitution of one's very self or autonomy/vulnerability as a mother, father, husband, wife or civil partner.

While the autonomy/vulnerability of all legal subjects is shaped in part by intersubjective recognition and situational reality, family law, by defending the distinctiveness of its so-called protective instinct, may be one area of law that is still able to – and still wants to – acknowledge and do something about the way that autonomy/vulnerability is experienced by its subjects. In this way, it corrects the standard common law's misunderstanding of autonomy that requires both context- and identity-stripping in order to be able to identify family law subjects as either equal, invulnerable autonomous subjects or always vulnerable subjects. It also corrects the problematic universal certainty created about family relations that is gender- and hetero-normative in which kinship based upon genetics is rendered natural and choices about the organisation of family life are rendered 'autonomous'. Family law pays attention to the complex autonomy and vulnerability of actual parents, children and partners. So, it may be true that the standard view sees family law historically as 'an assertion of the power of the state in an area of human affairs where the principle of autonomy has usually counted for much less'. But that may not always be a bad thing, not because it protects an outdated and patriarchal morality, sentimentality or specious separation of the privacy of family from the coldness, individuality and liberty-based justice of the public sphere and the market, but rather because it recognises the structural and material consequences of (gendered and heteronormative) family living and promotes a more realistic and humane understanding of autonomy and vulnerability. There are thus important particularities about the realities of family living, which its law wants to see, but which are becoming increasingly unacceptable as that law is forced through the standard lens.

Family law's history

The history family law does owe something to ecclesiastical law, as his Lordship told us, at least as far as marriage, nullity and divorce are concerned. But it owes as much, if not more, to the law of the household, of husband and wife and of master and servant: the law of domestic relations, which was always about production and distribution as much as it was about sacred relationships, love and care. Halley (2011a, p. 1; 2011b) offers in her genealogy of family law a review of the ideological conditions that facilitated the renaming and reconstruction of the law of domestic relations as family law, suggesting that family law today is what it is by virtue of its categorical distinction from contract and market but that each needs the other to exist.

'Life at home was once lived in a household,' she writes with Kerry Rittich (2010, p. 756), 'an explicitly economic unit housing both human reproduction and material production as well as a complex array of legal relationships. ... Slaves, indentured servants, and contract servants were as much a part of the household as husbands and wives. Food was not only cooked and eaten in the household, it was grown there; thread was spun and cloth woven there.' The household was a place of residence *and* of industry made up of people within and outside what later became the nuclear ideal, including apprentices, servants, parents and children.

Halley and Rittich (ibid.) go on, writing about families in the United States:

> Market modernization involved the breakup of these large semi-public spaces and the segregation of their functions into the notorious separate spheres. Productive work for pay moved out of the home, both in social life and in legal taxonomy. The law of master and servant – formerly adjunct to the law of husband and wife and the law of parent and child – gradually dissolved. Slavery and indentured servitude were abolished, and the legal relations governing employment, even where they retained vestiges of the master servant relationship, were transmuted and reframed within the law of contract.

Similar changes occurred in England. Lifecycle service and apprenticeship, once seen as providing both education and family status for adolescent men and women, changed with early marketization and industrialisation. When production moved from the household to the market, the factory or the shop, employers sought a less personal relationship with their workers and those relations became governed by a marketised exchange. Service work in the household became stigmatised as 'declasse', and the family's relation with those who remained in such work ceased being familial and became contractual (Cooper 2005), leaving only the husband and wife and the parent and child 'in the newly private, intimate, and affective space of the home' (Halley and Rittich 2010, p. 57).

And so, the consequent 'separation of the law of familial intimacy from the law of productive labour coincided with, among other things, the emergence of a market for labour, an ideology of laissez faire for the market and an ideology of domestic intimacy that was articulated as the opposite of the market' (Halley 2011a, pp. 2–3).

'Contract and tort [thus] became the law of everyone, – the faceless individual of liberalism – while the law of marriage became the law of special persons – abnormal persons' (ibid., 3). This idea of what Halley (ibid.) then labels 'family law exceptionalism', the law different from that meant for the rational individualistic and morally neutral market, was 'an intrinsic', not merely accidental, or natural, part of the emerging legal order. The law of contract, will theory, became the foundation of the common law and emblematic of progress rendering the law of marriage as status not contract as exceptional, yet fundamental to this new legal order (ibid., 94–95). Importantly, this separation also meant that 'all the ways in which contract law fosters solidarity and family law enables individual freedom are ruled out from the start.' As Halley goes on to (2011b, p. 291) say, 'this is a serious descriptive deficit. Even worse, it ratifies neoliberal fantasies about the freedom of contract' – autonomy and liberty.

A central point of Halley's (ibid., 288) genealogy 'is that the family/market, status/contract, marriage/contract distinction is not a natural or inevitable part of our legal order or even our legal consciousness. Humans invented it, and over time they have bestowed it with an array of ideological significances and deployed it for ever-changing ends.' Moreover, the two sides of the dichotomy are mutually sustaining. She cites Kennedy who argues that 'the characterization of marriage as status-not-contract both relieved contract of the values of regulation, paternalism, community and informality and cabined them in marriage (Halley 2011a, p. 86).

It is within this 'normative frame' that we see the emergence of the 'instincts' of the common law, in which 'doctrinal elaborations of contract and property law are understood as neutral and facilitative, merely providing background support for the free pursuit of individual transactions minimally constrained by law' (Conaghan 2013, p. 110). We see also those of family law which become the exceptional, abnormal law in which morality, regulation and paternalism are said to reign.

While Halley and other family law historians challenge both the naturalness and descriptive accuracy of this form of family law exceptionalism – family law was and still is connected to the market, to productivity, to social security, and to the distribution of economic resources – others challenge the narrative of progress in which family law then came to be understood, including its slow but positive move from morality and status to freedom and contract. This narrative says that while it is still seen as exceptional, family law has abandoned its status-based 'historical practices grounded in subordination and injustice' (Hasday 2014, p. 95). But critical legal historians 'focus on discontinuity rather than continuity' and 'disrupt any notion that law evolves in a natural, or conceptually coherent manner' (Conaghan 2013, p. 117). They challenge the normative idea of 'development'.

And so, Hasday (2014, p. 96) argues that the narrative of progress overstates both the extent and the nature of family law's historical transformations and underemphasises and obscures continuity in family law doctrines, practices and policies. The narrative of transformation permits decision-makers to 'direct attention away from persistent disparities and injustices, on the ground that family law has already left its support for problematic policies safely in the past'. For example, coverture's demise celebrates family law's commitment to sex equality and allows decision-makers to invoke the demise as an argument against focusing on the continued disparities, socially and legally, between men and women in families. They assume that the end of coverture is the same thing as women's legal, political and social equality, and so 'family law merely has to assume that equality rather than work to protect it' (ibid., 104). She points out, however, that the roots of coverture still shape the field. One example is family law's refusal to interfere in the finances of 'intact' families; it is for the household to decide how to allocate its wealth among its members, even though this usually gives that authority to the money earner. Another example of the narrative of progress obscuring problematic continuity is family law's recognition of same-sex parents, which is said to promote equality for non-normative families but which remains coupled with law's heteronormative insistence that a child may have only two legal parents (and one legal mother) at one time.

On the flipside, overemphasising the move from status to contract is problematic for two reasons: 'descriptively it is not always accurate and normatively it contains the presumption that [undertheorized] contract rules are better that status rules' (Hasday 2014). At the descriptive, doctrinal level, for example, marital or civil partnership status is what gives the courts discretion over financial settlements (even where it may not be wanted [Auchmuty 2016]), and parental status hugely affects determinations about the welfare of children (Hasday 2014). And at the normative level, we have seen that these elements of 'status' shape both the formation of family law's autonomous/vulnerable husbands, wives, mothers and fathers and their exercise of agency. The assumption that the abstract contractual subject is 'better' or more progressive discourages family law from recognizing its subjects' complex autonomy/ vulnerability.

Lifshitz (2012, p. 54) observes that the narrative of progress in family law contains three elements. It is interesting that they each eschew any elements of relationality and the autonomy/vulnerability it engenders. The first is privatisation, the retreat of the state and its values or 'paternalism' in favour of the individual. The second is the move from the family as the unit of concern to the individual, who is no longer viewed as a family member but as an abstract autonomous entity, and the third is the assumption of the achievement of gender equality.

We see all the elements of this narrative of progress in Lord Sumption's plea for family law's continued evolution towards the liberal ideal. But again, these moves are choices law has made rather than progressive developments that arose organically. More than that they are political-legal choices that often disadvantage some family members at the expense of others. While law must recognise the autonomy and agency of its subjects, we have seen that that autonomy can be seen as complex and entwined with both situational and recognitional vulnerability. Many argue, for example, that a move towards privatisation is retrogressive rather than progressive; the courts, the public gaze of the law and the social and legal values they impart (the rule of law or paternalism?), must be able to influence what justice means in intimate relationships (Eekelaar 2011; Diduck 2016). Further, there is some advantage not only to family law but to all law, acknowledging its subjects' 'status', in the sense of their situational and recognitional autonomous and vulnerable selves, rather than treating them as independent abstract entities removed from situational and recognitional relations. And finally, we must not accept the part of the narrative that says that the relationship between law and its patriarchal past is reducible to a simple before and after; gender still 'operates in law in other than formal categorical terms' (Conaghan 2013, p. 114; see, for example, Barlow 2015; Diduck 2016). It influences both situational and recognitional autonomy/vulnerability.

What we have in the narrative of historical progress, therefore, is an admonishment for family law to get in step, to ignore its gendered and particularised autonomous/vulnerable subjects in the way the common law ignores them as its standard ideas of autonomy and vulnerability come to define progress, fairness and justice.

If family law history tells us anything, however, it is, as Martha Minow (1985, p. 893) says, that 'the unfolding story of family law is not over.' Her study of women in family law history found 'complicated relationships between autonomy and connection' and 'offer[s] an additional source of criticism for the traditional history of family law' which 'treats autonomous rights-bearing individualism as the destiny of progress'. This traditional story 'fails to protect or advance an equally plausible view of the self as interdependent: needing others, and needing to be needed ... [which] seems to have animated the activities of women in their domestic and reform roles. Locating each individual within social networks, roles connecting with others, this alternate conception maintains that membership helps to constitute the "I," and belonging is essential to becoming' (ibid., 894).

Law's coherence (and cross-fertilisation to that end)

So far, I have examined the standard view that family law's and the common law's instincts are oppositional and that family law's history can be characterised as one of progress towards a liberal ideal. The other part of the standard view set out by Lord Sumption restates the descriptive and normative claims of law's coherence, consistency and rationality. On this view, legal decisions must be seen to make sense in 'the broader fabric of the legal order' in which they, or more particularly, their 'justification, coheres with – does not contradict, undermine or render out of place – the kinds of justificatory norms which have already found institutional acceptance; they must fit within the broad frames of those norms' (Conaghan 2013, p. 220). But, feminist and other critical analysis questions law's coherence; it reveals inconsistencies, contingencies and contradictions. It is concerned, as Lacey (1998, p. 11) says, 'to reconstruct the pretension to coherence' as part of the ideology of law's claim to authority, philosophical integrity and doctrinal legitimacy. Revelation and reconstruction must take place at the level of doctrine and at the prior level of the constitution of the subjects who are inserted into the doctrinal framework. One example of contradiction is the way in which the 'family' is perceived in law. At the same time as the family became the only legitimate repository for love and feelings and an increasingly private institution into which state intervention was abhorred, it 'suffered' from the intervention of state or moral values unlike the neutral freedom from such values said to inhere in the market.

Another example may be the way law deals with the family home. The family home is infused with different layers of meaning that render it incomprehensible in its entirety to either family or property law. To property law, the family home is fundamentally an item of capital. It is a commercial asset, interests in it and the value of which are measured in money. Property *law* is about the realisation of that value according to objective – market concerns; it is about rights, entitlements and arm's-length transactions. Any intangible, personal and sentimental value inherent in the property as a 'home' is meaningless to property law (Fox 2002, 2006) and so is disregarded: 'Only if an object is stripped of its particularity and history can it become a commodity and an exchange value. From the perspective of property [law], any value other than exchange value is *sentimental* value, a value of which the object must be stripped if it is to be freely exchanged on the market' (Stallybrass 1998, p. 195).

On the other hand, family is all about particularities, histories, emotions and sentiment. Family *law* is about the exercise of discretion and the assessment of justice in the light of these particularities. It claims to take into account intangibles such as love, sentiment and power. Family law subjects (like all subjects) have, as we have seen, a particular connection to each other and to their situational conditions, including their home that is more than a rights-based or marketised one. Their connections may be biological, emotional, historical, sexual, spiritual or psychological; they may be rooted in empathy, sympathy, compassion, duty, love or hate, but they reside outside the paradigmatic legal relationship to other persons or property.

And yet, while the principles of property law and family law may seem to be opposed, there may be less purity in each than appears at first blush. If it is true that 'sentimental' or non-legal attachments apply not only between people but also between people and possessions, including home, then they, like our other relations, also render us vulnerable to external happenings, and are a part of what contributes to a flourishing autonomous life. Our property is ours to dispose of as we wish; it has a market value, but it also has other important values. Both our autonomy and our vulnerability are in part constituted, and affected, by our relations with our possessions.[2]

Some cherished possessions, particularly 'home', might be seen as an expression of, or become bound up with, our sense of self. The work done on the meaning of the 'home' for elderly persons who lack legal capacity shows that the home is a 'meaningful context' that 'shapes and maintains seniors' self-identities' (Bedford 2018). The importance of home to seniors, but also, I would suggest, to all who feel it, is expressed in *Re: GC* [2008] EWHC 3402 (Fam), para 21: 'there is often an importance in place which is not generally recognised by others; not only physical place but also the relational structure that is associated with a place....' The literature on wills as narrative also points to how cherished possessions are not to be measured only in their

---

2 I am grateful to the editors for this discussion on sentimental relationship with possessions. As they note, this view contrasts with a more Kantian notion that would seek to protect our agency against the threats generated by emotional attachments.

economic value but also in the way that certain types of properties are part of the way we 'constitute ourselves as continuing personal entities in the world'. They carry memories, create connections to others and express who we are (Gordon 2017).

These observations on the way in which relations to property may constitute both autonomy and vulnerability are reflected in the ways that both property law and family law deal with 'home'. Sometimes property law attempts to recognise more than market rights and sees a subjective quality in 'home' to say that the family home is more than real estate, the value of which is measured solely in terms of the market. A non-titled spouse's occupancy of the marital home, for example, is a registerable interest in the property,[3] recognising that relations to another can create relationships to property. And, Article 8 of the European Convention on Human Rights demands recognition of a form of privacy and integrity that comes with 'home', rather than only of financial interests in it (*Qazi v London Borough of Harrow* [2003] 3 WLR 792, per Lord Bingham [8]). Article 8 has also successfully been invoked when the scope for one enjoying the *amenities* of home were affected, including the personal security and well-being it offers (*Hatton and Others v UK*, ECtHR, 8 July 2003; *Karner v Austria*, ECtHR, 24 July 2003). These relations – these situational and recognitional vulnerabilities – here become a part of the autonomy protected by human rights and property law.

And when family law deals specifically with the home, it knows it is dealing with irrationalities and is about recognising relationships and 'statuses'. Even an unmarried, nonregistered cohabitant's occupation of the family home in which they have no interest can be protected in situations of domestic violence.[4] But family law is also about taming the irrationalities of family living, in part by demanding conformity to institutional norms such as the market-based property rhetoric which is assumed to have a regularising effect upon those irrationalities, so, a non-entitled domestic violence victim's occupation of the family home is intended to be temporary, only.[5] Consider further the classic *Mesher* order (*Mesher v Mesher and Hall* [1980] 1 All ER 126). While promoting the welfare of the child and her caregiver by protecting their occupancy of and connection to the family home during a time of emotional, psychological stress, it merely postpones the sale of the home because as Thorpe LJ reminds us (*Dart v Dart* [1996] 2 FLR 286, p. 294):

> The scheme of the [MCA 1973] must also be set in the wider perspective of history and the general civil law. In this jurisdiction rights of property are not invaded or reduced by statutory powers save for specific and confined purposes.

3 Family Law Act 1996 s 31.
4 Family Law Act 1996 s 36.
5 In the case of cohabitants or former cohabitants, see Family Law Act 1996 s 36(10).

My point in reviewing these examples is the relatively uncontroversial one that family law and property law already are not as 'pure' as they are held out to be. Each contains elements or traces of the other so that as legal categories they are not closed. There are contradictions, contingencies and more open boundaries than may appear at first blush. These examples challenge formal law's claims to ontological and epistemological coherence and integrity and the standard view's accusation of family law's self-imposed segregation from it.

Once we reveal inconsistencies that can challenge law's pretence to coherence we can see that accusations of family law's divergence from a norm which is said to harm that coherence, and pleas for cross-fertilisation to promote it, fall away. Instead, we see not so much a plea for the enriching sharing of 'instincts' or principles (which occurs anyway), but rather for the wholesale colonisation of family law by those liberal precepts of autonomy, liberty and formal equality that have achieved longstanding institutional acceptance and thus have come to form 'the broad fabric of the legal order'. Recall Lord Sumption's words in the *Prest* case, para 37:

> The language of this provision [s. 24(1)(a) of the Matrimonial Causes Act] is clear. It empowers the court to order one party to the marriage to transfer to the other 'property to which the first-mentioned party is entitled, either in possession or reversion'. An 'entitlement' is a legal right in respect of the property in question. The words 'in possession or reversion' show that the right in question is a proprietary right, legal or equitable. This section is invoking concepts with an established legal meaning and recognised legal incidents under the general law. Courts exercising family jurisdiction do not occupy a desert island in which general legal concepts are suspended or mean something different.

In other words, his Lordship is directing the traffic only one way. In the uncritical narrative of liberal progress towards a coherent and 'whole' law, all law should evolve to look like 'real', instinctual, progressive law and all legal subjects should become the autonomous 'everyone and no one' of contract law. In the name of 'coherence', this move would bring a normalcy to abnormal, exceptional, family law and its abnormal, exceptional subjects. On this view, while family law's departure from the norm may once have been understandable, it is now seen as old-fashioned, as a primitive law from which we should have progressed.

But if we accept the idea that vulnerability/autonomy is universal then perhaps the enriching sharing of ideas can move the other way as well, as it already does, but now more honestly and comprehensively. Family law's understanding of its 'status' based on autonomous/vulnerable subject could inform all law, for example. But even this is not a plea for another version of coherence in law. While all relations create autonomous/vulnerable subjects, their autonomy/

vulnerability changes from time to time and from situation to situation, and family living creates specific kinds of autonomy/vulnerability that do not arise in other contexts. If we accept that contingency, contradiction and inconsistency are real and normal, this family-related particularity should not be a problem for law. There may therefore be a place in law for all contingent types of autonomy/vulnerability, including for those that inhere especially in intimate, and usually gendered, family relationships. On this view, family law is not an atypical, exceptional law; rather, it is just another part of all contingent and complicated law.

What family law can do, in other words, is reframe the 'accepted legal order' so that the 'logic of family living' becomes 'embedded and ordinary', rather than continuing to be seen as exceptional or extraordinary (Sverdrup 2015, p. 246).

Concluding thoughts on family law's instincts or 'exceptionalism'

It seems to me that family relationships and family law are distinctive, but not for the reasons and in the way they were rendered exceptional in the historical narrative that reinforces the standard view of the public/private, autonomy/vulnerability distinctions. They are distinctive in a new legal logic that resides in an autonomy/vulnerability discourse. If in every relationship and every transaction we are both situationally and recognitionally vulnerable/autonomous, then the standard view already continues injustice to the marginalised, the subjugated and the excluded, but to extend that view and its common instincts to family relationships would compound that injustice due to the particular autonomy/vulnerability inherent in family living.

I may at this point appear to be making a contradictory argument. On the one hand I am saying, like Halley, that the separation of family law from the law of the market was the result of human-made historical conditions that have resulted in a descriptively inaccurate state of affairs that is ideologically problematic. And, like Halley and Rittich (2010, p. 754), I see family law exceptionalism as both real and a fantasy. It can be deployed to support spurious claims 'that family law (or marriage, or "the family") should be different because of the unique, special, crucial, affective, altruistic, social-ordering, and/or sacred nature of the relationships that it houses' which accept the problematic conception of autonomy and legal relations that relational autonomy/vulnerability rejects. On the other hand, I think a case for accepting family law's distinctiveness, if not exceptionalism, can be based upon the liberatory possibility of promoting and protecting family law's concern to understand the gendered, heteronormative and material realities of family living and the particular situational and recognitional autonomy/vulnerability of its subjects.

The problematic 'instincts' of the common law were developed for relationships that were separated from family ones and indeed were counter-posed to them. They were thought to be inapplicable to the sacred, altruistic and patriarchal family. The claim is that now that family law has moved beyond that view of the family, it should fit itself within the common law's instincts. My point has been that family lawyers must think carefully about this move. The standard liberal 'instincts' of individualism, privatisation and liberty and the narratives of progress and coherence that come with them are based upon problematic presumptions of equality and liberty and impoverished ideas of autonomy and vulnerability. Family lawyers might also think carefully about accepting a characterisation of its law's 'instincts' as paternalistic and patronising. Rather its instincts to acknowledge complex autonomy/vulnerability could be characterised instead as 'sensible and realistic' (*Radmacher v Granatino* [2010] UKSC 42, per Lady Hale [135]), as what gives it its ability to understand and correct generational and gender-based disadvantages that arise from family living. Even in market situations, the standard view can exclude and disadvantage entire categories of people, but the plea in the name of progress and coherence to extend it to family law might give many family lawyers cause for concern.

Bibliography

Anderson J, 'Autonomy and vulnerability entwined' in C Mackenzie, W Rogers and S Dodds (eds), *Vulnerability: New Essays in Ethics and Feminist Philosophy* (Oxford University Press 2014).

Anderson J and Honneth A 'Autonomy, vulnerability, recognition, and justice' in J Christman and J Anderson (eds), *Autonomy and the Challenges to Liberalism New Essays* (Cambridge University Press 2005).

Auchmuty R, 'The experience of civil partnership dissolution: *not* "just like divorce"' (2016) 38 *Journal of Social Welfare and Family Law* 152.

Barlow A 'Solidarity, autonomy and equality: mixed messages for the family?' (2015) 27 *Child and Family Law Quarterly* 215.

Barlow A and Duncan S, 'New labour's communitariansim, supporting families and the "rationality mistake": part I' (2000) 22 *Journal of Social Welfare and Family Law* 23.

Barlow A and Smithson J, 'Legal assumptions, cohabitants' talk and the rocky road to reform' (2010) 22 *Child and Family Law Quarterly* 328.

Bedford D, 'Embracing vulnerability in ageing: *'our route to* flourishing?' in B Clough and J Herring (eds), *Ageing, Gender and Family Law* (Routledge 2018).

Boyd SB, Chunn DE, Kelly F and Wiegers W, *Autonomous Motherhood? A Socio-Legal Study of Choice and Constraint* (University of Toronto Press 2015).

Christman J, 'Relational autonomy, liberal individualism and the social constitution of selves' (2004) 117 *Philosophical Studies* 143.

Collier R, 'A hard time to be a father? Law, policy and family practices' (2001) 28 *Journal of Law and Society* 520.

Collier R, 'In search of the "good father": law, family practices and the normative reconstruction of parenthood' (2001) 22 *Studies in Law, Politics and Society* 133.

Collier R and Sheldon S, *Fragmenting Fatherhood. A Socio-Legal Study* (Hart 2008).

Conaghan J, *Law and Gender* (Oxford University Press 2013).

Cooper SM, 'Service to servitude? The decline and demise of life-cycle service in England' (2005) 10 *The History of the Family* 367.

Diduck A, *Law's Families* (Cambridge University Press 2003).

Diduck A, '"If only we can find the appropriate terms to use the issue will be solved": law, identity and parenthood' (2007) 19 *Child and Family Law Quarterly* 458.

Diduck A, 'Relationship fairness' in A Bottomley and S Wong (eds), *Changing Contours of Domestic Life, Family and Law. Caring and Sharing* (Hart Publishing 2009).

Diduck A 'Ancillary relief: complicating the search for principle' (2011) 38(2) *Journal of Law and Society* 272.

Diduck A, 'Autonomy and vulnerability in family law: the missing link' in J Wallbank and J Herring (eds), *Vulnerabilities, Care and Family Law* (Routledge 2014).

Diduck A, 'Autonomy and family justice' (2016) 28 *Child and Family Law Quarterly* 133.

Eekelaar J, *Family Law and Personal Life* (Oxford University Press 2006).

Eekelaar J, '"Not of the highest importance": family justice under threat' (2011) 33 *Journal of Social Welfare and Family Law* 311.

Eekelaar J, 'Family law and love' (2016) 28 *Child and Family Law Quarterly* 289.

Fineman MA, 'The vulnerable subject: anchoring equality in the human condition' in M A Fineman (ed), *Transcending the Boundaries of Law* (Routledge 2011).

Fox L, 'The meaning of home: a chimerical concept or a legal challenge?' (2002) 29 *Journal of Law and Society* 580.

Fox L, *Conceptualising Home* (Hart 2006).

Gordon DS, 'Mor[t]ality and identity: Wills, narratives, and cherished possessions' (2017) 28(2) *Yale Journal of Law & the Humanities* 265.

Halley J, 'What is family law?: a genealogy part I' (2011) 23(1) *Yale Journal of Law and the Humanities* 1.

Halley J, 'What is family law?: a genealogy part II' (2011) 23(2) *Yale Journal of Law and the Humanities* 189.

Halley J and Rittich K 'Introduction to critical directions in comparative family law: genealogies and contemporary studies of family law exceptionalism' (2010) 58 *American Journal of Comparative Law* 753.

Hasday JE, *Family Law Reimagined* (Harvard University Press 2014).

Herring J, 'Relational autonomy and family law' in J Wallbank, S Choudhry and J Herring (eds), *Rights, Gender and Family Law* (Routledge Cavendish 2010).

Herring J, *Relational Autonomy and Family Law* (Springer 2014).

Kaganas F and Day Sclater S, 'Contact disputes: narrative constructions of "good" parents' (2004) 12 *Feminist Legal Studies* 1.

Lacy N, *Unspeakable Subjects. Feminist Essays in Legal and Social Theory* (Hart 1998).

Lifshitz S, 'The liberal transformation of spousal law: past, present and future' (2012) 13 *Theoretical Inquires in Law* 15.

Mackenzie C and Stoljar N, 'Autonomy refigured' in C Mackenzie and N Stoljar (eds), *Relational Autonomy Feminist Perspectives on Autonomy, Agency and the Social Self* (Oxford University Press 2000).

Minow M, '"Forming underneath everything that grows": toward a history of family law' (1985) 4 *Wisconsin Law Review* 819.

Nedelsky J, *Law's Relations a Relational Theory of Self, Autonomy and Law* (Oxford University Press 2011).

Reece H, 'The pitfalls of positive parenting' (2013) 8 *Ethics and Education* 42.

Stallybrass P (1998) 'Marx's coat' in P Spyer (ed) *Border Fetishisms: Material Objects in Unstable Spaces* (Routledge 1998).

Straehle C, 'Vulnerability, autonomy and self-respect' in C Straehle (ed), *Vulnerability, Autonomy and Applied Ethics* (Routledge 2017).

Sverdrup T, 'Family solidarity and the mindset of private law' (2015) 27 *Child and Family Law Quarterly* 237.

Response

Reflections on 'family law's instincts': law's varied relationship with the vulnerabilities of family law's children

Jo Bridgeman

Family law's children

In her examination of vulnerability and family law, Alison Diduck focuses upon vulnerability as a challenge to the dominant norm of the legal subject as autonomous. Alison draws on the scholarship of Martha Fineman (2011, 46) who has argued that, in contrast to autonomy, which only those with certain characteristics attain, vulnerability is inherent and thus universal. As humans our vulnerability, according to Martha Fineman (ibid.), comes from our embodiment; it also arises from our relationality (Dodds 2007, 501; Bridgeman 2014). As Jennifer Parks (2010, 335) has observed, 'human beings are not best understood as individual rights bearers or property owners, but as vulnerable beings-in-relationship who rely on one another for care, concern, nurture and identity.' Vulnerability is life-long, and in Martha Fineman's (2011, 46) words, 'our bodily vulnerability is apparent at the beginning of life when we are totally dependent on others for our survival. Vulnerability in this sense accompanies us continually throughout life, as we age, become ill, disabled or need care from others and, finally, die.' Our embodiment, relationality and connectedness mean that humans are 'constantly susceptible to change in our well-being'; that is, both in a state of 'constant possibility of harm' (Fineman 2008, 11–12) and of constant potential for flourishing (Fineman 2017, 142). Further, as Martha Fineman (2011, 46) has observed, our vulnerability as humans comes not only from the natural world in which we live but also from the society and institutions that have been created.

In this short response to Alison's chapter on vulnerability and family law, which Alison analysed through consideration of the nature of law's instinct, understanding of its history and a view of law's coherence, I reflect upon three examples of family law's children to identify the insights each offers to our thinking about the relationship between law and vulnerability. This choice may seem to contribute little to the endeavour, but children are, it could be argued, particularly vulnerable in obvious ways; the 'other' to the autonomous adult, which vulnerability scholarship seeks to contest. From this perspective, to focus upon children does not advance our understanding of the ways in which we are universally vulnerable or of the consequences of being so. In contrast, Jonathan Herring (2012, 244) has argued that it is important to acknowledge the vulnerability of children while recognising that claims of childhood vulnerability are frequently exaggerated. But further he has argued that children's vulnerability should not be perceived as a difference from the adult norm but rather should lead to consideration of the ways in which adults are similarly vulnerable. I aim to build on Alison's conclusion that family law should resist narratives based upon 'misleading presumptions of equality and liberty, and a distorted idea of autonomy' and that family law's recognition of vulnerability as well as autonomy is necessary for the law to 'understand and correct generational and gender based disadvantages that arise from family living'. In this short response I am able to give just three, very different, examples of family law concerning children which offer reflections upon the relationship between vulnerability and the law. The first concerns an area of law in need of reform which could beneficially be approached from a vulnerability perspective. The second demonstrates that recognition of the vulnerabilities of children and a concern to promote their well-being may be instructive in consideration of the legal regulation of other aspects of family life. The third concerns an established area of law where, it is argued, the law exacerbates vulnerabilities.

Addressing vulnerabilities in reform of the law

The Children Act 1989, central to child law's modern history, as is well-understood, recognised that the primary carers of children may not be the child's genetic/gestational mother and her husband, and that it may be necessary for others to have the formal legal responsibility that enables them to provide day-to-day care and make important decisions about the child's upbringing. Yet the 2018 form of that legislation looks vastly, perhaps unimaginably, different from that conceived of by the law reformers three decades earlier, now that step-parents,[1] civil partners[2] and second female parents[3] can acquire formal legal responsibility for the upbringing of children in their care. The Children Act 1989 does not, however, address the allocation of parental responsibility to the intended parents of children born through surrogacy arrangements. Instead, the outdated Surrogacy Arrangements Act 1985, and the provisions in the Human Fertilisation and Embryology Act 1990 to enable the transfer of parental responsibility of a child born following a surrogacy arrangement, were responsive measures reflective of the type of arrangement considered at the time to be morally acceptable. Judges lament that the provisions on parental orders, now slightly amended and found in s.54 of the Human Fertilisation and Embryology Act 2008, which enable the transfer of parental responsibility for a child born as a result of a surrogacy arrangement to the intended parents, place them in the difficult position of trying to reconcile implementation of the

---

1 Children Act 1989, s.4A inserted by the Adoption and Children Act 2002.
2 Children Act 1989, s.4A(1) inserted by the Civil Partnership Act 2004.
3 Children Act 1989, s.4ZA inserted by the Human Fertilisation and Embryology Act 2008.

policy of that legislation with their duty to place the welfare of the child as the paramount consideration.[4]

The determination to place the welfare of the child, perceived as vulnerable, as the paramount consideration means that parental orders have been made following retrospective authorisation of payments which exceed 'reasonable expenses' (e.g. *Re PM* [2013] EWHC 2328), after the six-month time limit for making an application (e.g. *Re A (A Child)* [2015] EWHC 911), and in the absence of consent from the surrogate (e.g. *Re D (Children) (Surrogacy: Parental Order)* [2012] EWHC 2631). Unable to make an order upon application by a single father due to s.54(1), which permits an order to be made only upon the application of two people, Sir James Munby P made a declaration of incompatibility pursuant to s.4 of the Human Rights Act 1998 (*In the Matter of Z (A Child) (No 2)* [2016] EWHC 1191).

Critical comment upon the practice of surrogacy often refers to the vulnerabilities of the participants. Warnock (1984, paras 8.10–8.12), for example, raised concerns about the effect of surrogacy upon the marital relationship, the human dignity of the surrogate, the 'distortion' of the relationship between mother and child, and the degradation of a child exchanged for money. Yet the outmoded state of the current law, which does not address the complex issues of parenting, nationality, origin, identity, relationships or the additional issues arising from international surrogacy arrangements, leaves all in a legally uncertain and, hence, vulnerable position. Commentators such as Claire Fenton-Glynn (2016, 70) have proposed reform, in which 'the optimal conditions for autonomous decision-making are developed, and adequately enforced,' framed upon retrospective authorisation of agreements reached with free and informed consent. For the Law Commission consulting on review of the law (which has been subject to much recent academic critique, for example, Fenton-Glynn 2015; Alghrani and Griffiths 2017),[5] this is an opportunity to reflect upon the 'continued reach of autonomy in family law, with its concomitant pursuit of contractualisation and privatisation' (Diduck, this volume) and to ask what would a legal framework look like that is concerned to promote the well-being of all involved given the context, relationships and responsibilities of care that arise out of those relationships (Parks 2010).

Learning from law's recognition of the vulnerabilities of children

Within the child law aspects of family law, law's coherence lies in the perception of the child as 'other' to the autonomous adult individual, a becoming subject in relation to whom the law gives parents much freedom in their choices about educating, instilling with moral values, or disciplining, the child. When disputes between parents are brought before the court the welfare principle or best

---

4 The Human Fertilisation and Embryology (Parental Orders) Regulations 2010, No. 985.
5 Law Commission, 'Surrogacy' (*Law Commission*) <https://www.lawcom.gov.uk/surrogacy/> accessed 24 April 2018

interests of the child ensures a fact-based, particularistic determination. When those with parental responsibility cannot agree about their child's upbringing, judges seek to promote the welfare of the child in the widest sense with account taken of 'ethical, social, moral, religious, cultural, emotional and welfare considerations' and of everything relevant to the child's welfare and happiness, development, and present and future life, including 'the child's familial, educational, and social environment, and the child's social, cultural, ethnic and religious community' (*In the Matter of M (Children)* [2018] EWCA Civ 2164, [44]). Following previous case law, in *In the Matter of M*, Sir James Munby P (ibid., [49] quoting *Re G (Children)* [2012] EWCA Civ 1233, [26–27]) stressed that, 'fundamental to this is the need to have regard to the ever changing nature of our world: changes in our understanding of the natural world, technological changes, changes in social standards and, ..., changes in social attitudes.' Earlier in *Re G*, Munby LJ ([30]) had referred to the journal article by Jonathan Herring and Charles Foster, 'Welfare means rationality, virtue and altruism' (2012), agreeing with their view that

> relationships are central to our sense and understanding of ourselves. Our characters and understandings of ourselves from the earliest days are charted by reference to our relationships with others. It is only by considering the child's network of relationships that their well-being can be properly considered. So a child's relationships, both within and without the family, are always relevant to the child's interests; often they will be determinative.

The vulnerabilities that can arise from the complex web of relationships in which we live our lives were recognised in the judgment of the Court of Appeal *In the Matter of M* allowing the appeal of the father against the decision of Peter Jackson J to permit indirect, but not direct, contact with his five children. The Court of Appeal accepted the judge's determination that the children who had been, and continued to be, raised within the Charedi Jewish community, would suffer serious harm through deprivation of a relationship with their father who had been shunned by the community because she now lived as a woman. They would also suffer serious psychological harm by being marginalised and excluded by the community. The judge had observed that the children would adapt to the change to their father but that the difficulties arose from the response of their community; an example of recognition vulnerability explored by Alison in her chapter. The judge observed, 'Children are goodhearted and adaptable and, given sensitive support, I am sure that these children could adapt considerably to the changes in their father. The truth is that for the children to see their father would be too much for the adults' (*J v B (Ultra-Orthodox Judaism: Transgender* [2017] EWFC 4, [18]). The court reflected that 'The attentive reader of Peter Jackson J's judgment might well question how it is, if he was indeed acting as the "judicial reasonable parent" and adopting the reasonable parent's broadminded and tolerant approach, that he was nonetheless driven to a conclusion dictated by the practices of a community which he characterised as involving discrimination and victimisation' (*In the Matter of M*, [62]). Recognising that communities are, as Fineman (2008, 15) has observed, 'social assets' which can provide strength and support, but that communities can also exacerbate human vulnerability, the Court of Appeal sought to challenge the entrenched thinking of the adults in the community and encourage compromise through recognition of the needs of the other and the responsibilities of care which arose from relationships. The court emphasised that professional assistance had been offered to help the children come to terms with their father's decision and that this would undoubtedly help them to understand the need to be sensitive to the views of others, including those within their community unable to accommodate changes of identity given their religious views (*In the Matter of M*, [137]). *In the Matter of M* may seem unremarkable in the cannon of family law, applying an established approach to determination of child welfare to a novel set of facts. It does however provide an illustration of attention to context, relationships and responsibilities not only of parents but also of the community to care through recognition of vulnerabilities arising from changing relationships and a community resistant to a changing world. Consideration of the particular nature of the vulnerabilities of children and legal responses to them which promote their flourishing may enable us to reflect on legal solutions to the vulnerabilities of adults through approaches other than merely individualistic rights-based ones.

The potential for the law to exacerbate vulnerabilities

The exercise of parental responsibility that has recently received greatest public attention has concerned the determination of the parents of Charlie Gard (*Gosh v Yates* [2017] EWHC 972), Isaiah Haastrup (*King's College NHS Foundation Trust v Thomas & Haastrup* [2018] EWHC 127) and Alfie Evans (*Alder Hey Children's NHS Foundation Trust v Evans* [2018] EWHC 308) to secure the continued life-support of their child when the clinicians upon whom they depended for the provision of life-sustaining treatment concluded there was no further active treatment and that it was in the child's best interests for palliative care to be provided enabling them to die with dignity.[6] Such cases accord with the understanding of vulnerability as inherent arising from total dependency upon others at the beginning of life and vulnerability arising from illness and disability. As King LJ observed in one of the appeals surrounding the future care of Alfie Evans, dependent upon ventilation and artificial nutrition and hydration as a result of an undiagnosed neurodegenerative condition (*In the Matter of E (A Child)* [2018] EWCA Civ 550, [101]):

> The sort of devastating illness with which this court is concerned can and usually does come out of nowhere, regardless of whether the family is rich or

6 There are a number of reported judgments concerning the future medical treatment of all three infants. I include here the citation for the first Family Court judgment as in all cases the judgment of the best interests of the child reached at the initial hearing was upheld in all subsequent legal proceedings.

poor, educated or uneducated, reasonable or unreasonable. The one thing these disparate families have in common is that it is 'not their fault', and in my experience, even if their emotion is sometimes expressed inappropriately, they each and every one of them share a fierce devotion and protective instinct towards their vulnerable, often dying, child.

Alfie Evans and Charlie Gard may have been vulnerable in evident ways arising from their infancy and disability making them dependent upon the medical knowledge and skills of clinicians and then medical technology to sustain their life. The vulnerabilities of their parents arose from their relationship with their child. When the disagreement between the parents and clinicians over the child's best interests was brought into the legal arena by the application of the Trust for determination of the best interests of the child and legal authority for the cessation of life-sustaining ventilation and the provision of palliative care, all – child, parents, doctors and nurses – depended upon a legal process applying legal principles to achieve a resolution.

The parents of both children drew upon the discourse of parental rights and, in submissions to the appellate courts, argued that parental decisions should not be subject to challenge in the absence of significant harm. Such arguments were contrary to law's instincts to protect the interests of the child but, even more fundamentally, contrary to the parental instinct to protect arising from love, concern and responsibility to care for their dependent child. The individualistic approach of the court countered these claims with observations that the child also had rights and the child's interests were independently represented by the court-appointed Guardian positioning the child's interests in opposition to the parents. Furthermore, stays to the orders necessitated by unsuccessful appeals, brought about because of the failure of the court to address the genuine convictions of the parents and their inability to understand why they were not permitted to take up the offer of help from abroad, meant that the doctors and nurses had to continue to provide mechanical ventilation for months after they had concluded that there was no further active care available and the court had ruled that continued ventilation was not in the child's best interests. As Jonathan Herring (2012, 253) has observed, 'We readily class those who need care from others as vulnerable, without seeing the vulnerability that caring creates for the carer.'

When all involved – parents, clinical team, legal representatives, judges – were striving for what was best, the process did not appear very caring. This can be considered to be an example of the legal process creating pathogenic vulnerabilities (Rogers, Mackenzie and Dodds 2012), which, Catriona Mackenzie, Wendy Rogers and Susan Dodds (2014, 9) have argued, may occur when a response intended to ameliorate inherent or situational 'vulnerability has the paradoxical effect of exacerbating existing vulnerabilities or generating new ones' thereby 'exacerbat[ing] the sense of powerlessness engendered by vulnerability in general'. That the parents of Charlie Gard fought for what they felt was right for their son through the domestic appeal system to the European Court of Human Rights and back to the Family Division, and the parents of Alfie Evans took the same path twice, indicates a failing in the legal system to all involved – child, parents, doctors and nurses. Institutions such as the law need to give recognition to the complex and varied nature of the vulnerabilities that arise from relationships, responsibilities, love and care if the state is to respond to, rather than add to, the vulnerabilities created by interdependencies.

Vulnerability and family law's children

A vulnerabilities approach seeks to disrupt assumptions about the legal subject from the liberal tradition and associated reliance upon rights-based approaches. It has developed from feminist work on dependency, dependency work and derivative dependencies (Feder Kittay 1999; Fineman 2008, 10), care, and relationality, which Fineman (2008, 10) has argued has done little to disrupt the understanding of the legal subject: where dependency upon care is acknowledged, it is viewed as an episodic disruption to ordinary life, arising from bodily infirmity, and part of life's cycle in which care is briefly given and, in turn, taken. Children may too readily be viewed as vulnerable, but reflections upon the vulnerabilities of children offer a variety of insights into the relationship between the inherent and relational vulnerabilities of humans and specific rules and institutions that have developed to regulate our lives.

Martha Fineman (2008, 2) has argued that replacing the ideal of the autonomous individual subject with the vulnerable subject would not only be 'more representative of actual lived experience and the human condition' but would result in a more responsive state. Institutions, such as the law, can respond to – recognise, redress, remedy, adjust, compensate – our vulnerabilities or ignore, reinforce and increase our vulnerabilities. Legal responses, the principles and processes of the law, can address human vulnerabilities, but if the law fails to consider dependency, relationality and interdependency, it can instead exacerbate the vulnerabilities we face as already vulnerable humans.

Bibliography

Bridgeman J, 'Relational vulnerability, care and dependency' in J Wallbank and J Herring (eds), *Vulnerabilities, Care and Family Law* (Hart 2014).

Dodds S, 'Depending on care: recognition of vulnerability and the social contribution of care provision' (2007) 21(9) *Bioethics* 500.

Feder Kittay E, *Love's Labor: Essays on Women, Equality and Dependency* (Routledge 1999).

Fenton-Glynn C, 'Outsourcing ethical dilemmas: regulating international surrogacy arrangements' (2016) 24(1) *Medical Law Review* 59.

Fineman MA, 'The vulnerable subject: anchoring equality in the human condition' (2008) 20(1) *Yale Journal of Law and Feminism* 1.

Fineman MA, 'Responsibility, family and the limits of equality: an American perspective' in C Lind, H Keating and J Bridgeman (eds), *Taking Responsibility, Law and the Changing Family* (Ashgate 2011).

Fineman MA, 'Vulnerability and inevitable inequality' (2017) 4 *Oslo Law Review* 133.

Herring J, 'Vulnerability, children and the law' in M Freeman (ed), *Law and Childhood Studies: Current Legal Issues Volume 14* (Oxford University Press 2012).

Herring J and Foster C, 'Welfare means rationality, virtue and altruism' (2012) 32 *Legal Studies* 480.

Law Commission, 'Surrogacy' (*Law Commission*) <https://www.lawcom.gov.uk/surrogacy/> (access 24th April 2018).

Mackenzie C, Rogers W, Dodds S, 'Introduction: what is vulnerability and why does it matter for moral theory?' in C Mackenzie, W Rogers, S Dodds (eds), *Vulnerability: New Essays in Ethics and Feminist Philosophy* (Oxford University Press 2014).

Parks J, 'Care ethics and the global practice of commercial surrogacy' (2010) 24 *Bioethics* 333.

Rogers W, Mackenzie C and Dodds S, 'Why bioethics needs a concept of vulnerability' (2012) 5 *International Journal of Feminist Approaches to Bioethics* 11.

Warnock M, 'Report of the Committee of Inquiry into Human Fertilisation and Embryology' (London 1984) <https://www.hfea.gov.uk/media/2608/warnock-report-of-the-committee-of-inquiry-into-human-fertilisation-and-embryology-1984.pdf> (access 1st May 2018).

Part 2
Law and ageing

Ageing and universal beneficial vulnerability

Jonathan Herring

Introduction

This chapter will start by outlining two ways the concept of vulnerability is used. First, 'particular deficient vulnerability': vulnerability seen an undesirable condition suffered by a few, which we should eliminate or mitigate as much as possible. Second, 'universal beneficial vulnerability': vulnerability seen as a desirable attribute of all humankind, which we should embrace. The primary focus of this chapter is on older people, who are often presented under the 'particular deficient vulnerability' model as an archetype of vulnerable people. The chapter will explore four aspects of life for older people: bodies, autonomy, identity, and the role of the state. It will examine the consequence of applying the 'particular deficient vulnerability model' to older people and will then explain how the approach to these issues would change (for the better) under the 'universal beneficial vulnerability' model.

Two approaches to vulnerability

This section will very briefly outline the two approaches to vulnerability (Fineman 2008; Herring 2016a; 2018).

Particular deficient vulnerability

In the current public discourse, vulnerability is used to identify a particular group of people who are at risk of suffering harm or behaving in a way deemed undesirable. Typically, those regarded as vulnerable are seen as needing intervention or surveillance to protect them from suffering disadvantage. For example, if a medical researcher has a volunteer from a member of a vulnerable group, this will automatically trigger a set of mechanisms to ensure that the volunteer is protected and freely consenting, or may indeed prohibit a member of that group being involved. Children are commonly presented as being vulnerable and so in need of a wide range of protections and restrictions (Herring 2018a). Vulnerability is seen as undesirable because the vulnerable need help from others and cannot live up to the ideals of independence and self-sufficiency that we expect from 'normal citizens'. Margrit Shildrick (2002, 71) noted that 'in western modernity at least, vulnerability is figured as a shortcoming, an impending failure.' Being vulnerable is seen as a source of shame, which should be disguised.

England now has a Secretary of State for Vulnerability. Sarah Newton's full title is Parliamentary Under Secretary of State for Vulnerability, Safeguarding and Countering Extremism. The grouping of these three topics in her title is revealing. It reinforces the view that particular kinds of people ('the vulnerable') need to be safeguarded from harm because they cannot look after themselves. It can also be linked to moral harm: vulnerable people are at risk of becoming extremists or engaging in other undesirable activity. There is, therefore, a public interest in ensuring those who are vulnerable are empowered to escape that undesirable state.

A good example of the way that the designation 'vulnerable groups' has been used was a recent report from Public Health England and the National Institute for Health and Care Excellence (2017) warning of the danger of pollution in urban areas, particular by idling cars. The report suggests that 'the most vulnerable' need protecting from pollution and so idling outside care homes, schools and hospital should be forbidden. The assumption here, as so often with this discourse, is that 'normal people', that is 'non-vulnerable people' are able to look after themselves, but the authorities need to take care of the vulnerable. The example of air pollution is one where this approach seems manifestly absurd.

Universal beneficial vulnerability

I would argue for a very different understanding of vulnerability. That is that everyone is vulnerable and that is a really good thing. I will call this the 'universal and beneficial theory of vulnerability'. This is a view associated particularly with the writing of Martha Fineman (2008, 1). She argues:

> The vulnerability approach recognizes that individuals are anchored at each end of their lives by dependency and the absence of capacity. Of course, between these ends, loss of capacity and dependence may also occur, temporarily for many and permanently for some as a result of disability or illness. Constant and variable throughout life, individual vulnerability encompasses not only damage that has been done in the past and speculative harms of the distant future, but also the possibility of immediate harm. We are beings who live with the ever-present possibility that our needs and circumstances will change. On an individual level, the concept of vulnerability (unlike that of liberal autonomy) captures this present potential for each of us to become dependent based upon our persistent susceptibility to misfortune and catastrophe.

In that passage she is clear that vulnerability is a universal characteristic, but some of the language used might be seen to be negative about vulnerability, referring to it in terms of damage and harms. However, in more recent writing (Fineman 2017, 142) she takes a more positive approach to vulnerability:

> As embodied beings, we are universally and individually constantly susceptible to change in our well-being. Change can be positive or negative – we become ill and are injured or decline, but we also grow in abilities and develop new skills and relationships. The term 'vulnerable', used to connote the continuous susceptibility to change in both our bodily and social well-being that all human beings experience, makes it clear that there is no position of invulnerability – no conclusive way to prevent or avoid change

Vulnerability is an inherent part of being human (Beckett 2006). Admittedly, this is not how generally people understand themselves. We emphasise our capacity, independence and autonomy. But we puff ourselves up with such talk. In reality, we are all vulnerable because we are all profoundly dependant on others for our physical and psychological well-being (Gergen 2009). Our society has built up a wide range of structures and forms of assistance which disguise our vulnerability. That does mean that some people's vulnerability is mitigated to a greater extent than others, but does not undermine the universal vulnerability everyone has.

I would argue that our vulnerability emerges from three primary features of our nature. First, our embodied nature creates vulnerability. Experience teaches us that our bodies are vulnerable to sickness, illness and accidents (Matambanadzo 2012). Our health is frail. Our bodies are 'profoundly leaky' (Shildrick 1997). They are constantly changing with new material being added to them and old material being discarded. Inside our bodies are dependent on a wide range of non-human material to survive, and outside it is constantly interacting with the environment (Chau and Herring 2007). All of this means our bodies are mutable, porous and vulnerable.

Second, in a radical sense our relationships constitute our 'selves' (Gergen 2009; McLaughlin 2012). We primarily understand our selves in terms of how we relate to and are understood by others. It is only in response to others that our selves have meaning. The language we use and the way we understand our surroundings and perceive our place in the world is generated through our relationships. But this means we are in constant danger of our self being challenged by others rejecting us, not accepting us as members of a group, not providing the support we expect or using our relationships to harm us (Diduck, this volume; Herring 2017). As the self is constituted through relationships, and we only have limited control over these relationships, we lack 'masterful' control over the self (Herring 2018a).

Third, dependency is an inevitable facet of human life (Herring 2013). Because we are dependent, we must rely on others to survive, and this inevitably creates vulnerability. The care we require may cease or may be inadequate. Of course, for most people, there will be times when this overt kind of dependency will not be apparent.

However, at these times, others will often be dependent on us to meet their needs, be that as parents or carers for others. This itself creates a vulnerability. So there are two connections between care and vulnerability here. It is because we are vulnerable that we need care and because we care that we are vulnerable.

Much could be, and has been, said on all these themes. However, the focus of this chapter is the significance of this debate for older people. I will assume for now that the universal and desirable understanding of vulnerability is the correct one and consider what the significance of that approach is for older people. I will focus on four aspects of older people's lives.

1. Bodies

One aspect of ageing which gets considerable attention is the ageing body. It is commonly presented as being in decline: slower, wrinkled, liable to break, leaky and less dependable (Bergoffen 2014). Old age is associated with physical frailty and increased disease. Catherine Thompson (2015) is Head of Patient Experience for Acute Services at NHS England writes presenting the common assumption:

> For a significant number of older people, advancing age is associated with frailty. In medicine this is often defined as a reduction in physical capacity: a group of older people who are at the highest risk of adverse outcomes such as falls, disability, admission to hospital, or the need for long-term care.

The perception is not just that older bodies are more prone to illness but also that they are unsexy: greying; wrinkling and saggy: the body in decay (Chonody and Teater 2016). Sara Hofmeier and colleagues (2016, 12) quote one woman saying:

> I am ashamed of my aging body and ashamed that I am ashamed. I believe women pay an enormous price for cultural biases related to gender and age.

Older bodies are presented in contrast to the constrained, controlled bodies of the young. Older bodies droop, wrinkle and spill; while young bodies are taunt and ordered. Linn Sandberg (2013) writes:

> At the very heart of this discourse on old age as negation is the ageing body as unbounded, leaky, fragmented and lacking control. The ageing body has consequently been discussed as a threatening disruption to identity and self.

This perception generates fear and people take great steps to 'pass' as young. Notably, people throughout their adult lives report anxiety about the ageing of their bodies (Sargen-Cox et al. 2014). The *Daily Mail* recently had a headline: 'Would YOU dare ask a computer how old you look? Eight brave women try out the terrifyingly simple new internet craze' (Ley 2016). The bravery, presumably, is because you might be told you look (to the computer!) older than you really are. Notably, 'looking one's age' is rarely seen as a compliment.

The fear of the ageing body is reflected in the dramatic increase in the use of cosmetic surgery, much of it aimed to combat the 'signs of ageing' (Fernand 2008). In the US, between 2000 and 2015, there has been an 89% increase in the number of 'breast lifts' and a 4,959% increase in 'upper arm lifts'. Of the officially recorded procedures there were 1.7 million cosmetic surgical procedures in 2015 and 14.2 million 'minimally invasive' cosmetic procedures (American Society of Plastic Surgeons 2017). The Global Anti-Aging Market was worth $250 billion in 2016 and is predicted to reach $331.41 billion by 2021 (Orbis Research 2017). Newspapers repeatedly run articles on how a particular celebrity looks young or old for their age.

I believe these views about the older body being unhealthy and unsexy are both false, but not for the reasons commonly assumed: that older bodies can be as healthy and sexy as young bodies. Rather the image of older bodies provides a far more accurate image of the true nature of bodies, than that presented for younger ones. The body is commonly imaged to be constrained, controlled and owned, but this is the image challenged by the vulnerability analysis. The natural state of the body is to be leaky, mutable and fragile. At all stages of life, the body has these characteristics. Crucial parts of our bodies are made up of nonhuman material. Many non-human organisms play a central role to the maintenance of our bodies. We are less us than we like to think! (Chau and Herring 2014). The truth is that our bodies are constantly changing, dependent on others for survival and subject to environmental factors. Our true sense of self and identity is not found in our bounded, owned body, but in the breaking, mixing and interaction of our bodies with others and with the wider environment (Herring 2014a). As Kenneth Gergen (2009, 23) writes:

> [T]he idea of the skin as a container seems inappropriate. The metaphor of a sieve might be more relevant, with material moving in both directions. On the one hand we could say that nothing that passes through me is distinctly mine (my body); all that I call 'my body' belongs to the larger world out of which it is but a transient conglomerate.

In fact, the contrast between the firm youthful body and the wrinkled older body is a false contrast. The frail, impervious, mutable, fragile, interdependent body presented as an older body is in fact the truth for all bodies. But that is a more exciting and dynamic understanding of the body than the false claims of a 'youthful body' that is static, constrained and independent.

2. Lacking autonomy

One of the assumptions commonly made about old age is that it is a time when a person's capacity becomes impaired and so they fall short of the ideal of the autonomous liberal subject and become vulnerable. Autonomy is closely linked to being invulnerable. As Alison Diduck (2013, 102) argues, there is a strong message that 'autonomy is to be respected and promoted while vulnerability is to be pitied, remedied or alleviated.' Indeed, in legal thinking autonomy has come to play a central role, as a cornerstone of our understanding of rights (Herring 2016a). Our right to be able to make our own choices over how to act and to only be subject to those responsibilities we choose to take are seen as central pillars of economic, social and legal structures. The law's role is, under that image of the self, to protect the individual from unwanted intrusions and to protect the liberty to pursue one's goal for one's life. Those who most obviously fall outside the paradigm, such as older people, are described as 'vulnerable' because they cannot make decisions for themselves. That generates a need to monitor, supervise and discipline them (Fineman 2012).

It seems that older people are particularly prone to be found to lack capacity. This is indeed acknowledged in the Mental Capacity Act 2005 where it was thought necessary to specifically state that age alone cannot be used to established a lack of capacity. Section 2(3) states:

A lack of capacity cannot be established merely by reference to –

a   a person's age or appearance....

Yet the reference to 'merely' indicates that it is permissible to use age as a criteria on which to make a capacity assessment.

Even when older people are found to have capacity they can be found to fall into the inherent jurisdiction available to make orders in respect of vulnerable adults. This category includes those with capacity but who as Munby J put it in *re SA (Vulnerable Adult with Capacity: Marriage)* [2006] 1 FLR 867, para 77: 'either under constraint, or subject to coercion or undue influence, or for some other reason deprived of the capacity to make the relevant decision, or disabled from making a free choice, or incapacitated or disabled from giving or expressing a real and genuine consent'. It has been particularly used for older people (Herring 2016a, ch. 3). A good example being *DL v A Local Authority* [2012] EWCA 253 where a couple were 85 and 90. There were concerns over the way the couple were treated by their son and the local authority sought an order removing them from his home. They were assessed as having capacity and opposed the intervention. The Court of Appeal held that the inherent jurisdiction was available to make the order sought by the local authority, despite the fact the couple had capacity. Part of their reasoning was in terms of dealing with elder abuse, para 63:

> There is, in my view, a sound and strong public policy justification for this to be so. The existence of 'elder abuse', as described by Professor Williams, is sadly all too easy to contemplate. Indeed the use of the term 'elder' in that label may inadvertently limit it to a particular age group whereas, as the cases demonstrate, the will of a vulnerable adult of any age may, in certain circumstances, be overborne.

Despite emphasising that the jurisdiction is not limited to older people, Laura Pritchard Jones (2016) argues that older people are particularly likely to have orders made under the Inherent Jurisdiction or Mental Capacity Act 2005 because age is linked to perceived need to protect (Bailey et al. 2013). To give an example, In *London Borough of Redbridge v G* [2014] EWCOP 17, Russell J describes G as an 'old, vulnerable lady' and justified reporting restrictions on the basis of protecting the privacy of G who was 'old, frail and vulnerable'. ([12]) In *LLBC v TG* [2007] EWHC 2640 the man subject to the proceedings was described as 'elderly and infirm' ([40]).

The use of the Mental Capacity Act and the inherent jurisdiction have proved highly controversial. There are certainly those who see it as opening a door to unjustified paternalism. Those deemed vulnerable, such as older people, can be subject to paternalistic interventions which others would not be subject to. I am much more sympathetic to the use of these jurisdictions than others (Herring 2016a). My concern is that their use seems particularly focused on older people. In fact, even if we technically have mental capacity, all of us have flawed decision-making processes. We take into account falsehoods; we are unduly influenced by others; we act in irrational ways. The idea that we are governed by rational thought plans we pursue to develop our vision of the good life seems palpably false. That means that autonomy for everyone is hugely overrated as a principle. We are all muddled, irrational, irascible, emotionally driven, incoherent thinkers and deciders. These characteristics are commonly associated with older people, but are in fact true for us all (Herring 2016b). As the universal and beneficial model of vulnerability theory of vulnerability would claim we are not, thank goodness, slaves of our mind or rational thought or logic. We are creatures of blood, love, wildness and eccentricity. We are not the product of rational thought, nor do we want to be. The emphasis on individualised autonomy unduly restricts us. Our only hope for autonomy is found in and through our relationships with others, as advocates of relational autonomy have suggested (Diduck this volume, Herring 2014b).

Critics of this argument fear that it will lead to rampant paternalism. I think, however, that this fear is misplaced. First, if we are all flawed vulnerable decision-makers, that is as true for doctors, judges and social workers and everyone else. Indeed, the universal beneficial vulnerability theory seems to be the most powerful critique of paternalism available. Second, it assumes autonomy is the only basis of respecting someone's decisions and there are other good reasons in respecting a person's decision which do not rest in a claim they have capacity. For example, treating someone in a dignified way may involve respecting their decision, irrespective of capacity (Herring 2009). If, however, we start with a norm of vulnerable, interdependent, caring people, as the universal beneficial vulnerability model would suggest, then the nature of legal intervention becomes different. The importance of upholding and maintaining those relationships becomes key. The law does not emphasise independence, liberty and autonomy but rather seeks to uphold relationships and care.

Indeed, a refusal to recognise our mutual vulnerability creates paternalism. As Daniel Bedford (2018) notes, the evidence from nursing literature is that 'seeing vulnerability as a deficiency that leads to suffering can result in a refusal on the part of a care-worker to experience vulnerability, which, in turn, can lead to the dehumanisation of older adults.' Ironically, as Bedford points out, 'those who are incapable of being vulnerable with themselves and others can lack empathy – unable to engage in fellow-feeling and perceive the pain of others. Worse still, it is through being immune to the feelings of others that care workers can fail to see how they create hurt, and can go on to inflict harm.' The failure to recognise one's own vulnerability creates a failure in care which is itself a cause of vulnerability to the other.

3. Identity

Under the particular and deficient model of vulnerability, older people are seen as the archetype of vulnerable people. It assumes that old age is a loss: of vigour, autonomy, capacity and independence. The standard message of old age is not positive: 'Getting old sucks!' (Taylor 2013); 'old age is not a time for sissies' (Linkletter 1990); old age is 'a hideous inverted childhood' (Larkin 2003). It is not surprising that it is common to read of a fear of growing old. That can lead to dramatic outcomes. In *Kings College Hospital NHS Foundation Trust v C* [2015] EWCOP 59 80 C attempted suicide and refused a kidney transplant because she did not want to become poor, ugly and old. The *Daily Telegraph* (Donnelly 2015) reported a healthy woman aged 73 ended her life in Dignitas with this explanation:

> I have looked after people who are old, on and off, all my life. I have always said, 'I am not getting old. I do not think old age is fun.' I know that I have gone just over the hill now. It is not going to start getting better. I do not want people to remember me as a sort of old lady hobbling up the road with a trolley.

This fear of old age can create a crisis of identity for older people (Herring 2018b). They seek to defeat or, at least, slow down the ageing process (Sze 2015).

In the gerontological literature this is sometimes expressed in terms of there being a tension between the 'youthful self' in the 'ageing body'. This results in the use of masks or masquerades, whereby the older person seeks to take on the appearance of a younger person and so escape the negative stereotypes associated with age (Featherstone and Hepworth 1989). These masks can range from cosmetic surgery to styles of dress, speech or behaviour. Simon Biggs (1997) writes that the way 'we "story" or "perform" our way through structure and experience helps us to understand relations between generations and between genders.'

This response is undesirable for two reasons. The first is that it creates a tension for older people. They reject the label of being older and do not want to adopt the role that is expected for older people. They therefore seek to deny that they belong to the group older people, or at least disguise the fact the do. Interestingly, the description of old age is accepted, as it is 'natural, and thus beyond dispute' (Calasanti and Slevin 2006). It is just that the older person does not accept it for themselves (Hummert et al. 1994). They do not 'feel old'. Hence, the need for the 'mask' and 'masquerade' to deceive others into thinking they are young. This presentation, that the older body is a distortion of the true self, downplays the relational and bodily nature of the self. The body is presented as an enemy: it poses the risk of the mask slipping or the masquerade become farcical. Yet the presentation of the body as the enemy of the mind seems clearly based on the Cartesian divide between the mind and body which is rejected in modern thought. To argue that there is a 'youthful self trapped beneath an ageing mask' (Biggs 1997, 2004) suggests that the 'real us' is always young and the ageing bodies are not reflective of the real us. In reality, our identity and our bodies are intertwined.

Second, the mask/masquerade analogy perpetuates a highly individualised understanding of the self. The message of the universal beneficial vulnerability model is that our identity and self emerges from our relationships and interactions with others. The self, hiding from others, is a fictional idea (Foster and Herring 2017). We are how we are held by others. We cannot, therefore, separate out the real us from the us as we are treated as and related to. There is no self that can exist outside the relational and social context we live in.

This, then, shows the particular evil of ageism. The false assumptions made by others about someone challenges the self. It infects relationships that older people have with others and prevents people being honest about themselves. It is only by breaking down these false assumptions about bodies and our identities and being open to each other that the self can emerge. An interesting illustration of this can be seen in the research of Weiss and Lang (2012) who found that the negative stereotypes appear associated with chronological age, rather than generational identity. This was demonstrated by the fact that when people were asked about their generation (a war-time baby, a child of the 1960s etc.) people spoke in far more positive terms than when they were asked about people in relation to age (e.g. people in their 80s). This suggests that it is not actually belonging to a particular group born in a particular time which creates the negative assumptions, but the assumptions tied to being a particular age. This may be that the ties to a generation are communal. You are identified with a group of others about whom one may have positive feelings, rather than being associated with the number of age, and the more abstract negative images that are associated with that.

Third, the distinction drawn between the young and the old accepts the story that the older self is an impoverished version of the autonomous, self-sufficient, able younger self. Under the particular deficient view of vulnerability younger people emphasise the distinction between the young and the old in order to maintain the fiction that they are not vulnerable. The 'young' must ensure they look completely different to the 'elderly'. As Simone de Beauvoir (1970, 13) writes:

> When we look at the image of our own future provided by the old we do not believe it: an absurd inner voice whispers that that will never happen to us – when that happens it will no longer be ourselves that it happens to.

I would argue that the stereotype of old age – mental and physical frailty, dependence on others, gullibility, terror of loneliness – are entirely justified (Bullington 2006). But they are the reality we all face and cope with throughout our lives. The universal and beneficial model of vulnerability suggests that we all, regardless of age, seek to present an image of good physical and mental health, emotional security, sound judgement, controlled bodies. It is, ironically, only in old age that the stereotypes match the reality and we can then be authentic to our bodies and ourselves. We can come to accept our vulnerable nature and give up our hapless attempts to escape our inevitable vulnerability. Yet by then we have been hiding and denying that reality for too long. I suggest, therefore, not that we need to change the stereotypes of old age, so much as change our stereotypes of middle age and youth.

Once we recognise that vulnerability and dependence are part of the essence of human life, we can rethink old age. No longer is it a time when we lose our abilities and independence; rather, we are just as we always have been. It is rather that our vulnerable natures are better disguised by the provision of social service and a wide range of social structures. This may explain why it is that, despite the common perception of old age being a time of misery, sociologists have found that old age tends to bring with it increases in well-being (Ryff et al. 2004). Many studies of well-being have found that those aged around 40 as being at the bottom of a U-shaped curve of assessments of well-being (Blanchflower and Oswald 2004). The common assumption that in our 40s you are in the 'prime of your life' seems misguided. One explanation for the increase in well-being for older people is that older people have better coping mechanisms or resilience than younger people, rather than seeing any positives in old age (Diener and Suh 1997). That explanation is itself revealing because it assumes that old age brings with it negatives, with which people need to cope. I would suggest a rather different explanation. Perhaps the comfort of old age is that the need to pretend is less. We can be honest with ourselves and others and no longer strive to the unachievable fiction of being self-sufficient and autonomous.

4. *The responsive state*

The dominant narratives about the state and old age in the media and legal literature are negative. Ageing is seen as a crisis or a burden; becoming old is a pathology (Kesby 2017). This creates not only a personal problem for individuals but is also seen as creating a problem of wider significance. Considerable concern is expressed at the predictions of a growing percentage of the population aged over 60 (UN Department of Economic and Social Affairs 2013). Respectable bodies and writers talk of the 'old age crisis' (World Bank 1994), 'a grey tsunami' (Segal 2013) and a 'demographic time bomb' (Weicht 2013). Frost (2012) claims 'global aging is "a far bigger threat to the world economy than the Eurozone debt crisis, US unemployment and the Chinese slowdown combined."' One *Guardian* article claims

> an 85-year-old man costs the NHS about seven times more on average than a man in his late 30s. Health spending per person steeply increases after the age of 50, with people aged 85 and over costing the NHS an average of £7,000 a year.
>
> (Robineau 2016)

The crisis is also seen as a social one as younger people are required to take on the tasks of caring for the older people, and there is discussion of intergenerational conflict (Kesby 2017).

One way of challenging such claims is to question them on their own terms. The assumption that ageing produces economic harms is based on a wide range of questionable assumptions, such as the assumption that ageing will cause increased health and care costs (rather than delay their start) and that older people are not economically productive. While it is true that death is commonly associated with old age and death is commonly preceded by decline and disease, there is no reason to think these need to be associated with old age as such. In other words, that the overall rates of disease and infirmity may be the same for a given person whether they die at age 60 or 80 or 100. The primary difference being the point in time the particular costs or infirmities arise, rather than their extent. As Stephen Watkins (2016) puts it:

> For every extra year of life woe is delayed by a year but there is no change in the amount of woe. We live longer and the extra time is spent living – we spend no extra time on dying.... In such a case there would be no increase in the disease burden incurred by the individual. At a population level the health and social care costs will be delayed and the proportion of the population incurring them at any one time may therefore be reduced.

Further, the argument, even on its own terms, assumes that older people cannot be economically productive and ignores the wide range of economic and social forces excluding older people from the workplace (Biggs 2011). Also, some commentators have suggested there is an 'aging enterprise' in whose interests it is to emphasise and even exaggerate the needs of older people in order to boost the sectors 'servicing them', such as retirement home, care service and pension providers (Estes 1993).

However, I suggest a different challenge to the so-called 'crisis of aging' for the state. It assumes that only certain kinds of productivity are important for the state: work in the formal economy. This means that work which is unrecognised in the formal economy, such as volunteering, care work, informal child care and so on, is not valued. But even taking that on board we should not assume that an individual's contribution to society must be seen in terms of productivity. As Alison Kesby (2017, 381) writes, it 'adopts a conception of aging which places the responsibility for aging "successfully" firmly onto the older person who is presumed to have the resources to achieve the idealized benchmarks'. It can leave success as available for an elite, but not accessible by the disadvantaged groups, who will be seen as failing to ensure they have aged well. Being a successful citizen as defined in the terms set by capitalism. Kesby (2017, 382) writes:

> Of particular concern is the potential for positive aging to further reinforce the idea that frailty, illness and disability are to be shunned, are in some unspoken way the fault and 'failure' of the individual concerned and do not belong within modern society. To be visibly old, ill or disabled is to age 'unsuccessfully' or be unproductive. A new form of ageism emerges: the 'dread of aging' is replaced with the 'dread of aging with a disability'.

The requirements of productivity, and the crisis of the 'non-productive' makes no room for individuals having value to a society for simply being; for 'being held' (Lindemann 2013). It is important that we value existence in terms of the 'individual's location within webs of social, economic, political, and institutional relationships' (Fineman 2012), and that we realise that for all of us our role in society is not the subject of choice and control (Boudiny 2013). Our human nature becomes richer and acquires more meaning than the production of things as a result.

It is the failure to recognise this that writers on caring relationship have argued that care of the 'vulnerable' is downgraded in modern legal and social thought (Herring 2013). It is seen as a private matter for individuals and their families to organise.

The acknowledgement of universal vulnerability also creates a different image of the legal relationship between the individual and the state. Rather than seeing the obligations of the state as owed towards a few particularly vulnerable citizens to meet their needs, it acknowledges that the institutions and provision of the state are used to meet the needs of all (Fineman 2012). The question then becomes the extent to which the state meets all of our needs and those needs that it chooses not to meet. It recognises that the values and goods of a society are found in our interaction and mutual endeavours, which cannot be broken down into the contributions that each person makes on their own.

Conclusion

This chapter has argued that the shift from seeing vulnerability as resting in few people who are in need of particular state assistance in order to escape from that undesirable state, to seeing vulnerability as a beneficial state that is an inevitable part of being human. I have argued this has particular benefits in relation to old age.

First, we can see a similar point in relation to ageing bodies. Our bodies are constantly changing and porous. Our attempt to maintain what is called a 'youthful' body is an attempt to maintain a fiction which never was true: that our bodies are contained and controlled. The presentation of older bodies as frail and weak is no more than an attempt to deny the frailty and weakness of all bodies.

Second, old age is commonly regarded as a time of loss of capacity and autonomy – a departure from the ideal liberal autonomous self. I have argued, however, that the universal beneficial vulnerability model would claim that those characteristics sometimes associated with old age – irrationality, irascibility, emotionality and eccentricity – are in fact the characteristics we always have. In our nature, we are not autonomous, at least not in rationally-driven way commonly presented.

Third, acceptance of universal beneficial vulnerability enables us to move beyond the image of 'old age' being a characteristic to avoid by wearing masks to maintain an image of perpetual youth. The error in that presentation is not that the assumptions made about old age are wrong, but that the assumptions made about youth are in error. In old age, we become most apparently what we always have been: vulnerable, frail and mutable.

Finally, vulnerable older people are commonly seen as needing particular assistance from the state. A vision of the universal beneficial responsibility opens up the image of the state which puts caring relationships at its heart and the primary duty of the state being not the maximising of GDP, but the maximisation of care. Our value lies in what we are together, not in the productivity of individuals. Society should recognise the value every citizen has because it is in our mutual interlocking lives of care, mutual vulnerability and interdependency that the true value of human is found.

Bibliography

American Society of Plastic Surgeons (2017) *Statistics* (ASPS).

de Beauvoir S, *Old Age* (Penguin 1970).

Bailey C, Clarke C, Gibb C, Haining S, Wilkinson H and Tiplady S, 'Risky and resilient life with dementia: review of and reflections on the literature' (2013) 15 *Health, Risk & Society* 390.

Beckett A, *Citizenship and Vulnerability* (Palgrave 2006).

Bedford D, 'Embracing vulnerability in ageing: our route to flourishing?' in B Clough and J Herring (eds), *Ageing, Gender and Family Law* (Routledge 2018).

Bergoffen D, 'The dignity of finitude' in S Stoller (ed), *Simone de Beauvoir's Philosophy of Age: Gender, Ethics, and Time* (Walter de Gruyter 2014).

Biggs S, 'Choosing not to be old? Masks, bodies and identity management in later life' (1997) 17 *Ageing and Society* 553.

Biggs S, 'Toward critical narrativity: stories of aging in contemporary social policy' (2001) 15 *Journal of Aging Studies* 303.

Biggs S, 'Age, gender, narratives, and masquerades' (2004) 18 *Journal of Ageing Studies* 45.

Blanchflower D and Oswald A, 'Well-being over time in Britain and the USA' (2004) 88 *Journal of Public Economics* 1356.

Boudiny K, "Active ageing': from empty rhetoric to effective policy tool' (2013) 33 *Ageing Society* 1077.

Bullington J, 'Body and self: a phenomenological study on the ageing body and identity' (2006) 32 *Medical Humanities* 25.

Calasanti T and Slevin K, *Age Matters* (Routledge 2006).

Chau P-L and Herring J, 'My body, your body, our bodies' (2007) 15 *Medical Law Review* 34.

Chau P-L and Herring J, 'Interconnected, inhabited and insecure: why bodies should not be property' (2014) 44 *Journal of Medical Ethics* 39.

Chonody J and Teater B, 'Why do I dread looking old?: a test of social identity theory, terror management theory, and the double standard of aging' (2016) 28 *Journal of Women & Aging* 112.

Diduck A, 'Autonomy and vulnerability in family law: the missing link' in J Wallbank and J Herring (eds), *Vulnerabilities, Care and Family Law* (Routledge 2013).

Diener E and Suh E, 'Subjective well-being and age. an international perspective' (1997) 17 *Annual Review of Gerontology and Geriatrics* 304.

Donnelly L,(2015) 'Health retired nurse ends her life because old age 'is awful" *The Daily Telegraph* (London, 2 August 2015) <https://www.telegraph.co.uk/news/health/11778859/Healthy-retired-nurse-ends-her-life-because-old-age-is-awful.html> (access 29th October 2019).

Estes C, 'The aging enterprise revisited' (1993) 33 *The Gerontologist* 292.

Featherstone M and Hepworth M, 'Ageing and old age: reflections on the postmodern life course' in B Bytheway, T Keil, P Allatt and A Bryman (eds), *Becoming and Being Old: Sociological Approaches to Later Life* (Sage 1989).

Fernand D, 'Women who date younger men' *The Sunday Times* (London, 18 May 2008) https://www.thetimes.co.uk/article/women-who-date-younger-men-lhxb95nfc99 (access 29th October 2019).

Fineman MA, 'The vulnerable subject: anchoring equality in the human condition' (2008) 20 *Yale Journal of Law and Feminism* 1.

Fineman MA, "Elderly' as vulnerable: rethinking the nature of individual and societal responsibility' (2012) 20 *Elder Law Journal* 71.

Fineman MA, 'Vulnerability and inevitable inequality' (2017) 3 *Oslo Law Review* 2.

Foster C and Herring J, *Identity, Personhood and the Law* (Springer 2017).

Frost J, 'Greying is the biggest threat' *The Australian* (New South Wales, 4 August 2012).

Gergen K, *Relational Being* (Oxford University Press 2009).

Herring J, 'Losing it? Losing what? The law and dementia' (2009) 3 *Child and Family Law Quarterly* 21.

Herring J, *Caring and the Law* (Hart 2013).

Herring J, 'Why we need a statute for bodily material' in I Goold, K Greasley, J Herring and L Skene (eds), *Persons, Parts and Property* (Hart 2014).

Herring J, *Relational Autonomy and Family Law* (Springer 2014).

Herring J, *Vulnerable Adults and the Law* (Oxford University Press 2016).

Herring J, 'Peter Skegg and the question no-one asks: why presume capacity?' in M Henaghan and J Wall (eds), *Law, Ethics, and Medicine: Essays in Honour of Peter Skegg* (Thompson 2016).

Herring J, 'The serious wrong of domestic abuse and the loss of control defence' in A Reed and M Bohlander (eds), *Loss of Control and Diminished Responsibility* (Ashgate 2017).

Herring J, *Childhood, Vulnerability and the Law* (Springer 2018).

Herring J, 'Ageing, love and family law' in B Clough and J Herring (eds), *Ageing, Gender and Family Law* (Routledge 2018).

Hofmeier S, Runfola C, Sala M, Gagne D, Bronley K and Bulik C, 'Body image, aging, and identity in women over 50' (2016) 29 *Journal of Women and Aging* 3.

Hummert G, Garstka T, Shaner J and Strahm S, 'Stereotypes of the elderly held by young, middle-aged, and elderly adults' (1994) 49 *Journal of Gerentology* 240.

Kesby A, 'Narratives of aging and the human rights of older persons' (2017) 18 *Human Rights Review* 371.

Larkin P, *The Old Fools* (Faber and Faber 2003).

Ley R, 'Would YOU dare ask a computer how old you look? Eight brave women try out the terrifyingly simple new internet craze' *Daily Mail* (London, 10 October 2016) <https://www.dailymail.co.uk/femail/article-3868712/Would-dare-ask-computer-old-look-Eight-brave-women-try-terrifyingly-simple-new-internet-craze.html> (access 29th October 2019).

Lindemann H, *Holding and Letting Go: The Social Practice of Personal Identities* (Oxford University Press 2014).

Linkletter A, *Old Age Is Not for Sissies* (Bookthrift 1990).

Matambanadzo S, 'Embodying vulnerability: a feminist theory of the person' (2012) 20 *Duke Journal of Gender Law & Policy* 45.

McLaughlin K, *Surviving Identity: Vulnerability and the Psychology of Recognition* (Routledge 2012).

National Institute for Health and Care Excellence, 'No idling' zones can help to protect vulnerable people from air pollution, says NICE' NICE (2017) http://indepth.nice. org.uk/no-idle-zones-can-help-protect-vulnerable-people-from-air-pollution-says-nice/index.html (access 29th October 2019).

Orbis Research, 'Global anti-aging market 2017 is growing rapidly and expected to reach $331.41 billion by 2021' *Reuters* (Dallas, 19 June 2017) https://www.reuters.com/brandfeatures/venture-capital/article?id=11480.

Pritchard-Jones L, 'The good, the bad, and the 'vulnerable older adult'' (2016) 38 *Journal of Social Welfare and Family Law* 51.

Robineau D, 'Ageing Britain: two-fifths of NHS budget is spent on over-65s' *The Guardian* (London, 1 February 2016) https://www.theguardian.com/society/2016/feb/01/ageing-britain-two-fifths-nhs-budget-spent-over-65s (access 29th October 2019).

Ryff C, Singer B and Love G, 'Positive health: connecting well-being with biology' (2004) 259 *Philosophical Transactions, Royal Society* 1383.

Sandberg L, 'Affirmative old age: the ageing body and feminist theories on difference' (2013) 8 *International Journal of Ageing and Later Life* 11.

Sargent-Cox K, Rippon M and Burns R, 'Measuring anxiety about aging across the adult lifespan' (2014) 26 *International Psychogeriatrics* 135.

Segal L, *Out of Time: The Pleasures and the Perils of Ageing* (Verso 2013).

Shildrick M, *Leaky Bodies and Boundaries* (Routledge 1997).

Shildrick M, *Embodying The Monster: Encounters With The Vulnerable Self* (Routledge 2002).

Sze L, 'How can we slow the ageing process?' *British Council* (24 April 2015) https://www.britishcouncil.org/voices-magazine/how-can-we-slow-ageing-process (access 29th October 2019).

Taylor J, 'Getting old sucks!' *Psychology Today* (13 December 2013) https://www.psychologytoday.com/gb/blog/the-power-prime/201312/getting-old-sucks (access 29th October 2019).

Thompson C, 'Meeting the needs of an ageing population' *NHS* (11 February 2015) < https://www.england.nhs.uk/blog/catherine-thompson/> (access 29th October 2019).

UN Department of Economic and Social Affairs, 'World population prospects' *United Nations* (New York, 2013) <https://population.un.org/wpp/Publications/Files/WPP2012_HIGHLIGHTS.pdf> (access 29th October 2019).

Watkins S, 'Does an "ageing population" make it harder to afford our NHS? A look behind the rhetoric' *Open Democracy* (30 November 2016) https://www.opendemocracy.net/en/ournhs/does-ageing-population-make-it-harder-to-afford-our-nhs-look-behind-rhetoric/ (access 29th October 2019).

Weicht B, 'The making of 'the elderly': constructing the subject of care' (2013) 27 *Journal of Aging Studies* 188.

Weiss D and Lang F, 'The two faces of age identity' (2012) 25 *Journal of Gerontopsychology and Geriatric Psychiatry* 5.

World Bank, *Averting the Old Age Crisis: Policies to Protect the Old and Promote Growth* (Oxford University Press 1994).

Response

Reflections on ageing and the binaries of vulnerability

Rosie Harding

Introduction

Jonathan Herring's chapter in this volume begins with a characterisation of two understandings of vulnerability, which he calls 'particular deficient vulnerability' and 'universal beneficial vulnerability'. He locates the first of these contrasting accounts in public discourse. His own (Herring 2016) and Martha Fineman's (2008) contributions to understanding vulnerability underpin his understanding of the latter. In this response, I challenge this binary construction of conceptual and popular understandings of vulnerability and explore what it might mean to think of vulnerability as both universal and particular; as both beneficial and troublesome. I then go on to focus on the challenge of ageism in the context of vulnerability and resilience, exploring how individualised responsibility for health dominates so much of the discourse of ageing. I argue that rather than, as Herring suggests, changing our thinking to consider vulnerability as a positive attribute, we need to focus our attention on the wider relational contexts that help some people to develop resilience in the face of their vulnerability.

Challenging the binaries of vulnerability: universal/particular; beneficial/deficient

When working with concepts like vulnerability to help explain social life, dichotomies like universal versus particular or beneficial versus deficient are both helpful and constraining. In Herring's contribution, he leads us through different interpretations of the concept of vulnerability, contrasting public policy interpretations of the vulnerability of specified groups or individuals with recent theoretical approaches to vulnerability (Fineman 2008; Herring 2016). Through this theoretical approach, the concept of vulnerability becomes a productive space in which the universal fragility of the human condition can be theorised.

I agree with both Herring and Fineman that vulnerability is a productive concept and that vulnerability theory can help critical scholars to articulate justifications for political and legal responses to human frailty. It is important, however, to be careful of the unintended consequences of setting vulnerability up within polarised binaries which have positive and negative connotations. Here, I take a little space to work through just how much distance there is between the polarised interpretations of vulnerability Herring offers and to ask whether it is substantively possible to separate the two in the way that those of us who consider vulnerability to be a productive concept might want to do.

The first question that we need to explore is whether vulnerability, when considered an individual trait, is *negative*. Certainly, this is the way vulnerability was most often constructed in work that pre-dates Fineman's (2008; 2010; 2012; Fineman and Grear 2016) approach to vulnerability and the human condition. Yet if an individual or a group of individuals who share similar characteristics are categorised as 'vulnerable', does this necessarily mean that we are constructing that individual or group in a negative manner? This is not as straightforward as it may initially seem. If we understand vulnerable groups or persons as either responsible for their own vulnerability or of 'behaving in a way deemed undesirable' (as Herring has decoded this account of vulnerability), then certainly we seem to populate the word *vulnerable* with negative traits.

A helpful example of this (predominantly negative) construction of vulnerability is the one set out by Vanessa Munro and Jane Scoular (2012) in their article about vulnerability and prostitution policy in the UK. In that work, Munro and Scoular highlighted the complex ways that 'vulnerability' has been used in UK political discourse, through the example of a group of women who are both at risk of harm (women engaged in sex work have significantly higher risk of being the victim of violence and have higher rates of sexually transmitted infections than the general population) and are constructed as the source of vulnerability for others (those who are negatively affected by proximity to sex work). At the heart of the tension they expose in the political operation of the concept of vulnerability is that (ibid., 194):

> Exactly what it means not only to be vulnerable but to suffer an 'abuse' of that vulnerability – though crucial in triggering a formal state response in this context – is left markedly ill-defined, and the question of exactly what it is that a person is vulnerable to is often marginalised, as the mere designation of vulnerability is afforded central stage.

While Fineman (2008) would dispute the usefulness of considering particular groups to be more or less vulnerable than others, there is an important kernel of critique in Munro and Scoular's analysis. To be vulnerable is to be exposed to the potentiality of harm, but that vulnerability becomes actionable, in a political sense, only when the harm shifts from an abstract potentiality to a substantive and immediate harm or risk of harm. In other words, the state only responds to immanent harm, not general risk.

Another use of the term, more closely related to ageing, is helpful in excavating this meaning. In the original Department of Health 'No Secrets' guidance (2000), which precipitated the founding of the 'safeguarding adults' regime in England and Wales (Brammer 2014), a 'vulnerable adult' was defined as a person over the age of 18 (Department of Health 2000, 3):

> Who is or may be in need of community care serves by reason of mental or other disability, age or illness; and who is or may be unable to take care of him or herself, or unable to protect him or herself against significant harm or exploitation.

Here, we see that there were two elements to the original definition of 'vulnerable adult' in the safeguarding context: that the person themselves has some internal reason for needing community care (disability, age, illness); they are unable to look after themselves (so therefore require assistance to do so) or they are unable to protect themselves from 'significant harm', which could include both self-neglect and harm caused by others, or they are unable to protect themselves from exploitation by others. Vulnerability, as constructed in the *No Secrets* guidance, therefore utilised a definition which is very close to the inherent/situational/pathogenic taxonomy outlined by Catriona Mackenzie, Wendy Rogers and Susan Dodds (2014). It focused on inherent characteristics (disability, age, illness), alongside situational contexts (unable to take care of themselves) and pathogenic relations (unable to protect themselves from significant harm or exploitation).

Interestingly, the use of the term 'vulnerable' does not appear in the more recent statutory restatement of safeguarding in the Care Act 2014. In the Law Commission report (2011, 114) that preceded the Care Act 2014, they noted that 'the term *vulnerable adult* appears to locate the cause of abuse with the victim, rather than placing responsibility with the actions or omissions of others.' The new definition of adults who fall into the safeguarding remit remains very similar, focusing on a combination of inherent, situational and pathogenic vulnerabilities, while simultaneously removing the reference to individual 'groups'. It does this by restating the definitional threshold in more universal language in the primary legislation:

S. 42(1) This section applies where a local authority has reasonable cause to suspect that an adult in its area (whether or not ordinarily resident there) –

   a   has needs for care and support (whether or not the authority is meeting any of those needs),
   b   is experiencing, or is at risk of, abuse or neglect, and
   c   as a result of those needs is unable to protect himself or herself against the abuse or neglect or risk of it.

In this new definition, we appear to have moved away, in the statutory safeguarding landscape, from a focus on harm that discursively locates the negative emphasis on the individual. Instead, the new definition focuses on 'abuse' or 'neglect', both of which imply a relational context. Clearly both 'abuse' and 'neglect' are negative concepts, but the language of the new definition does seem to point more in the direction of this arising from negative relationships or situations, rather than within an individual's inability to look after themselves. This suggests that vulnerability has been recognised, within this new definition, to be rooted within the broader social context an individual finds themselves in, rather than their inherent characteristics.

We also appear, at least at first glance, to have moved from a situation where only particular groups (disabled people, older people, ill people) were constructed as vulnerable and in need of safeguarding to a definition that appears to be universal. It looks, therefore, if we only explore the primary legislation, that the adult safeguarding framework has been recast from a focus on 'particular deficient vulnerability' to a universal approach. The universality of this definition has to be understood, however, within the constraints of the overall regulatory regime. Under the Care Act 2014, individuals only fall into the safeguarding definition if they have 'needs for care and support'. These 'needs' are quite strictly defined through The Care and Support (Eligibility Criteria) Regulations 2015,[1] and only apply where a) the needs 'arise from or are related to a physical or mental impairment or illness'; b) relate to specific 'outcomes';[2] and c) iterate a 'significant impact on the adult's well-being'.[3] As a result, despite the discursive shift away from the explicit language of vulnerability, the safeguarding regime continues to apply only to specific groups: those whose well-being is at risk as a result of their 'impairment or illness'. Importantly, however, even this specificity is no longer grounded in identarian categories (disability, age) but captures all those who experience illness or impairment, howsoever caused.

The universal language of the statute is therefore modified by the secondary legislation that sets the criteria for access to state support to a 'particular' approach, founded on specific needs and circumstance. This new 'safeguarding adults' framework, I think, demonstrates that vulnerability as a legal concept needs to be both universal, in the sense that all humans are vulnerable, and also attentive to variability across the life course and between individuals. As Fineman (2008, 1) put it, vulnerability is 'universal and constant, inherent in the human condition'. This does not, however, mean that everyone at all times experiences that vulnerability in the same way. Instead, the experience of vulnerability, and resilience to the multiple harms that our universally vulnerable human condition iterates, vary from person to person because of goods like resources, education

---

1 SI 2015/313.

2 The outcomes are listed at Paragraph 2(2) and include inherent characteristics like managing nutrition, personal hygiene, toileting, 'being appropriately clothed' being safe at home, 'maintaining a habitable home environment' as well as more relational contexts like developing and maintaining personal relationships, accessing community facilities and services, engaging in education or employment, and caring for their own children. A person who in unable to achieve two of the 12 outcomes would satisfy the safeguarding needs threshold.

3 The Care and Support (Eligibility Criteria) Regulations 2015 SI 2015/313 paragraph 2. Well-being for the purposes of the Care Act is defined in s. 1 of the Act itself.

level, geographical location, interpersonal relationships and even simple luck. State responses to vulnerability, however, often (perhaps always) require some form of threshold, definition or means testing. Resources are always finite, and redistribution of them is most properly done on the basis of need, with regard to individual circumstances. In the particular case of adult safeguarding, there are also questions of interference with a person's private and family life, or their choices. As a result, the state response to universal human vulnerability cannot always be universal. Instead, we need to ensure that the response to vulnerability is directed, proportionate and free from stigma.

A vulnerability approach, in my view, does not require us to lose sight of the particular. My understanding of universal vulnerability is that it provides a persuasive basis for arguing that the state has a responsibility to be both attentive and responsive to the dependencies that arise from vulnerability when it is experienced, and to have universal policies in place, which provide access to that response at the appropriate moment in a particular life.

Similarly, while political engagements with the concept of vulnerability (like that identified by the Law Commission [2011]) have often been negative, it seems to me that it does not necessarily follow that universal vulnerability is either beneficial or deficient. Fineman's concept of vulnerability does not seek to tell us anything in particular about individuals or groups of individuals organised by identity category or individual characteristics. Universal vulnerability simply seeks to demonstrate a basic commonality across all (fragile) human life: that we are all vulnerable and that we all live with the potential for that vulnerability to translate into individual needs, dependencies and changes. As a consequence, the liberal construction of individuality or human autonomy is a dangerous myth that obscures our ability to respond to genuine human needs.

Vulnerability can be potential (in that we all hold the possibility of change) or actual (in that conditions in a person's life have given rise to one or more needs or dependencies), but the key point is that it is universal. My reading of Fineman's work on vulnerability does not, however, lead me to consider vulnerability to be a positive or beneficial human trait. Rather, it makes more sense to propose universal vulnerability as value-free, inherently neither positive or negative, simply an unavoidable facet of the human condition, that provides an impetus for the responsive state to provide the means to develop resilience.

There is, of course, a great deal of political and rhetorical potential in suggesting that we should repopulate the term *vulnerability*, away from negative 'particular deficiencies', and away from a value-neutral construction like that proposed by Fineman, into a positive trait. Herring's contribution to this collection demonstrates that potential. Yet by recasting universal vulnerability as beneficial (and in opposition to an understanding of vulnerability as a personal deficiency), Herring is, I think, taking vulnerability theory in a new direction, one which I am not convinced is necessary. In contrast, I consider that we do not need to valorise the fragility of humanity to harness the productive potential of vulnerability as a concept. Rather, I consider that vulnerability is useful in thinking about state responses to ageing precisely because of its value-neutral universality.

Vulnerability and ageing: challenging ageism

In Herring's chapter, he drew attention to bodies, loss of autonomy, identity and the responsive state. In focusing on these issues, he highlighted the valorisation of youth, and the stereotype of ageing as decline. In this section, rather than directly respond to Herring's arguments, I want to focus on how ageism, in combination with the contemporary focus on individual responsibility for health, creates at least some of the negativity that Herring outlines.

Ageism is understood as discrimination against older people simply because they are old (Butler 1969) and also includes a reliance on stereotypes (whether positive or negative) about age (Iversen et al. 2009). Not all ageism is focused on older people – the young also often experience ageism in employment, in relation to both pay and promotion. Ageism is, in many respects, different from other categories of social difference or 'protected characteristics' as these are expressed in equality law. In part, this is because age does not correlate to identity in the ways that other characteristics (like gender, ethnicity, sexuality, religion/belief or disability) do. Instead, chronological age is a universal phenomenon, which does not so easily connect with identarian politics or social movements.

Ageing does not work well as an identity category because it is both fluid and universal. Fluid, because the numerical age at which a person becomes 'old' or 'older' is relative (to the others around them) – in my daughter's primary school class, she is one of the younger ones – some children in her class are nearly a year older than her. When she started school that was 25% older. As she gets older that year will become progressively less significant. But the proportionate relationship is interesting. By the age of 40, 25% is a decade; at 80 it is two decades. If we translate those numbers across different contexts, numerical age becomes meaningless as a signifier of vulnerability.

Different social contexts mean that a man who was born in Glasgow has a life expectancy of just over 69 years, whereas a man born at the same time on the same day in the same year in Kensington and Chelsea would be expected to live 82 years (Office for National Statistics 2014). These differences are exacerbated if we take a global, rather than local, view with differences of over three decades between the countries with the highest and lowest life expectancy.[4] These geographical variations further complicate any attempt to construct identity categories around age. Indeed, the idea of particular rights for 'older persons', as is one focus of the UN's open-ended working group on ageing, often struggles to make headway, in part because equality discourse is not effective in tackling the issues that ageing and ageism generate (Harding 2018).

Yet there remain significant and substantive gaps, internationally, in the protection of older people's rights. I have argued elsewhere (Harding 2018) that a capabilities approach may offer a more useful conceptual basis than in/equality for a new international convention on the rights of older people (Sen 1985; 1995; 1999; 2010; Nussbaum 1999; 2013). Here, the question is whether a vulnerability approach might similarly offer a starting point for tackling the

---

4 See www.worldlifeexpectancy.com for figures and analysis.

substantive disadvantages experienced by older people, such as those negative constructions of ageing identified by Herring, and also the significant gaps in protection of older people identified by the UN High Commissioner for Human Rights (UN High Commissioner on Human Rights 2012).

In order for vulnerability to provide a useful conceptual starting point for addressing the substantive disadvantage experienced by (some) older people (being aware that this is often refracted through gender, class, 'race'/ethnicity, poverty and other life contexts and experiences), we need to be attentive to both the positive *and* negative consequences of vulnerability. As Fineman (2012, 96) put it:

> Sometimes, and perhaps even ultimately, our vulnerability results in weakness, or physical or emotional decline. But properly understood in the context of the human condition, vulnerability is also generative. Importantly, our vulnerability presents opportunities for innovation and growth, creativity and fulfilment. It makes us reach out to others, form relationships, and build institutions. Human beings are vulnerable because as embodied beings we have physical and emotional needs for love, respect, challenge, amusement and desire.

Challenging ageism requires a move away from a political understanding of older people as especially vulnerable, to focusing on responding to those cases and instances when people have additional needs for support. The real difficulty, however, will come in addressing the continued stigma that attaches to having those needs for support.

Contemporary public health messages are often iterated through 'nudge' politics (Thaler and Sunstein 2008; Vallgårda 2012; Carter 2015). This neoliberal, governmentalising approach places responsibility for 'successful ageing', 'active ageing', 'healthy ageing' or any number of variations on this theme, onto the individual (Lamb, Robbins-Ruszkowski and Corwin 2017). Rather than assume an element of decline, contemporary politics 'says *you* can be the crafter of your own successful aging – through diet, exercise, productive activities, attitude, self-control and choice' (ibid., 2). The personalisation of responsibility for ageing well, and the recent rise in neoliberal discourse around individualised responsibility for health is, in my view, a particularly noxious iteration of the autonomous liberal subject. It is this discourse that a vulnerability approach needs to undermine, if it is to offer an alternative view of ageing.

A direct consequence of this active/healthy/successful ageing discourse is that positive social and political attention becomes focused only on those who age successfully – who avoid becoming disabled, ill or dependent. Vulnerability theory offers us an alternative approach. Instead of focusing on those older people who have the good fortune[5] to maintain good health and personal independence

---

5 I do not consider good fortune here to be a consequence of mere 'luck' – it is a consequence of a wide range of indicators of social capital, including access to quality healthcare, financial stability, relational support networks and so on.

into their later years, vulnerability theory reminds the state to be responsive to those who need additional support to secure their well-being. By emphasising universal vulnerability, we remind the state that anyone can require extra support, irrespective of their personal attributes or situations. Vulnerability as a universal aspect of the human condition requires us to look at the complex, nested relationalities that combine to create collective and individual experiences of life and care (Nedelsky 2011; Harding 2017). In turning to and interrogating these complex networks of social attributes, life experiences, norms, policies and laws, the different ways that these affect individual experience can be drawn out. Opportunities for state intervention, targeted at helping individuals develop resilience to the consequences of our universal human vulnerability, can then come into view.

Concluding remarks

In contrast to Herring, I do not see vulnerability through the lens of binaries (positive/deficient; universal/particular). For me, the universal vulnerability of the human condition is neither positive nor negative; it just is. Universal vulnerability also does not obscure individual, particular experiences of harm or risk. Instead, it offers us a way of thinking through how the state could and should respond to the constant potentialities of vulnerability within the human condition.

Bibliography

Brammer A, *Safeguarding Adults* (Palgrave Macmillan 2014).

Butler R. N, 'Age-ism: another form of bigotry' (1969) 9(4) *The Gerontologist* 243.

Carter ED, 'Making the blue zones: neoliberalism and nudges in public health promotion' (2015) 133 *Social Science & Medicine* 374.

Department of Health, 'No secrets: guidance on developing and implementing multi-agency policies and procedures to protect vulnerable adults from abuse' (London 2000) <https://assets.publishing.service.gov.uk/government/uploads/system/uploads/attachment_data/file/194272/No_secrets__guidance_on_developing_and_implementing_multi-agency_policies_and_procedures_to_protect_vulnerable_adults_from_abuse.pdf>.

Fineman MA, 'The vulnerable subject: anchoring equality in the human condition' (2008) 20 *Yale Journal of Law and Feminism* 1.

Fineman MA, 'The vulnerable subject: Anchoring equality in the human condition' in MA Fineman (ed), *Transcending the Boundaries of Law* (Routledge-Cavendish 2010).

Fineman MA, 'Elderly as vulnerable: rethinking the nature of individual and societal responsibility' (2012) 20 *Elder Law Journal* 71.

Fineman MA and Grear A, 'Equality, autonomy, and the vulnerable subject in law and politics' in MA Fineman and A Grear (eds), *Vulnerability: Reflections on a New Ethical Foundation for Law and Politics* (Routledge 2016).

Harding R, *Duties to Care: Dementia, relationality and law* (Cambridge University Press 2017).

Harding R, 'Equality, social justice and older people' in I Doron and N Georgantzi (eds), *Ageing, Ageism and the Law* (Edward Elgar 2018).

Herring J, *Vulnerable Adults and the Law* (Oxford University Press 2016).

Iversen TN, Larsen L, and Solem PE, 'A conceptual analysis of ageism' (2009) 61(3) *Nordic Psychology* 4.

Lamb S, Robbins-Ruszkowski J, and Corwin A. I, 'Introduction: successful aging as a twenty-first-century obsession' in S Lamb (ed), *Successful Aging as a Contemporary Obsession* (Rutgers University Press 2017).

Law Commission, *Adult Social Care* (Law Com No 326, 2011).

Mackenzie C, Rogers, W, and Dodds S, *Vulnerability: New Essays in Ethics and Feminist Philosophy* (Oxford University Press 2014).

Munro VE and Scoular J, 'Abusing vulnerability? Contemporary law and policy responses to sex work in the UK' (2012) 20(3) *Feminist Legal Studies* 189.

Nedelsky J, *Law's Relations: A Relational Theory of Self, Autonomy and Law* (Oxford University Press 2011).

Nussbaum MC, 'Women and equality: the capabilities approach' (1999) 138(3) *International Labor Review* 227.

Nussbaum MC, *Creating Capabilities: The Human Development Approach* (Harvard University Press 2013).

Office for National Statistics, 'Life expectancy at birth and age 65 by local areas in the united kingdom: 2006-08 to 2010-12' (*Office for National Statistics* 16 April 2014) <https://www.ons.gov.uk/peoplepopulationandcommunity/birthsdeathsandmarriages/lifeexpectancies/bulletins/lifeexpectancyatbirthandatage65bylocalareasintheunitedkingdom/2014-04-16#local-area-life-expectancy>

Sen A, *Commodities and Capabilities* (Oxford University Press 1985).

Sen A, *Inequality Reexamined* (Oxford University Press 1995).

Sen A, *Development as Freedom* (Oxford University Press 1999).

Sen A, *The Idea of Justice* (Oxford University Press 2010).

Thaler RS and Sunstein CR, *Nudge: Improving Decisions about Health, Wealth, and Happiness* (Penguin 2008).

United Nations Economic and Social Council, 'Report of the UN High Commissioner on Human Rights'.

UN High Commissioner on Human Rights, 'Report of the UN High Commissioner on Human Rights' (Geneva 2012) <https://www.un.org/ga/search/view_doc.asp?symbol=E/2012/51>

Vallgårda S 'Nudge—a new and better way to improve health?' 2012 104(2) *Health Policy* 200.

Part 3
Healthcare law

The idea of vulnerability in healthcare law and ethics: from the margins to the mainstream?

Mary Neal[1]

Introduction

Without vulnerability, there would be no need for healthcare, or law, or ethics. Each of these systems owes its existence to the fact that human beings are open, fragile and fallible. The idea of vulnerability might seem to deserve a prominent place in thinking and writing about healthcare law and ethics (HCLE), therefore. But what exactly do we mean by 'vulnerability' when we refer to it in the context of HCLE, and what *should* we mean by it? Must the theory and practice of HCLE adopt an understanding of vulnerability that applies in other contexts too, or should we be seeking a bespoke concept of vulnerability particular to the HCLE setting?

The idea of vulnerability has had a chequered history in HCLE literature. It has figured mainly at the margins of the discourse, where it has tended to be associated with risk, harm and exploitation and seen as something undesirable to be minimised or eliminated. Since the turn of the millennium, however, there has been a pronounced shift towards more direct, explicit engagement with the idea of vulnerability.

In this chapter, I will begin by using a Wittgensteinian approach to enquire into what 'vulnerability' currently means in the context of HCLE.[2] I will observe that the meaning of vulnerability in HCLE is in flux and suggest that, although our thinking, talking and writing about healthcare *seems* to be progressing towards a more appropriate engagement with the idea of vulnerability, now would be an appropriate moment to take stock of developments. In the latter part of the chapter, I will offer some clarifications, draw some key distinctions and emphasise some important themes, in order to facilitate the development of our understanding.

1 School of Law, University of Strathclyde. I am grateful to the participants at the roundtable event *Vulnerability Is Good: The Implications for Law of Positive Accounts of Vulnerability*, held at Exeter College, Oxford, on 5 July 2017, and to the editors for their very helpful feedback on an earlier draft of this chapter.

2 I will use the terms 'bioethics' and 'healthcare law and ethics' ('HCLE') interchangeably when discussing the discourse that embraces both law and ethics, but when referring to the law only, I will use 'medical law'.

Setting the scene: language-games and 'meaning is use'

It is necessary to begin by enquiring into what vulnerability *currently* means in HCLE, before we can reflect critically on this and consider whether we want it to retain this meaning, or to mean something else. In relation to enquiries about (current) meaning, Ludwig Wittgenstein (2009, para 43) famously declared: 'For a *large* class of cases of the employment of the word "meaning" – though not for all – this word can be explained in this way: the meaning of a word is its use in the language.' In other words, if we want to know what we currently understand a word to mean, we must start by gathering examples of the ways in which we use it (as opposed to attempting to construct a definition in the abstract). This is one of Wittgenstein's most well-known and discussed philosophical claims, and it is often summarised in the slogan 'meaning is use.' In order to put this insight into practice, however, we must combine it with another of Wittgenstein's (ibid., para 23) most influential ideas, the notion of the 'language-game'. This is because the context in which we ought to be looking for examples of use is the particular 'language-game' in which we are searching for meaning.

If words have meaning in the context of particular 'language-games', we need to be able to recognise language-games (and identify the relevant one) in order to discover meaning by observing use. As we might expect, given Wittgenstein's approach to meaning, he never attempts to provide an abstract definition of the term 'language-game' itself, but instead offers examples, dotted throughout the *Philosophical Investigations*, of situations in which language-games are being played. Wittgenstein's examples are small-scale: small acts of describing, telling, lying, explaining, instructing and so on count as 'language-games', presumably because Wittgenstein's aim is to show us how language-games are in operation in even the most mundane exchanges. In previous work, I have argued for extending the label 'language-game' to much larger and more complex linguistic enterprises like fields of academic inquiry (specifically, legal inquiry; Neal 2012, 110–11). As I have noted (ibid., 110), it seems reasonable to interpret Wittgenstein as meaning that '[a]ny instance of language-use in which the participants are sharing a purpose or are "playing" by shared rules will probably count as a language-game. Language-games will inevitably overlap, and words may have different meanings within different language-games.'

The final point here is of critical importance: since all terms except narrow 'terms of art' are used in a plurality of language-games, and since words derive their meanings from their use in particular language-games, it follows that the same word *may* turn out to have different (perhaps very subtly different) meanings within these different contexts. An example which springs immediately to mind is 'dignity', which is often observed to have a number of different possible meanings, including 'the intrinsic worth of human beings' (which seems to be its primary use in human rights discourse) and 'noble bearing' (arguably its primary use in lay discourse). Accordingly, we need to know which language-game is the relevant one before we can gather *relevant* examples for the purposes of inquiring into the term's meaning (how it is used in the context in question).

Sometimes, controversy about the meaning of a word will arise – or *seem* to arise – *within* a particular language-game. 'Dignity' is again illustrative here: even within the context of human rights discourse, different writers use 'dignity' to signify different things, and the question arises as to whether one of these uses is correct, and the others mistaken. It might be argued that this is because human rights discourse is not a single language-game at all, but the nexus at which numerous other political, legal and philosophical language-games intersect; if so, that would explain the difficulty with persuading all participants to converge on one meaning of a word like 'dignity'. If human rights discourse *is* a single language-game, however – or has *become* a distinct language-game over time – then I would argue, following Wittgenstein, that it is necessary to agree upon *one* way of using dignity – one meaning of 'dignity' – that all players of the game abide by. This is, obviously, no mean task, given the centrality the notion of dignity is assumed to have in human rights discourse and the enormous literature devoted to *dis*agreeing about its 'meaning' in that context, but it is a task that we cannot abandon if human rights discourse is to be conducted other than at cross purposes.

Just as different putative meanings may jostle for primacy within the space of a single language-game, conversely the meaning of a word or phrase (like 'vulnerability', for example) may be shared across different language-games because they share roots, purposes or other relevant features. As I have observed in the context of an argument about the meaning of 'dignity' (ibid.):

> Of course the various language-games within law will share a proportion of their terminology, rules, and so forth, in common – some of the terms and concepts used may even mean the same things across different language-games, given the fact that some of the language-games within law may actually be offshoots from a common trunk. In many cases, then, the language-games of law will be very closely related and have some of their purposes, rules and concepts in common, but this will be true to varying degrees, and in some cases what seems like a concept occurring in two language-games may instead be two separate concepts sharing the same terminology.

Thus, a word like 'vulnerability' might turn out to mean the same thing across different language-games, or it might not. One thing to bear in mind, however, is that if, following Wittgenstein, 'meaning is use' (rather than words having fixed meanings that are external to our dealings with them), then we are not 'stuck' with whatever the historical or current meaning of 'vulnerability' turns out to be, since we can agree to use it in a different way in future. This does not mean that we can use it in any way we like, of course, and the condition of widespread agreement would presumably preclude all but a narrow range of potentially reasonable uses.

Vulnerability as a marginal idea in healthcare law and ethics

What has 'vulnerability' traditionally signified, then, in HCLE? In light of my Wittgensteinian approach to meaning, this can be translated as asking: how has the term been used, and how is it presently used, in the context of the HCLE language-game? Given that the landscape of healthcare is largely populated by subjects whose physical and mental health is threatened or compromised, and those caring for them, it would be natural to assume that a widespread recognition of the ubiquity of human vulnerability must always have been central in the HCLE literature. This is far from the case, however. Although 'reference to vulnerability is used widely in bioethics' (Wrigley 2015, 478), nevertheless as Florencia Luna and Sheryl Vanderpoel (2013, 325) note,

> In the categorical (or traditional) approach to vulnerability in medical and research ethics, those considered 'vulnerable' seem to be drawn up from a list of 'usual suspects': persons with mental or behavioral disorders, prisoners, residents of nursing homes, people receiving benefits or social assistance, the unemployed, patients in emergency rooms, some ethnic and racial minority groups, homeless persons, nomads, refugees.

Vulnerability, these authors argue, has been regarded as a *marginal* phenomenon in HCLE, something that affects 'a list of identifiable subpopulations' rather than human beings generally (ibid.). The Belmont Report (1978), commissioned by the US government in the wake of high-profile ethical failures by medical researchers, is one early, and notable, example of this tendency to regard only certain individuals or subpopulations as 'vulnerable'. So what might explain the tendency to marginalise vulnerability in HCLE?

The liberal, autonomous subject of healthcare law and ethics

Commentators have often observed that the human subject, as conceived by law in general, is a 'liberal subject', assumed to be rational, autonomous and independent. As Jonathan Herring (2016, 1) has put it recently in the context of a comprehensive discussion of vulnerability in law:

> The law is built around the ideal of legal personhood: a man who is autonomous, self-sufficient, in control, capacitous, and independent. For such a man the law gives the legal tools he needs to maintain his status: the rights of autonomy, privacy, liberty, and freedom from state interference. For him, legal rights are designed to keep him free from intrusion. Rights are designed to keep people apart, to give people their space.

Herring (ibid., 14, 1) warns that the assumption about selfhood that underpins law – 'the assumption that we are competent, detached, independent people who are entitled to have our rights of self-determination and autonomy fiercely protected'– is false; in fact, it is 'all a dangerous fiction'. This should lead us to wonder: if it is a dangerous fiction in law generally, how much *more* fictitious (and dangerous) is the image of the liberal self in the context of HCLE? Yet in HCLE, too, liberal assumptions about selfhood have exerted powerful gravitational force.

Relatively early in the late-twentieth-century flourishing of HCLE as a discipline, one ethical approach quickly gained prominence in the US, coming to dominate teaching and theorising about medical ethics there during the decades that followed. 'Principlism', or the 'four principles approach', describes four key ethical principles – respect for autonomy, beneficence (acting in the patient's best interests), non-maleficence ('do no harm'), and justice (fairness and equality) – and understands ethical decision-making in healthcare as being a matter of balancing whichever of the principles are applicable to a given decision (which may be a decision about an individual patient's treatment, or a governance decision, for example, about how health resources should be distributed; Beauchamp and Childress 2013). Although it has been criticised from a variety of rival perspectives (Holm 1995; see also the various contributions to a Festschrift edition of the *Journal of Medical Ethics* in honour of Raanan Gillon volume 29(5), 2003), principlism has, nevertheless, had an enduring appeal in medical ethics, probably because it offers a user-friendly framework for making complex decisions which, for some, seems to chime with widespread intuitions about morality.

Although the architects of principlism do not explicitly 'rank' the four principles, the principle of respect for autonomy has assumed particular prominence, both within the framework of principlism (one notable proponent of the approach has called it the 'first among equals'; Gillon 2003), and – importantly – apart from it. The latter point is important because, as Chadwick and Wilson (2018, 195) have recently noted, 'prominent UK bioethicists largely rejected the principles-based approach endorsed by the majority of their counterparts in the USA,' and bioethics in the UK was 'generally regarded less as a stable discipline and more as what Onora O'Neill (2002, 1) calls "a meeting ground for a different number of disciplines, discourses and organisations"'. (A small but vocal utilitarian cohort is perhaps the main exception to the general distrust of 'systematic' ethics in the UK.) Nevertheless, the ideal of the autonomous patient and disapproval of the paternalistic professional may be as powerful in the UK as the US, albeit that here, autonomy seems to exist more as a standalone ethical principle in the classical liberal mould, and as a challenge to utilitarianism. Writing about the US context, Carl Schneider (1998, 3) remarked in 1998 that 'the law and ethics of medicine are today dominated by one paradigm – the autonomy of the patient,' and few would claim that things have changed substantially since then, on either side of the Atlantic.

Perhaps because it appears to align neatly with the rational, autonomous image of the subject enshrined in liberal law (described by Herring 2016), the principle of respect for autonomy has also been influential in the courts' development of medical law, especially in relation to issues like consent and the right to refuse treatment. The absolute right of a competent patient to refuse treatment for any reason or for none (articulated by Lord Donaldson in the case of *Re T* [1992] EWCA Civ 18 and reaffirmed in various subsequent cases, including *St George's Healthcare NHS Trust v S* [1999] Fam 26), even when that will result in death, is probably the most potent symbol of the idea's dominance in medical law.

At first glance, all of this emphasis on autonomy and self-determination in healthcare might seem surprising: patients are often (but not always) more than usually dependent, and more than usually susceptible to being hurt and harmed, so that it might seem more natural to regard them as vulnerable than as independent 'liberal subjects'. Would not a model of subjecthood in which vulnerability is foregrounded be more apt in HCLE? One need not be a particular critic of the liberal model of subjecthood *in general* to question its application to the subject in *this* context, surely?

The emphasis on the autonomy of the patient and her ability to decide for herself must be understood in the context of the fact that modern HCLE emerged in the late twentieth century *in significant part* as a corrective to the 'doctor knows best' paternalism of previous eras. In America, bioethics seems to have emerged as both an academic discipline and a social movement after the 1950s, having as its key figures writers like Paul Ramsey (1970), who questioned the prerogative power of the clinician and the expectation that patients and the public would be passive in the face of it. In the UK, where the equivalent movement happened decades later (beginning in the 1980s), the most influential actors included the legal academic Ian Kennedy (who had been very influenced by American bioethics during his time in the US, and who became a vocal – yet constructive – academic critic of medical paternalism in the UK), and the campaigning Patients' Association, which challenged the profession's 'ownership' of medicine by debating issues of medical ethics in the public square. The anti-paternalists who drove the development of HCLE were well aware of professional power but chose to counter it by minimising talk of vulnerability, instead emphasising 'patient power' and the model of the patient as a rational, autonomous rights-holder, entitled to participate in decision-making and, ultimately, to choose for himself. Accordingly, the image of the patient as autonomous and self-determining might be understood more as a rhetorical/political strategy than as an attempt to reflect the realities of the healthcare encounter.

Vulnerability as a marginal/background phenomenon

Vulnerability has figured in this autonomy-heavy picture as a background theme. Although not explicit in the 'four principles' approach, nevertheless the idea of vulnerability can be said to be omnipresent in healthcare ethics in a foundational sense, since vulnerability is presupposed by *all* ethics. As Martha Nussbaum (1998, 275) has observed, 'moral excellence is about taking risks to protect human vulnerability: if vulnerability is denied, then the traditional virtues lose their point.' Writing specifically in the context of healthcare ethics, Margrit Shildrick (2002, 102) has claimed that 'it is vulnerability itself, of the one and of the other, and the responsibility that it engenders in the one and for the other, that is the provocation of ethical subjectivity,' and Jacob Dahl Rendtorff (2002, 237) considers that 'respect for the vulnerability of the other is the foundation of ethics in our time.'

As noted earlier in this section, however, explicit concern with vulnerability has tended to be confined to cases involving those identified as 'vulnerable subjects' and 'vulnerable groups'. And this approach is mirrored in law: as Herring (2016, 45) explains, in healthcare law and in law generally the concept of *capacity* – which Herring defines as the ability to make legally binding decisions for oneself – operates to draw convenient lines that confine the label 'vulnerable' to narrow subsets of population. 'Capacity', he writes, 'is used by the law as a key marker between the vulnerable and the non-vulnerable'. Because of liberal law's commitment to freedom, its starting point is to *assume* (ibid., 41)

> that adults have capacity, are autonomous, and are able to make decisions for their life which are worthy of respect. The general law's rules apply to such people. There are then special areas of the law which are marked off for those lacking capacity.

Thus, in healthcare law as in other areas of law, 'vulnerability' is understood as a characteristic of those whose formal legal capacity is absent, or less than fully present, such as children and people with mental illnesses or disabilities. Everyone else is dealt with under the default paradigm of independent, autonomous subjecthood. When Herring (ibid., 45) tells us that 'those who lack capacity are seen as vulnerable and need protection from themselves and from others,' the obvious implication is that the majority who are assumed to be capable are seen as 'not-vulnerable' and as able to protect their own interests. According to Herring, then, vulnerability is confined, in healthcare *law*, at least, to specialist areas, its zone of relevance apparently coterminous with the zone of impaired capacity. Although there has historically been a willingness to discuss vulnerability in relation to research subjects, therefore, in the context of ordinary healthcare practice vulnerability seems to have been regarded as a marginal phenomenon.

This is not to say that there were *no* accounts of medical ethics in the formative decades of HCLE which sought to foreground vulnerability in everyday medical practice. Notably, for example, Edmund Pellegrino and David Thomasma (1990, 250, 249) discussed how 'the fact of illness creates vulnerabilities in people that a concerned professional is sworn to address' and insisted it was an axiom of medical ethics that 'care must be taken for the vulnerable individual.' As Henk Ten Have (2012, 400) has observed, however, in Pellegrino and Thomasma's ethics, vulnerability – although applied more widely – is still understood in the context of '[illness] threatening the essential unity of the person...wounding and harming the person'. In other words, it is still a negative view in which vulnerability is something harmful and undesirable. Roberto Andorno (2016, 265) has complained that 'modern medical science gives sometimes the impression of being obsessively focused in reducing human vulnerability' as if it was 'an absolute evil to be eradicated'.

It is also worth making explicit here that when vulnerability *is* discussed, it is much more frequently associated with the *recipients* of healthcare – that is, with patients (and their families) and with 'vulnerable groups' or 'vulnerable populations' who may be more 'at risk' of harm than others – than with healthcare *providers*. Again, understanding HCLE as (at least historically) an anti-paternalist project renders this entirely predictable: by definition, an anti-paternalistic approach regards doctors as relatively powerful and patients as relatively powerless, so that it is the vulnerability of the *patient* that primarily concerns anti-paternalists.

There are some signs, however, that this tendency to regard vulnerability as applying only to patients/populations is changing. For decades now, literature produced by clinicians themselves, notably by scholars of nursing such as Joyce Travelbee (1971) and Mary Ellen Lashley (1994), and physician-scholars such as Eric Cassell (2004), has offered us powerful images of the professional as humanised, vulnerable carer. More recently, a substantial academic literature has described and theorised phenomena like 'moral distress' and 'burnout' in relation to health professionals (sometimes, but not always, in relation to debates about conscientious objection in healthcare; Glasberg et al. 2007; 2008; Gustafsson et al. 2010; Morley et al. 2017), and, against the background of pressure on the UK's National Health Service, contributors to the *British Medical Journal* have engaged in discussion about the vulnerability of doctors (Dyer 2013; Munro 2014; Limb 2016).

Overwhelmingly, however, and almost unbelievably given the realities of the healthcare environment, vulnerability in HCLE has been seen as a marginal phenomenon, thought to be attention-worthy only in particular kinds of case. And a marginal view of vulnerability goes hand in hand with a negative view of it: when we confine vulnerability to the margins, we thereby associate it with the circumstances in which harm, risk, exploitation, and helplessness are most pronounced. As Angela Martin and colleagues (2014, 52) noted as recently as 2014, in the healthcare context,

> those are considered as vulnerable who are more likely to be exploited, are unable to protect or safeguard their own interests, lack basic rights, are susceptible to additional harm, or are at risk of unequal opportunity to achieve maximum possible health and quality of life.

In the next section, however, I will argue that HCLE is in the process of developing *other* ways of discussing vulnerability, and that its usage – and therefore its meaning – is currently in flux.

Vulnerability: meaning in flux

Post-millennial reconsideration of the role of vulnerability

As noted in the previous section, 'vulnerability' has historically been used in HCLE discourse primarily in relation to particular groups and individuals who are regarded as being particularly 'at risk', susceptible to harm and/or less able to defend their own interests because of impaired capacity. This entails a negative view of vulnerability and leads to a focus on attempting to reduce or eliminate it. Even some theories in which vulnerability is acknowledged to be relevant in a wider sense, such as that of Pellegrino and Thomasma, still regard vulnerability as a property of 'patients rather than persons in general...located in the state of being ill, not in the human condition as such', and seek to minimise it (Ten Have 2012, 400). Thus, vulnerability has traditionally been understood in HCLE through the lens of the 'ideal' of the autonomous, self-determining patient, and seen as an obstacle to that ideal.

Since the turn of the millennium, however, there have been signs that this is changing and that the alternative, positive accounts of vulnerability that have been developed by feminist writers are beginning to be embraced by mainstream HCLE discourse in a way that disturbs certain key assumptions about vulnerability (in particular, that it is a feature of only some and not all people, and that it is something undesirable that we should seek to reduce or eliminate).

In 1998, as the culmination of a three-year project, a group of experts in bioethics and biolaw from 22 European Union countries ('the EU group') published the Barcelona Declaration (1998), a document containing an agreed set of ethical principles and policy proposals which were subsequently expounded in the group's Report to the European Commission titled *Basic Ethical Principles in European Bioethics and Biolaw. Autonomy, Dignity, Integrity and Vulnerability* (2000). As the titles suggest, the Declaration and the Report recognised four 'basic ethical principles' in healthcare ethics: autonomy, dignity, integrity and vulnerability. In the intervening period, these have come to be known as the 're-vised four principles' and contrasted with the classic principlist approach of Tom Beauchamp and James Childress (sometimes called 'Georgetown principlism' because its originators were, at the time they developed it, based at the Kennedy Institute of Ethics at Georgetown University in the US).

Most noteworthy for present purposes is that 'vulnerability' appears as a principle in its own right in the revised list, given equal billing with autonomy (the only principle common to both lists), in stark contrast with its backstage role in classic principlism, presupposed by beneficence and non-maleficence but never to the fore. Jacob Dahl Rendtorff (2002, 242), one of the signatories of the Barcelona Declaration and the ethicist who, with Peter Kemp, is most closely associated with the 'revised four principles' approach, has noted that, although there was 'considerable disagreement' between members of the group about many matters, 'in particular the notion of dignity', nevertheless there was 'total agreement on the importance of articulating the notion of vulnerability' in the document.

The prominence given to vulnerability by the EU group is a radical departure in itself, but the way 'vulnerability' is articulated within the revised four principles approach also raises a number of questions. This articulation by Kemp and Rendtorff in 2008 (2008, 240) is representative:

> [vulnerability] expresses the condition of all life as able to be hurt, wounded and killed...[and] must be considered as a universal expression of the human condition. The idea of the protection of vulnerability can therefore create a bridge between moral strangers in a pluralistic society, and respect for vulnerability should be essential to policy making in the modern welfare state. Respect for vulnerability is not a demand for perfect and immortal life, but recognition of the finitude of life and in particular the earthly suffering presence of human beings.

Here, vulnerability is clearly understood both as '*universal*' (applying to all human beings) and as *normative* (capable of 'creat[ing] a bridge between moral strangers'); note that Kemp refers not merely to 'vulnerability' but to '*protection of* vulnerability' and '*respect for* vulnerability'. The idea that vulnerability is something to be 'protected' and 'respected' also indicates a less negative view of vulnerability than is traditionally found in bioethics and seems to suggest a departure from the 'vulnerability-reducing agenda' and a willingness to embrace vulnerability in some sense.

There is a great deal to unpack here, and in the wake of the EU project, and the academic outputs in which Rendtorff and Kemp advocated their approach, numerous writers have been provoked to reflect afresh on the role and meaning of the idea of vulnerability in the healthcare context. In the first section of this chapter, I claimed that one of the main advantages of a Wittgensteinian approach to meaning, which regards 'meaning as use', is that we are never stuck with whatever the current meaning of a term happens to be; we can alter the meaning of a term like 'vulnerability' by using it differently in future. Since meaning is not an objective 'given', we have some element of *choice* regarding what words will mean. In fact, in the case of vulnerability, we are faced with *several* decisions about use/meaning.

In the remainder of this chapter, I will seek to explore whether we should understand vulnerability as '*universal*' or '*particular*'/'*situational*', or whether we can understand it as *both*; whether we should understand vulnerability simply as a *fact* about the human condition, or as also having some degree of *normative* force; and how we should understand the relationship between vulnerability and autonomy – does focusing on vulnerability necessarily involve a de-prioritising of autonomy, or a different understanding of it? As will become clear, these questions are interlinked.

Universal or particular?

I noted earlier that the 'predominant' use of the term 'vulnerability' in HCLE has been its use to refer to the heightened susceptibility to harm that individuals or groups experience in conditions of particular risk or helplessness, so that those who are 'vulnerable' are 'those who should be afforded *special* protection and *additional* attention in medical research and health care' (Martin et al. 2014, 52, emphasis added). This has had the effects of (i) marginalising the idea of vulnerability in healthcare by treating it as something that arises in 'special cases' and (ii) embedding a view of vulnerability as undesirable, a threat to individual autonomy, and thus something that should be reduced or eliminated where possible.

In the postmillennial literature, however, the hitherto 'predominant' use – signified by terms such as 'particular vulnerability', 'specific vulnerability', 'situational vulnerability', 'variable/selective vulnerability' and/or 'susceptibility' – has been criticised on a number of grounds. Kate Brown (2011, 315–316), for example, notes the potential for *particular* vulnerability to be deployed in ways that are 'oppressive, controlling, and exclusive' and summarises academic criticism of it as

> [centring] predominantly around three objections: (i) that it is a paternalistic and oppressive idea, (ii) that it functions as a mechanism of widening social control and (iii) that calling individuals or groups 'vulnerable' can act to exclude and stigmatise them, particularly where people's behaviour may not conform to accepted notions of victimhood or innocence. Some authors also note that vulnerability is not necessarily a label that those being singled out as such would identify with.

A concern for many writers is 'the deficit-oriented nature of the term [vulnerability] and its link with stigma' (ibid., 319). Levine and colleagues (2004, 47) caution that 'the concept of vulnerability stereotypes whole categories of individuals without distinguishing between individuals in the group.'

Martin and colleagues (2014, 52, emphasis added) point out the potential for 'oversight of some individuals who are inappropriately *not* regarded as vulnerable'. Conversely, other commentators worry that the lack of a settled definition of 'vulnerable' allows for 'almost everyone [to] be classified as vulnerable in some way', so that the idea of vulnerability is becoming 'useless as a means of picking out special status' (Wrigley 2015, 478). In the healthcare context specifically, it has been observed that '[s]ince its first mention in the Belmont Report (1979), an ever wider range of categories and sub-categories of vulnerable persons has been identified, resulting in seemingly exhaustive lists of vulnerable populations' (Ten Have 2012, 398). On a slightly different note, I have previously wondered whether a 'vulnerable groups' approach, combined with a 'vulnerability-reducing agenda', might (Neal 2012, 186)

> provide incentives for individuals to perceive and represent themselves as vulnerable in order to qualify for and benefit from enhanced protections or allowances, which in turn could result in a 'competitive vulnerability' wherein different groups and their advocates strive to secure the best 'deals'.

These criticisms all focus on the potential *harms* that might be caused by a 'particular' approach to vulnerability, but such an approach might also be criticised on *conceptual* grounds, on the basis that it fails to acknowledge – and may even *mask* – the reality of the human condition. The reality, according to an increasing number of contemporary writers, is that vulnerability is a 'fundamental human constant', an 'essential attribute of mankind' (Kottow 2004, 285, 284) and 'an intrinsic element of human life' (Andorno 2016, 265). Michael Kottow (2004, 283) has observed that, in the most recent literature on vulnerability in healthcare, '*two* distinct forms of vulnerability need to be unravelled,' as what Luna and Vanderpoel (2013) call the 'traditional' (particular) account is increasingly juxtaposed with references to 'universal', 'inherent' or 'essential' vulnerability.

Ten Have (2012, 401), for whom 'vulnerability is...a fundamental expression of the human condition' credits Onora O'Neill (1996) with having 'introduced' the distinction between 'persistent' (universal) and 'variable' (particular) vulnerability in 1996. Whatever its origins, the distinction is now widely observed, and many influential writers advocate for a 'universal' understanding of human vulnerability. The Vulnerability Theory of feminist legal theorist Martha Fineman (2008, 1) is one of the best-known examples of a comprehensive theory that proceeds upon the insistence that vulnerability is 'universal and constant, inherent in the human condition', but there is increasing support for an acknowledgement of 'universal' vulnerability among those who write about HCLE now too. As mentioned already, the 'revised four principles' approach undoubtedly sees vulnerability in that way, and many other writers are happy to embrace the idea of vulnerability as universal. Ten Have, Roberto Andorno, Kottow and Herring are just a few notable cases in point; likewise, Wendy Rogers, Catriona Mackenzie and Susan Dodds (2012, 12) recently acknowledged that 'all human life is conditioned by vulnerability, as a result of our embodied, finite, and socially contingent existence.'

The idea that vulnerability is universal has undeniable intuitive appeal: after all, who can deny that all human beings are susceptible to harm, and dependent on others for our survival? But agreement that universal vulnerability is an *anthropological fact* is one thing; positing vulnerability as a 'basic ethical principle' and something that deserves our 'respect' and 'protection' (as the revised four principles approach does) is another (Rendtorff 2002, 241).

Fact or value?

The distinction between *fact* and *value* is a prominent theme in discussions of universal vulnerability. Rendtorff and Kemp (2000, 46), key academic proponents of the revised four principles approach, insist that 'in ordinary language [vulnerability] is not only descriptive but at the same time explicitly normative. Thus, in the discussion of vulnerability we cannot maintain a sharp distinction between fact and norm because vulnerability is mostly always already an ethical concept.' For Rendtorff and Kemp, then, as Ebbesen (2011, 241) observes, 'the fact that a person is vulnerable entails a demand to respect the vulnerability of that person.' But this is robustly contradicted by a number of critics. Kottow (2004, 28), for example, warns that '[b]y stating that humans are vulnerable and that this constitutes an ethical principle, a naturalistic fallacy is being committed.' Andorno (2016, 265), too, is adamant that '[o]ur shared vulnerability is a *fact*, which cannot have per se any normative effect.'

Martin and colleagues (2014, 62, emphasis added) agree that vulnerability cannot 'ground any direct obligation' in and of itself, but point out that it 'exists because we have welfare and agency interests which can be frustrated', and *'the moral importance of these interests*, rather than vulnerability itself' is capable of generating moral obligations. Andorno (2016, 270) makes the same point when he acknowledges that, although vulnerability *per se* is purely descriptive and 'deprived of any normative value,' nevertheless it has normative implications in combination with the recognition that human beings have intrinsic worth:

> legal systems take into account the fact that we are ontologically vulnerable and, for that reason, recognize rights and establish procedures for ensuring their respect. But they have previously assumed that we have inherent dignity. In sum, if the fact that we are vulnerable leads to the recognition of human rights, it is because we are dealing with the vulnerability of a kind of beings that possess inherent worth.

This insight is important, as it explains how observations about 'universal vulnerability', while undoubtedly descriptive of an anthropological fact, can – in theory, at least – have normative implications/generate moral obligations when combined with evaluative premises about human worth (I will return to this point later). Some other criticisms of the idea of 'universal vulnerability' as an ethical principle must also be mentioned, however.

One of the most frequent criticisms is that 'vulnerability' is an inescapably vague and meaningless term. As Ten Have (2012, 397) acknowledges, 'the notion of vulnerability is criticised as being too vague, too narrow, and too broad. It is often used as a "conversation stopper." There is no commonly accepted definition.' Because there is no simple, uncontroversial way of defining vulnerability, he agrees, the idea 'does not provide clear moral guidance' (ibid.).

Anthony Wrigley (2015, 478) argues that the we should stop attempting to use the term 'vulnerability' in normatively load-bearing ways; he claims that it is not a normatively substantive concept and has 'no genuinely explanatory role' since it does not express anything about the world which is not already captured more usefully by other familiar concepts. We should use vulnerability 'only as a kind of warning or signal', he says, 'a linguistic marker drawing our attention towards already well-understood ethical concepts and concerns such as physical harms or exploitation' (ibid., 479).

Very similar sorts of criticism have also been levelled against the idea of 'dignity'. Dignity, too, has been criticised on the basis that it is 'difficult to fathom' (Advocate-General Christine Stix-Hackl in the case of *Omega Spielhallen und Automatenaufstellung GmbH v Oberbürgermeisterin der Bundesstadt Bonn*

[2004] ECR I-9609, [74]), that it is too subjective and 'hardly up to the heavy-weight moral demands assigned to it' (Pinker 2008), and that it means nothing that is not captured more effectively by other values (like autonomy and respect for persons; Macklin 2003). Even some of its supporters have acknowledged that dignity is essentially a 'rhetorical ornament' (Barroso 2012, 333) – something people mention 'when they want to sound serious but are not sure what to say' (Waldron 2012, 201) – and that conceptually, it is 'in such disarray that it does not provide even a minimally stable frame for global discourse and action' (Mattson and Clark 2011, 305). All of this has led me to observe, elsewhere, that 'a number of academic commentators… deny that [dignity] is normatively meaningful or that it can have anything other than a polemical value in ethical debates' (Neal 2016, 83). Yet I was – and still am – unconvinced by these denials, since (Neal 2012, 117)

> A range of vague and contested concepts, such as justice, fairness, reason-ableness, mercy and compassion, are arguably indispensable to an under-standing of what 'law' is (as distinct from force, power, control, tyranny, and so on)…. [A]ny claim that dignity should be ignored or derided simply because it appears vague and contested ought to make us ask whether we may also ignore similarly vague/contested concepts such as justice, fairness, mercy and compassion…. In practice, we base a great deal on unscientific, contested concepts all the time.

I tend to agree with Jeremy Waldron (1988, 31), therefore, that

> Conceptual definition is a complicated business and the idea that it always involves the precise specification of necessary and sufficient conditions must be regarded as naive and outdated. A term which cannot be given a water-tight definition in analytic jurisprudence may nevertheless be useful and important for social and political theory; we must not assume in advance that the imprecision or indeterminacy which frustrates the legal technician is fatal to the concept in every context in which it is deployed.

Ideas can be indeterminate and resist agreed definition, yet still express some-thing indispensable. 'Dignity' seems to be one such concept, and 'vulnerability' (in its universal sense) is arguably another. Indeed, as Ten Have (2012, 397) remarks, '[i]t is striking that nearly all scholars, critical or not, concur that the notion of vulnerability should not be abandoned since it is already so common.'

However, a couple of the points Wrigley (2015, 482) makes can lead us to some important insights about universal vulnerability. First, he says that

> The problem with [universal vulnerability] is that if we are all vulnerable and we are vulnerable in virtue of this being a natural fact about us, then trying to avoid it or seeking special protection because of it becomes largely futile as it is simply a natural part of everyone's existence.

This is only a problem with universal vulnerability if we *are* 'trying to avoid it or seeking special protection because of it'. But those who appeal to *universal* vulnerability seem not to use the idea in this way, that is, as a marker of special concern existing in the context of a vulnerability-reducing agenda. That is how *particular* vulnerability is used, so as noted earlier, it is fair to criticise accounts of *particular* vulnerability in which the label 'vulnerable' is attached so indiscriminately as to render almost everyone 'vulnerable', and the status itself essentially meaningless (if everyone is *particularly* vulnerable, then no one is). But the criticism is only valid in that context because there is a clear need to *restrict* the scope of that kind of vulnerability. In the case of universal vulnerability, there is no such need, since the point is not to highlight the particular vulnerability of *only some* people: quite the contrary. As such, criticisms of overextension can be legitimate *only* in the context of particular vulnerability. It is important to be clear about this, and Wrigley's critique helps to bring it out.

Wrigley (ibid.) also makes the following point about what *kind* of ethical function he thinks universal vulnerability can, and cannot, perform:

> [universal vulnerability] is far too broad to act as anything other than an underlying presumption about all human beings and is unable to generate ethical duties that go beyond what we would owe to every human in virtue of their being human. This is problematic....

But *is* it problematic? What if the proper role of *universal* vulnerability is far more foundational, and the work that we need it to do is *not* to generate any specific ethical rule(s) or principle(s), but rather to describe more accurately the foundations of our ethical selfhood in relationship with one another – to reposition/recalibrate our understanding of ourselves and one another, as a corrective to liberal myths? This may sound like a purely descriptive role, but insofar as our normative conclusions are premised on perceived 'facts' about ourselves, a serious acceptance of universal human vulnerability would have normative implications. This links back to the insight that, although acknowledgement of universal vulnerability is a recognition of anthropological fact, it can be a legitimate basis for moral claims when combined with normative premises (e.g. that all human beings possess are intrinsically morally valuable).

Such a 'foundational' function alone may not be enough, however. Wrigley (ibid.), for example, insists that if 'vulnerability' is to be analytically useful (and ultimately he concludes that it is not), we also need it to do the work of 'identify[ing] cases where people or groups are open to harm in ways that are different to a standard norm for humans'. In other words, there is a need for the marking-out function that 'particular' vulnerability can perform, whether or not vulnerability also has a foundational role in our ethics. This seems to be supported by Rogers and colleagues (2012, 12) when they acknowledge that 'vulnerability is universal; at the same time, many vulnerabilities are context-dependent and demand ethical responses because of their significance within a particular setting.'

Perhaps, then, we want to use vulnerability in *both* of its 'two forms'; perhaps we need to 'unravel' them *not* in order to choose one usage over the other, but in order to understand and use them *both*. Is it open to us to choose this? Several commentators see no issue with using vulnerability in both ways simultaneously. Martin and colleagues (2014, 53), for example, regard the difference between the two uses as quantitative rather than qualitative:

> the two apparently disparate views of vulnerability are neither competitive nor contradictory. In fact, they depend on each other, since they refer to the very same concept with different likelihoods of manifestation: the notion of vulnerability requiring protection just for some needs to be embedded into the view that vulnerability encompasses everyone.

As such, in their view, 'the controversy concerning the scope of vulnerability does not represent a true problem but rather a philosophical *pseudo* problem' (ibid., emphasis added). Herring (2016, 7) agrees that there is no contradiction in using vulnerability in both the universal and particular senses 'once it is recognised that the second understanding is seeking to identify a category of people who are vulnerable in a way *above and beyond* the way we are all vulnerable'.

As has been mentioned already, however, any proposal for a dual-use approach must contend with the fact that the use of vulnerability to mark out particular at-risk groups or individuals has been challenged, and not only on the basis of over-extension leading to meaninglessness. As touched on above, some critics argue that this usage paints vulnerability as negative/undesirable/to be minimised, thus stigmatising those who are said to possess it and that it can be deployed in paternalistic or controlling ways. But I want to offer a suggestion up for consideration, namely, that while these pitfalls may apply to the 'particular' form of vulnerability when it is the *only* sense in which 'vulnerability' is used, they may be less likely to materialise if 'particular' and 'universal' senses of vulnerability are *both* used within an analytical framework. This is admittedly no more than speculation on my part at the moment, but I wonder whether the presence of a foundational acknowledgement that we are *all* inescapably vulnerable, and that 'particular' vulnerability is simply a heightening of the vulnerability that characterises all of us all of the time, might work to mitigate any tendency to overextend particular vulnerability, to adopt an overly negative view of it and to stigmatise those said to possess it. If the universal/particular distinction were to be seen as merely a 'matter of degree', these problems *may* be less pronounced.

Before concluding, it is necessary to return to a subject raised earlier, namely, Andorno's insight that in order for a statement about human vulnerability to have normative force and generate moral obligations, as opposed to being a simple description of anthropological fact, it must be combined with a normative premise about human beings. Note that this point applies to statements about universal and particular vulnerability alike. The vulnerability of humans makes ethical claims on us because we hold pre-existing evaluative beliefs about human beings (e.g. that they possess dignity or intrinsic value), so that their vulnerability, when we encounter it, is appreciated as the vulnerability of morally relevant or morally important beings and demands a response from us because we value the beings whose interests are threatened by it. Catriona Mackenzie (2016, 92) makes essentially the same point when she writes about the 'entwinement' of our vulnerability and neediness with the 'morally salient' characteristics of human beings such as 'our rational, emotional and agential capacities, as well as our capacities to suffer and to experience well-being' and claims that '[t]he aim of developing an ethics of vulnerability...is to highlight this entwinement and hence the moral salience of vulnerability.'

An immediate issue here is that the main candidates for the normative premises that might be conjoined with the fact of vulnerability to yield ethical obligations are *themselves* often criticised as indeterminate, multiply valent ideas. The examples Andorno cites – dignity and intrinsic worth – are cases in point: concepts endowed with a range of contradictory, controversial meanings. I have already said that I do not regard ideas as useless or purely polemical on this basis; on the contrary, I believe that essentially contested concepts can and do perform important functions in our ethical and legal discourse. Nevertheless, if our aim is to 'cash out' the idea of vulnerability into practical normative guidance, trying to do so by reference to other contested concepts *without defining precisely what we mean by them* is unlikely to take us very far. It seems like common sense to look for normative premises that are as clearly defined as possible.

Vulnerability and autonomy

Another concern arises if the normative premises we cite ultimately make the normativity of vulnerability depend on *individual autonomy*, because this would create the risk that our theorising about vulnerability, and our application of it, would slip full-circle back into the liberal mythology that the mainstreaming of vulnerability is an attempt to redress. This risk would arise, for example, if we were to take, as our normative premise, a version of human dignity or intrinsic worth that is too closely bound up with individualistic or atomistic notions of autonomy, or an idea like 'personhood' which tends to draw heavily on cognitive capacities and the capacity for self-determination.

How, then, can we theorise vulnerability in a way that minimises the risk of sliding back into an overemphasis on individual autonomy? One option is to choose normative premises in which autonomy is not the focus. There are accounts of human dignity, for example, which do not particularly emphasise autonomy. In my own previous writing, I have argued that what we value when we respect 'human dignity' is the apparently unique sense in which humanity, and human life, embodies a balancing of the fragile/material/finite and the transcendent/sublime/immortal (Neal 2012, 198):

> [W]hat is distinctive about dignity and differentiates it from other 'grand' principles of ethics, like autonomy, or sanctity, is...that it gives vulnerability a place of honor...what we value when we invoke 'dignity' is a kind of

balancing, or equilibrium, which is only valuable, or admirable, *because we are vulnerable*...[N]ot only is vulnerability a necessary condition without which this kind of good would not be possible; it is *an essential part of the good* of dignity. Other ethical principles respond to vulnerability too, but they value entities and actions either in spite of vulnerability, regardless of it, or to the extent that it is overcome. Dignity, on the other hand, treats vulnerability as a *source* of value.

In claiming this, I am arguing for a unique form of what Mackenzie (2016) calls the 'entwinement' of vulnerability with a morally salient characteristic, namely, that vulnerability is a prerequisite for, and a component of, the value of human dignity. Various others have also recognised that autonomy is only *part* of the dignity picture and have appreciated the importance of respecting dignity in conditions of reduced or absent autonomy (Hale 2009).

Arguably, however, there is a need, when theorising vulnerability, to 'pay sufficient attention to obligations to foster agency and autonomy' alongside the obvious focus on meeting needs and protecting against harm, in order to avoid paternalism (Rogers et al. 2012, 22–23). As Rogers and colleagues (ibid) argue:

> If human persons are both vulnerable and capable of autonomy, then we need an account of autonomy that is premised on recognition of human vulnerability, and we need an analysis of vulnerability that explains why we have obligations not only to protect vulnerable persons from harm, but to do so in a way that promotes, whenever possible, their capacities for autonomy.

The key, they say, is to strike the appropriate *balance* between protection and support for autonomy, and they consider that *relational* theories of autonomy are best suited to this task, since (ibid., 24)

> [Relational] autonomy is...premised on the fact of our inescapable dependency on, and hence vulnerability to, others. Moreover, because relational theorists regard agency and some degree of autonomy as important for a flourishing human life, a relational approach is committed to the view that the obligations arising from vulnerability extend beyond protection from harm to the provision of the social support necessary to promote the autonomy of persons who are more than ordinarily vulnerable.

What we might seek to avoid, then, may not be normative premises that emphasise autonomy *at all*, but ones that emphasise the individualistic liberal-legal vision of autonomy that helped to edge the idea of vulnerability out to the margins of HCLE discourse in the first place. Relational accounts of autonomy seem to offer a particularly promising alternative vision, since any foregrounding of relationships necessitates a focus on the sorts of factors – such as openness and interdependence – that are also bound to be central to discussions of vulnerability (see Mackenzie and Stoljar 2000; Dove et al. 2017). Relational accounts may also be particularly useful in the healthcare context because they tend to emphasise the embodied nature of the subject (Walter and Ross 2014).

Another kind of 'alternative' account of autonomy is Onora O'Neill's (2002) 'principled autonomy'. In contrast with many contemporary accounts, O'Neill understands autonomy *not* as being about 'independence or self-determination or self-expression' (ibid., 62), but rather, following Kant, as a matter of 'acting on...principles of obligation' (ibid., 84). This is, she says, 'a different and older view of autonomy' than the individual autonomy emphasised within classic principlism (ibid., 73–74). A key feature of O'Neill's account is its strong emphasis on *trustworthiness.* Claudia Wiesemann (2017) notes that vulnerability is a prerequisite for trust. She quotes Carolyn McLeod's observation that someone who trusts 'must be able to accept that by trusting, s/he is vulnerable, in particular to betrayal' (ibid., 162) and reflects that, this notwithstanding, relationships involving vulnerability and trust – she cites the parent–child relationship and romantic partnerships, among other examples – are 'considered very rewarding types of human relationship' (ibid., 156). Moreover, this is '*because* of the vulnerability involved, not *despite* it. Since we cherish the idea that someone is committed to promote our personal good we welcome relationships that are characterized by vulnerability and trust' (ibid., 164). Vulnerability cannot be 'bad per se', (ibid.) therefore, because it is a prerequisite for something 'we all value,' namely, relationships of trust (ibid., 162).

When we understand vulnerability through the lens of trust, according to Wiesemann, this also enables us both to appreciate vulnerable people as active moral agents and to better understand the nature of our moral obligations towards them. First, Wiesemann (ibid., 164) argues that 'by bestowing and refusing trust', a vulnerable person 'actively engages in relationships with those who are to protect her in her vulnerability' and so 'should be considered an active moral agent in her relationships'. Thus, for Wiesemann (ibid., 161–162), '[c]onceptualizing vulnerability in terms of trust helps to orientate the decision-making process toward the (potentially) vulnerable as moral agents' instead of them being 'patronized and reduced to passive objects of care' (ibid., 161–162).

Moreover, making the relationship between vulnerability and trust explicit helps clarify that the *kind* of obligations that are owed to vulnerable people are obligations owed 'to persons who trust' (ibid., 165). This does not give us precise information about the content of our obligations, since the appropriate moral response to trust will be person- and context-specific. But Wiesemann's key point is that when we encounter vulnerability, the most appropriate moral response will not necessarily be to seek to reduce or eliminate it, even where that is possible. There are two possible responses to vulnerability: one is 'to minimize the need to trust', but the other is 'to invest in those factors assuring and maintaining trustworthiness' (ibid., 167). In the healthcare context, specifically, minimising vulnerability and the need to trust 'is not realizable in every situation given the complexities of medical progress and the natural limitations of (patient) autonomy' (ibid.). Therefore, trusting in the 'integrity and goodwill of a health care practitioner' will often be a reasonable way (and indeed, may be the only possible way) for a patient to respond to her vulnerability and face 'the complexities of medical treatment' (ibid.).

Wiesemann (ibid., 167) concludes that each of both types of response to vulnerability can be appropriate in different contexts; sometimes, we should respond to vulnerability by seeking to minimise it, and at other times by trusting, or encouraging trust. If, as she argues, each is 'indispensable for controlling vulnerability' (including in healthcare), this entails that it is necessary to create and sustain a culture wherein trust is encouraged and rewarded (ibid.). As Wiesemann's work makes explicit, relationships of trust inevitably involve vulnerability, so that accounts which emphasise trustworthiness are accounts in which the subject is necessarily understood as vulnerable (even while her autonomy is being emphasised). In both 'relational' and 'principled' accounts of autonomy, therefore, we find autonomy theorised in ways that acknowledge the subject as simultaneously autonomous *and* vulnerable. Just as it seems there is no need to choose between the universal and particular understandings of vulnerability, then, neither does there appear to be any need to choose between valuing vulnerability and valuing autonomy.

Conclusion

When analysing engagement with the idea of vulnerability in HCLE scholarship, it is analytically useful to identify two distinct periods. In the late twentieth-century, the dominant voices in HCLE were those that promoted an ideology of the patient as *individually* autonomous and self-determining, with a resultant marginalisation of vulnerability to 'special cases' in which autonomy was significantly impaired. By contrast, the early postmillennial literature has seen many HCLE scholars – led by feminist theorists both inside and outside healthcare scholarship – seeking to reclaim the idea of vulnerability from the margins and to place it front and centre in theorising healthcare. This new willingness to reflect on vulnerability has latterly included a willingness to discuss the vulnerability of healthcare *professionals* as well as patients.

In this chapter, I have used a Wittgensteinian approach to meaning to argue that the use, and therefore the meaning of 'vulnerability' in HCLE, is in flux and that we have a choice about what it will mean in future. My purpose here has not been to advocate for any particular use of the term but rather (i) to note that we have a choice and (ii) to offer some observations that I hope may inform the debates to come.

I have argued that we do not necessarily need to choose *between* the 'particular' and 'universal' senses of 'vulnerability'; we do not need to decide that vulnerability will *either* continue in its marginal role *or* cease to be used in relation to particularly vulnerable individuals and groups altogether. I have suggested – tentatively – that the particular and universal senses of vulnerability can be used in combination and that they might even turn out to be complementary.

Observations about human vulnerability (either particular or universal) can only generate normative conclusions, however, in combination with evaluative premises about the importance of human beings' interests (and so ultimately about the importance of human beings themselves). I have cautioned here against appealing to premises that are themselves dependent on indeterminate or contested ideas, since this will decrease the likelihood of reaching agreement about what the term 'vulnerability' ought to signify in HCLE discourse. I have also cautioned against premises that would render the meaning of 'vulnerability' dependent on a liberal-individualistic conception of autonomy, since that image of the subject seems to have contributed to the marginalisation of vulnerability in the first place, and I have suggested that 'relational' and 'principled' accounts of autonomy are more naturally compatible with vulnerability.

Ultimately, it is for us – the participants in the HCLE language-game – to determine the future meaning of 'vulnerability' within that context, by agreeing how we will use it. That, in turn, will depend on what work we want the idea to do.

Bibliography

Andorno R, 'Is vulnerability the foundation of human rights?' in A Masferrer and E García Sánchez (eds), *Human Dignity of the Vulnerable in the Age of Rights* (Springer 2016).

Barroso LR, 'Here, there and everywhere: human dignity in contemporary law and in the transnational discourse' (2012) 35(2) *Boston College International and Comparative Law Review* 331.

Beauchamp TL and Childress JF, *Principles of Biomedical Ethics* (7th edn, Oxford University Press 2013).

Cassell E, *The Nature of Suffering and the Goals of Medicine* (2dn edn, Oxford University Press 2004).

Chadwick R and Wilson D, 'The emergence and development of bioethics in the UK' (2018) 26(2) *Medical Law Review* 183.

Dove ES, Kelly SE, Lucivero F, Machirori M, Dheensa S and Prainsack B, 'Beyond individualism: is there a place for relational autonomy in clinical practice and research?' (2017) 12(3) *Clinical Ethics* 150.

Dyer C 'GMC and vulnerable doctors: too blunt an instrument?' (2013) 347 *British Medical Journal* 6230.

Ebbesen M, 'Two different approaches to principles of biomedical ethics: a philosophical analysis and discussion of the theories of the American ethicists Tom L Beauchamp and James F Childress and the Danish philosophers Jakob Rendtorff and Peter Kemp' (2011) 7(3/4) *International Journal of Ethics* 233.

Fineman MA, 'The vulnerable subject: anchoring equality in the human condition' (2008) 20(1) *Yale Journal of Law and Feminism* 1.

Gillon R, 'Ethics need principles – four can encompass the rest – and respect for autonomy should be "first among equals"' (2003) 29(5) *Journal of Medical Ethics* 307.

Glasberg A-L, Eriksson S and Norberg A, 'Burnout and "stress of conscience" among healthcare personnel' (2007) 57(4) *Journal of Advanced Nursing* 392.

Glasberg A-L, Eriksson S and Norberg A, 'Factors associated with "stress of conscience" in healthcare' (2008) 22(2) *Scandinavian Journal of Caring Sciences* 249.

Gustafsson G, Eriksson S, Stranberg G and Norberg A, 'Burnout and perceptions of conscience among health care personnel: a pilot study' (2010) 17(1) *Nursing Ethics* 23.

Hale B, 'Dignity' (2009) 31(2) *Journal of Social Welfare and Family Law* 101.

Herring J, *Vulnerable Adults and the Law* (Oxford University Press 2016).

Holm S, 'Not just autonomy - the principles of American biomedical ethics' (1995) 21(6) *Journal of Medical Ethics* 332.

Kemp P and Rendtorff JD, 'The Barcelona declaration' (2008) 46(2) *Synthesis Philosophica* 239.

Kottow M, 'Vulnerability: what kind of principle is it?' (2004) 7(3) *Medicine, Health Care and Philosophy* 281.

Lashley ME, 'Vulnerability: the call to woundedness' in ME Lashley, MT Neal, ET Slunt, LM Bergman and FH Hultgren (eds), *Being Called to Care* (State University of New York Press 1994).

Levine C, Faden R, Grady C, Hammerschmidt D, Eckenwiler L and Sugarman J, 'The limitations of "vulnerability" as a protection for human research participants' (2004) 4(3) *The American Journal of Bioethics* 44.

Limb M, 'Doctors are emotionally "damaged" by complaints, analysis finds' (2016) 354 *British Medical Journal* 3732.

Luna F and Vanderpoel S, 'Not the usual suspects: addressing layers of vulnerability' (2013) 27(6) *Bioethics* 325.

Mackenzie C and Stoljar N (eds), *Relational Autonomy: Feminist Perspectives on Autonomy, Agency, and the Social Self* (Oxford University Press 2000).

Mackenzie C, 'Vulnerability, needs, and moral obligation' in C Straehle (ed), *Vulnerability, Autonomy and Applied Ethics* (Routledge 2016).

Macklin R 'Dignity is a useless concept' (2003) 327 *British Medical Journal* 1419.

Martin AK, Tavaglione N, and Hurst S, 'Resolving the conflict: clarifying "vulnerability" in health care ethics' (2014) 24(1) *Kennedy Institute of Ethics Journal* 51.

Mattson D and Clark S, 'Human dignity in concept and practice' (2011) 44(4) *Policy Sciences* 303.

Morley G, Ives J, Bradbury-Jones C, and Irvine F, 'What is "moral distress"? A narrative synthesis of the literature' [2017] *Nursing Ethics* 1.

Munro J, 'What I know I owe to patients' (2014) 349 *British Medical Journal* 6734.

National Commission for the Protection of Human Subjects of Research, 'The Belmont report: ethical principles and guidelines for the protection of human subjects of research' (1978) (Department of Health Education and Welfare Publication No. (OS) 78-0012)) https://videocast.nih.gov/pdf/ohrp_belmont_report.pdf.

Neal M, '"Not Gods but animals": human dignity and vulnerable subjecthood' (2012) 23(3) *Liverpool Law Review* 177.

Neal M, 'Dignity, law and language-games' (2012) 25(1) *International Journal of the Semiotics of Law* 107.

Neal M, 'Discovering dignity: unpacking the emotional content of "killing narratives"' in H Conway and J Stannard (eds), *The Emotional Dynamics of Law and Legal Discourse* (Hart 2016).

Nussbaum M, 'Political animals: luck, love, and dignity' (1998) 29(4) *Metaphilosophy* 273.

O'Neill O, *Towards Justice and Virtue* (Cambridge University Press 1996).

O'Neill O, *Autonomy and Trust in Bioethics* (Cambridge University Press 2002).

Partners in the BIOMED II Project, 'The Barcelona Declaration on Policy Proposals to the European Commission on Basic Ethical Principles in Bioethics and Biolaw' (adopted in November 1998) <hrlibrary.umn.edu/instree/barcelona.html> (access 16th January 2019).

Pinker S (2008), 'The stupidity of dignity' *The New Republic* (New York, 28 May 2008) <https://newrepublic.com/article/64674/the-stupidity-dignity> (access 16th January 2019).

Ramsey P, *The Patient as Person: Explorations in Medical Ethics* (Yale University Press 1970).

Rendtorff JD, 'Basic ethical principles in European bioethics and biolaw: Autonomy, dignity, integrity and vulnerability – towards a foundation of bioethics and biolaw' (2002) 5(3) *Medicine, Health Care and Philosophy* 235.

Rendtorff JD and Kemp P, *Basic Ethical Principles in European Bioethics and Biolaw. Vol. 1: Autonomy, Dignity, Integrity and Vulnerability* (Centre for Ethics and Law 2000).

Rogers W, Mackenzie C and Dodds S, 'Why bioethics needs a concept of vulnerability' (2012) 5(2) *International Journal of Feminist Approaches to Bioethics* 11.

Schneider CE, *The Practice of Autonomy: Patients, Doctors and Medical Decisions* (Oxford University Press 1998).

Shildrick M, *Embodying the Monster: Encounters with the Vulnerable Self* (Sage 2002).

Ten Have H, 'Respect for human vulnerability: the emergence of a new principle in bioethics' (2015) 12(3) *Bioethical Inquiry* 395.

Partners in the BIOMED II Project, 'The Barcelona Declaration on Policy Proposals to the European Commission on Basic Ethical Principles in Bioethics and Biolaw' (adopted in November 1998) <hrlibrary.umn.edu/instree/barcelona.html> (access 16th January 2019).

Thomasma D, 'Establishing the moral basis of medicine: Edmund D Pellegrino's philosophy of medicine' (1990) 15(3) *The Journal of Medicine and Philosophy* 245.

Travelbee J, *Interpersonal Aspects of Nursing* (2nd edn, FA Davis Company 1971).

Waldron J, *The Right to Private Property* (Clarendon 1988).

Waldron J, 'How law protects dignity' (2012) 71(1) *Cambridge Law Journal* 200.

Walter JK and Ross LF, 'Relational autonomy: moving beyond the limits of isolated individualism' (2014) 133 *Supplement 1 Pediatrics* S16.

Wiesemann C, 'On the interrelationship of vulnerability and trust' in C Straehle (ed), *Vulnerability, Autonomy and Applied Ethics* (Routledge 2017).

Wittgenstein L, *Philosophical Investigations* translated by GEM Anscombe, PMS Hacker, and J Schulte (4th edn, Blackwell Publishing 2009).

Response

Challenging the frames of healthcare law

Dr Beverley Clough

Mary Neal's chapter provides an excellent overview of the historical place of vulnerability within healthcare law discourse and provokes some interesting challenges to those who seek to utilise vulnerability theory in order to rethink the field. This response will engage with some of these challenges in the hope of pushing forward these debates and demonstrating the productive and generative capacity of the concept of vulnerability. It will focus on three key areas – defining vulnerability; moving beyond definition; and challenging dominant frames in healthcare law.

Defining vulnerability

Much of the focus of the chapter is on the ways in which vulnerability both has been used in the past, and can be used in the future, to refer to a particular ontological position and experience. Neal provides the historical context for the positioning of vulnerability in bioethics discourse as antithetical to autonomy and as such marginal to healthcare law. The emergence of healthcare law as a corrective to the idea of 'doctor knows best' is charted by Neal as a key juncture in this pre-eminence of autonomy in the field. One of the interesting points to reflect on here is the idea that the centrality of 'patient power' and the rational, autonomous patient was in some ways a political and rhetorical strategy taken by those who wished to counter the paternalistic ethos of the delivery of modern healthcare. The minimising of any recognition of vulnerability or power imbalances in the doctor–patient (or, more accurately, healthcare system–patient) relationship as part of this strategy was thus simply collateral damage in the political and rhetorical framing of bioethics.

In some ways, we can see the continuation of this strategy in the landmark *Montgomery v Lanarkshire Health Board* [2015] UKSC 11 Supreme Court decision, which has been seen by some as heralding a new era for patient autonomy in consenting to medical treatment, and the end of the paternalism of the *Bolam* standard in relation to the law surrounding informed consent (*Bolam v Friern Hospital Management Committee* [1957] 1 WLR 582).

Notwithstanding doubts as to the extent to which this change has occurred in subsequent judgments (see, for example, *Grimstone v Epsom and St Helier*

University Hospitals NHS Trust [2015] EWHC 3756; *A v East Kent Hospitals NHS Foundation Trust* [2015] EWHC 1038; *XYZ v Warrington and Halton NHS Foundation Trust* [2016] EWHC 331), some of the judicial dicta in *Montgomery v Lanarkshire* run the risk of further entrenching the problematic liberal legal subject and further marginalising recognition of vulnerability in the healthcare encounter. Lords Kerr and Reed emphasised that ([75,76])

> One development which is particularly significant in the present context is that patients are now widely regarded as persons holding rights, rather than as the passive recipients of the care of the medical profession. They are also widely treated as **consumers** exercising **choices**: a viewpoint which has underpinned some of the developments in the provision of healthcare services...Other changes in society, and in the provision of healthcare services, should also be borne in mind. One which is particularly relevant in the present context is that it has become far easier, and far more common, **for members of the public to obtain information about symptoms, investigations, treatment options, risks and side-effects via such media as the Internet** (where, although the information available is of variable quality, reliable sources of information can readily be found), patient support groups and leaflets issued by healthcare institutions. The labelling of pharmaceutical products and the provision of information sheets is a further example, which is of particular significance because it is required by laws premised on the ability of the citizen to comprehend the information provided. **It would therefore be a mistake to view patients as uninformed, incapable of understanding medical matters or wholly dependent upon a flow of information from doctors**. The idea that patients were medically uninformed and incapable of understanding medical matters was always a questionable generalisation, as Lord Diplock implicitly acknowledged by making an exception for highly educated men of experience. To make it the default assumption on which the law is to be based is now manifestly untenable.

As will be discussed further below, the impact of this framing of the empowered consumer patient is not merely rhetorical. It does impact more broadly on the structure of healthcare law and the responses both of the healthcare system *and* of the judiciary. For example, in *Montgomery v Lanarkshire*, there is an implicit assumption that this recognition of patient autonomy and the consumer patient goes hand in hand with recognition of patient responsibilities and the consequent lack of recourse to a remedy through a claim for a lack of consent if things do go wrong ([81]):

> The social and legal developments which we have mentioned point away from a model of the relationship between the doctor and the patient based upon medical paternalism. They also point away from a model based upon a view of the patient as being entirely dependent on information provided

by the doctor. What they point towards is an approach to the law which, instead of treating patients as placing themselves in the hands of their doctors (and then being prone to sue their doctors in the event of a disappointing outcome), treats them so far as possible as adults who are capable of understanding that medical treatment is uncertain of success and may involve risks, **accepting responsibility for the taking of risks affecting their own lives, and living with the consequences of their choices**.

Yet, while the vulnerability of patients has been marginalised and arguably erased from the framing provided in *Montgomery v Lanarkshire*, it is important to recognise that this does not make it disappear. Moreover, the dominant frame of autonomy in fact results in the exacerbation of the experience of vulnerability in different ways in healthcare encounters, given that the systems become configured around a model of the patient (the liberal legal subject) which does not reflect the experience of patients.

In response to concerns about the problematic absence of the recognition of vulnerability in healthcare law and bioethics, a number of scholars have been utilising Fineman's vulnerability theory to expose the consequences of the centrality of autonomy and the liberal legal subject, as Neal outlines. The challenges in doing so in this context have been listed by Neal, including whether a universal or a more particular/situational account of vulnerability is needed, as well as where the normative force or consequences of this recognition can stem from.

The discussion of the universal/particular debate demonstrates the difficulties that theorists have encountered when seeking to utilise the insights from vulnerability theory. Neal highlights, for example, Kate Brown's (2011, 315–316) concern that focusing on particular vulnerabilities can entrench paternalism, function as a mechanism of widening social control and that it entrenches the idea of different groups as 'vulnerable' (Neal this volume, 117). Such an argument however conflates current understandings of vulnerability (as 'other', and requiring a particular sort of policy or legal response) with the suggestions being made by Fineman and others. Similarly, Neal highlights Anthony Wrigley's argument that we should not use vulnerability as a normative concept. He sees universal vulnerability as too broad to generate any ethical duties. Neal rightly points out that the concept of vulnerability captures both the universal and particular elements. I would add here that it is indeed central to the concept of vulnerability that this must be the case. It allows us to focus not only on how, as human and social beings, we are all interdependent and vulnerable (as a central challenge to the liberal legal subject and underpinning assumptions) but also to be attentive to how the particular experience of this has been shaped by particular social, institutional and cultural configurations we are embedded in. The definitional focus (i.e. who can we class as vulnerable) of much of the debate both here and elsewhere in the literature however seems to have become an unwarranted and unnecessary preoccupation which serves to close down the development and engagement with the more productive aspect of vulnerability theory – the idea of the responsive state.

Beyond definition

The responsive state is a central strand of Fineman's vulnerability theory. In many ways, this concept of the state holds much of the generative and creative potential of a shift to recognising vulnerability in healthcare law. The call is for states and institutions to be reconfigured in a way which is attentive to the vulnerable (as opposed to the liberal) legal subject. Being responsive to such a subject – one who is embedded in multiple relations of interdependence – thus entails different renderings of power and legal response. In the healthcare context, for example, it entails recognising power imbalances and the ways in which these are built into the very structures of bioethical and legal frames and how these have been built upon a fictional ideal of autonomy. Recognition of vulnerability as a shared, universal characteristic is thus an almost banal point in vulnerability theory, with the more radical and transformative potential residing in the call to change the structural and institutional scaffolding in law, policy and ethics more broadly. As such, it is not merely about shifting language use but thinking through in a deeper way how the recognition of ontological vulnerability requires a more wholesale reconfiguration of accepted ideas around obligations and responsibility. Interestingly, Neal frames the discussion in the chapter using Wittgenstein's concept of 'language games', which she uses to suggest that in the context of vulnerability discourse, vulnerability is deployed in different contexts with different meaning, yet meaning is not fixed or static and can be changed. In a sense, the discussion of the definitional challenges around vulnerability which have preoccupied much of the healthcare law debate to date can be seen as an instance of this language game. However, it is also important to pay attention to the context and historicity of these language games and to question these linguistic manoeuvres and shifts. For example, we might ask: what spatial, institutional, material and structural context do they occur within? Who gets a say in how such language is used? What are the material impacts of such shifts in language use? Moreover, what other language games are they entangled with? Coming back to the vulnerability discussion here, aside from rethinking what vulnerability means in the healthcare context, we must also be cognisant of *how* this meaning can shift and, more importantly, what the broader effects of this must be.

This is considered to a certain degree by Neal in her discussion of the fact/value distinction and the challenge to the normativity of vulnerability theory posed by scholars such as Wrigley, Kottow and Adorno. The thrust of such arguments is that simply stating that humans are vulnerable does not thereby have any normative force or warrant an ethical response to this. Again, such arguments have become commonplace in the healthcare law literature and in many ways miss the core argument of vulnerability theory. One of the potential insights from recognising universal vulnerability is recognising the constant role of the state, institutions and structures (I would also add culture, discourse and materiality here) in shaping the experience of vulnerability. Such factors are entangled within the very ontology which vulnerability theory begins with. So the issue is less 'why should the state (or ethics) step in to respond to this vulnerable subject?' and more 'what role has the state and institutions played in the experience of vulnerability, and how can this be changed?'

Again, there has been a tendency in the literature to debate vulnerability at the level of discourse or semantics, rather than engaging more fully with the structural, institutional changes which must occur if vulnerability is to emerge from the margins. The following section will consider in more detail some of the specific challenges posed to the structural frames in healthcare law should this shift occur.

Challenging the frames in healthcare law

As Neal discussed in setting out the development of healthcare law and bio-ethics, principlism, while not widely supported, has played an important and enduring role in the framing of bioethics debates. Beauchamp and Childress' (1979) four principles – respect for autonomy; beneficence; non-maleficence; and justice – have been utilised as tools for ensuring a range of different considerations that are discussed as part of ethical debates in this context. Despite the authors' intentions for all of the principles to hold equal weight, autonomy has emerged as the dominant principle – perhaps due to the strong anti-paternalism politics and rhetoric. While the UK has not been as enthusiastic in the embrace of principlism, autonomy *has* similarly become dominant in healthcare law and ethics. One potentially productive way to engage with vulnerability theory and its generative potential is to consider how vulnerability might re-orientate the debates in relation to what have come to be seen as the core principles of bioethics.

It could be argued that such a task is not novel, given that 'vulnerability' has been included in some key bioethics documents such as the EU *Basic Ethical Principles in European Bioethics and Biolaw. Autonomy, Dignity, Integrity and Vulnerability* (2009). Yet is this 'revised four principles' approach enough? Or, would it be enough to simply add 'vulnerability' to Beauchamp and Childress' original four principles? Arguably, this 'add vulnerability and stir' approach misses the opportunity that vulnerability theory offers to rethink the very foundations of healthcare law and ethics. Rather than simply adding vulnerability as an additional consideration alongside the traditional preoccupations which have shaped law and ethics in recent times, fully engaging with the theory instead suggests a more fundamental rethinking of the very status and meaning of concepts such as autonomy, beneficence, non-maleficence and justice.

Autonomy has tended to attract the most criticism from vulnerability scholars in this field, as well as from feminist legal theorists more broadly. This is hardly surprising given its pre-eminence as an organising feature of healthcare law and the contrasting ideal of the legal subject which underpins liberal notions of autonomy and vulnerability theory, respectively. As Neal points out, the debates around autonomy and vulnerability often distil into a questioning of whether autonomy can survive as a principle if vulnerability is taken seriously. Can autonomy be re-orientated so as to become more relational and more attuned to interdependence? If relational autonomy is rejected, and seen as simply clinging to a fictional rendering of the subject, then how else can we conceptualise and exert choice within the structures of healthcare provision and decision-making? Does the informed or individual consent model then require rethinking? Importantly, vulnerability theory calls not just for a shift in thinking about autonomy, but deploying this within a framework built upon liberal ideas of the state and legal subject. To begin with, choice, as part of informed consent, would need to be more carefully considered through the lens of institutional relations, rather than a more abstract, singular and individualised event. Such consent would need to be situated within the broader context, and as an ongoing practice, and the power relations which are institutionally created would need to become more central to our legal analysis. For example, recognising that the healthcare professions are institutions and are socially produced brings an alternative vision of the doctor–patient relationship. The current power relations within these professional–patient interactions will similarly be recognised for their constructed nature and the ways in which these relations are mediated and entrenched through, for example, models of consent. It also entails the recognition that they are not static and thus call for more attention to the role that healthcare law (and law more broadly) has played in structuring such relations and the means through which these could be different. Despite the critique of *Montgomery v Lanarkshire* propounded above, there is an interesting passage within this which provides recognition of this broader structural context ([75]):

> [A] wider range of healthcare professionals now provide treatment and advice of one kind or another to members of the public, either as individuals, or as members of a team drawn from different professional backgrounds (with the consequence that, although this judgment is concerned particularly with doctors, it is also relevant, mutatis mutandis, to other healthcare providers). The treatment which they can offer is now understood to depend not only upon their clinical judgment, but upon bureaucratic decisions as to such matters as resource allocation, cost-containment and hospital administration: decisions which are taken by non-medical professionals. Such decisions are generally understood within a framework of institutional rather than personal responsibilities, and are in principle susceptible to challenge under public law rather than, or in addition to, the law of delict or tort.

This signals the need for a realignment in healthcare law to enable more analysis of these inter-institutional relations, as well as the different legal structures and frameworks which impact upon the more traditional scope of healthcare law, and the decision-making processes taking place within it. Such processes ultimately shape the professional–patient encounter and are too often overlooked in debates around consent and autonomy. In *Montgomery v Lanarkshire*, the problematic erasure of vulnerability through the concept of the (already empowered) consumer patient seemingly mitigates against this broader recognition, however. Moreover, considering the role of the state and institutional obligations, vulnerability theory here suggests a move away from individualising responsibility – both for patients and for professionals – through recognition of our shared interdependence and embeddedness within these institutional structures. This calls into question the broader legal frameworks which are associated with healthcare law – such as tort and criminal law – and their (in)ability to move beyond an adversarial approach to individual obligations.

These debates around autonomy and vulnerability, as noted previously, are fairly common in the literature. Yet what is not often discussed is the impact that vulnerability theory might have on our understanding of concepts such as beneficence, non-maleficence and justice. Importantly, if we do begin to reconsider these concepts through the lens of vulnerability theory then the challenge to autonomy (and its entanglement within these broader concepts or principles) becomes even more critical. Beneficence, or acting in the best interests of the patient(s), can take on a less individualistic hue when considered in relation to a subject who is embedded within a number of different relations, including interpersonal ones. Doing good for the patient in the context of such relations might require different legal or medical responses than those which are entailed within the current frame. Indeed, doing good for the patient or patients may require a response which is not individualised at all; instead, it takes place at a more macro scale. Similarly, non-maleficence, or doing no harm to the patient, would require significant rethinking if vulnerability theory was a foundational, rather than an add-on, concept. The very understanding of harm would be open to change here as the broader contextual positioning of the patient, and their historical and contingent connections and relations, would be brought in with a fuller view of their interdependence. Harm could be recognised not just as an intentional and individually located act done by a healthcare professional to a patient but as more structural and diffuse and taking place at different levels. Again, this would require different responses to those which are currently considered necessary in healthcare law and ethics.

Vulnerability similarly poses some interesting and productive challenges to how justice is currently understood in healthcare law. Justice tends to be relatively overlooked in most bioethical debates, perhaps with the exception of discussion as to the allocation of resources. Often, such discussion put individuals or groups against the 'broader public'. Vulnerability theory instead contains a central challenge to understandings of justice and social justice much more broadly. It brings the state and institutional analysis back in to expose a number of interesting things about power relations, access to resources (not simply monetary, but resources to produce resilience) and the broader structural relations beyond the doctor–patient relationship which often shape such encounters. Moreover, the institutional analysis, and recognition of the role of institutional relations in the creation of particular circumstances, points to a broader concern not just with individual encounters or patients but with a range of different actors and institutions within healthcare processes and their vulnerability.

As can be seen, we should not limit our analysis of vulnerability in healthcare to an additional concept to consider or as something which only poses a challenge to autonomy. Vulnerability theory here must be understood not as marginal but as central and as reconfiguring the ethical concepts which currently dominate this terrain. In engaging with vulnerability, we can trace the frameworks and concepts which currently work together to create a particular vision of healthcare law and disentangle these by considering the broader implications of recognising vulnerability as both embodied and embedded.

Conclusion

The response sought to build upon the foundations laid by Mary Neal in her chapter and to respond to some of the challenges she indicated that have emerged in engaging with vulnerability in the context of healthcare law. The response argues that we need to move beyond the definitional wrangling about who is vulnerable and instead look at the deeper challenge that vulnerability poses for the frameworks of healthcare law. The potential of vulnerability theory goes beyond semantics and instead requires us to shift a number of aspects of the conceptual landscape which are mutually intertwined with autonomy, which is often (wrongly) portrayed at the core target of vulnerability theory. In doing so, we can more clearly see the creative and generative potential that vulnerability has in terms of both discursive and material shifts in the structures of healthcare law. The vulnerable legal subject in this analysis is no longer the passive, negative subject but instead an active agent for broader change.

Bibliography

Brown K, '"Vulnerability": handle with care' (2011) 5(3) *Ethics and Social Welfare* 313.
Beauchamp T, Childress J, *Principles of Biomedical Ethics* (Oxford University Press 1979).
EU *Basic Ethical Principles in European Bioethics and Biolaw. Autonomy, Dignity, Integrity and Vulnerability* (2009).

Part 4
Labour law

The potential and limitations of the vulnerability approach for labour law

Lisa Rodgers

Introduction

Vulnerability theory is a theory of social justice which challenges the ideals and premises of liberal law (MA Fineman 2017, 141). It exposes the unequal outcomes which result from basing law on the liberal notions of liberty, autonomy and, ironically, equality. It suggests that the 'liberal' subject at the heart of liberal law does not reflect the reality of the human condition, and hence law neither protects those actually in need, and those that it does protect are viewed as the opposite of the liberal ideal: dependent, weak and lacking in self-reliance. The vulnerability approach attempts to shift the view of the liberal subject at the heart of law to that of the vulnerable subject (MA Fineman 2010, 263). It is suggested that this vulnerable subject reflects the reality that we are all vulnerable, all of the time. This enables the law and law-making to be viewed more positively; its aim is not to target certain 'vulnerable' persons or groups but to work to enable all persons to build resilience and fulfil their own personal potential. Indeed, recent literature on the vulnerability approach has focussed on recognising vulnerability itself as a positive trait (Gilson 2011, 310; Boubil 2018, 184). While vulnerability may expose us to negative change, it also allows the potential for growth, both personal and institutional (MA Fineman 2012, 116). Vulnerability is viewed as 'generative' as it creates in human beings the 'desire to reach out to others, form relationships, and build institutions' (ibid.). This suggests new potentialities for the law in responding and supporting human interdependency. It is this potentiality of vulnerability which is the main focus of this book.

A number of connections can be made between this vulnerability approach and theoretical approaches to labour law. Indeed, the social justice approach of the classical labour law scholars, Hugo Sinzheimer (1927) and Otto Kahn-Freund (Davis and Freedland, 1983), displays a number of similarities with the vulnerability approach. These authors rejected many of the liberal legal institutions which had come to determine the management of employment relationships and (for that reason) were sceptical of the ability of the law to really improve the lives of workers. They suggested for example that the contract of employment acted as a legal fiction to obscure the reality of the inequalities existing in employment relationships (Davies and Freedland 1983, 24). As a result, they designed a solution which rested not on building law but on building relationships. The building of these relationships was viewed as essential in promoting social justice for workers because it was only this action which could serve to readdress the inevitable power imbalance in existence in employment relationships.

Of course, the language of the early social justice theorists in labour law did not include reference to 'vulnerability' as such, and there are areas of divergence as well as convergence between these two approaches. What is more perplexing is the continuance of the liberal legal approach to the design of labour law despite the existence of these social justice theories both in labour law and beyond. The contract of employment is alive and well as the basic methodology for determining the rights and obligations which arise out of an employment relationship. Liberal theorisations shape, increasingly, our understanding of the labour law world and the allocation of legal and social resources. The aim of this chapter is first to identify this legal problematic and the very negative implications of this problematic for labour. The second section of this chapter will outline the potential of vulnerability theory to challenge some of the assumptions inherent in this liberal approach and the possible outcomes for the development of labour law. The next section looks in more detail at the classical labour law approach to social justice and the vulnerability approach. It highlights where they overlap and where they diverge. The final section sets out the possible limitations of embracing the vulnerability approach in labour law, and, hence, its potential for bolstering social justice.

Liberal legal models and the eclipse of social justice

Despite the tradition of social justice in labour law, liberal models of justice continue to dominate labour law development. Moreover, theoretical innovation in the labour law field has, to a large extent, focussed on the application of liberal legal theorisations to the labour relationship. A good example is the attempt to include labour rights within a human rights theorisation (Adams 2001; Alston 2005). Traditionally, the human rights theorisation follows a liberal argumentation. This argumentation requires the promotion of 'negative' rights, those (civil and political) rights which can be enacted without 'excessive' state interference in individual liberty. Although some labour rights do fall within the civil and political rights category, many fall within the social and economic rights category and require positive state action. For example, minimum wage legislation appears to have more in common with the character of a social rather than a civil or political right, given that the level of the minimum wage will vary over time and according to what the relevant society can afford (Collins 2011, 14). As a result, human rights arguments do not support a number of labour law institutions and tend to be raised successfully only in extreme cases of individual abuse (a good example is the use of human rights arguments to challenge 'slavery' in employment relationships; see *CN v United Kingdom* [2013] 56 EHRR 24). Indeed, the relationship between human rights and trade unions is ambivalent at best, given the difficulties posed to the human rights model of the recognition of collective rather than individual rights (Fudge 2007–2008). In practical terms, trade unions have found it increasingly difficult to gain access to the relevant court systems, particularly when arguing their case under the jurisdiction of human rights (see Ewing and Hendy 2017).

Certainly there have been attempts to challenge the liberal foundations of human rights and move towards a more social justice-orientated approach (see Grear 2010; Turner 2006). Indeed, this can be seen in the contribution of Anna Grear in this volume, which attempts to put vulnerability and the vulnerability approach at the heart of human rights. Likewise, in the labour law field there have been suggestions that 'social' rights can also represent universal, urgent and compelling moral claims and create stringent entitlements that all countries ought to respect (Mantouvalou 2012, 164). However, it appears impossible to surmount the argument that while some labour rights are human rights on the normative analysis, others involve detailed regulation of the labour relationship and hence are not normatively akin to human rights. These rights must be considered 'labour standards' rather than human rights (ibid., 169). There are still other authors who specifically reject the contention that (all) social rights should have the same status as human rights (Gearty 2011, 1). It is argued that this leads to a watering-down of other more urgent and compelling human rights claims and the distortion of the judicial process. Social rights should be enforced through 'politics rather than law' (ibid., 84).

Another example of the persistence and expansion of 'liberal' approaches to labour law is the turn towards arguments based on economic efficiency as the basis for labour law development. These theories assume that employers and employees are free contracting individuals who can use their market position to achieve the best possible allocation of resources between themselves. The ultimate aim of regulation is to ensure the smooth functioning of the market and contractual freedom. It is the belief in this theory that a well-functioning market will bring benefits not just for the individuals entering into market transactions but society as a whole. The wealth generated from economic processes will trickle down to those who need it most (Davies 2009, 27). Arguments based on economic efficiency often have negative consequences for labour law. On this scheme the role of legislation is to stay out of employment relationships as far as possible to allow the parties the greatest freedom to manage their affairs. Labour law represents a 'cost' and generally prevents business from taking full advantage of market opportunities (Davidov 2007, 117). As a result, economic efficiency arguments have been used specifically to downgrade employment protection in the UK and beyond.[1]

1 The current UK government committed to a series of 'Cutting Red Tape Reviews' which aim to free firms from 'over-regulation' and make them more productive. The government programme is available at http://webarchive.nationalarchives.gov.uk/20170613104700/https://cutting-red-tape.cabinetoffice.gov.uk/ last accessed 10 February 2018.

A stark example is that in the wake of the financial crisis, national governments within the Eurozone have been required to reduce the protective content of employment regulation in the name of flexibility and the promotion of employment growth. For example, Portugal committed to a number of deregulatory measures as part of its bail-out package following the financial crisis. A number of reforms were undertaken, including aligning severance payments of open-ended contracts with those of fixed-term contracts, and also reducing the total severance payments for new open-ended contracts. The Portuguese government also committed to reform the law on individual dismissals, and subsequently new laws were introduced to reduce both the notification period for individual dismissals and dismissal compensation payments.[2] Likewise, the Fornero reform in Italy,[3] implemented in 2012, exempted companies from complying with technical requirements in the use of temporary employment contracts and increased the possibility of recourse to contracts of a fixed-term nature. Flexibility was cited as one of the primary motivations of this action. In 2014, the Jobs Act introduced a new open-ended contract with significantly reduced unfair dismissal protection and reduced the compliance requirements for fixed-term and apprenticeship contracts in the name of job creation and stimulation of the economy (see Pizzoferrato 2015, 196). This pattern has been repeated in a number of other countries (see Kilpatrick and de Witte 2014).

It appears that the turn to liberal legal approaches in the field of labour law is either of marginal help or actually proves detrimental to labour law protection. What is surprising is that despite the identification of these negative trends, these liberal legal approaches to law continue to dominate the labour law scene. Certainly, classical social justice theories in the field of labour law do not seem to have provided a successful alternative narrative through which to direct the development of labour law. The question arises whether the vulnerability approach can provide a serious and more sustained critique of these liberal approaches and whether it could be used to boost other social justice theories which have been side-lined by the hegemony of liberal legal discourse. The next section of this chapter will outline the vulnerability critique and how it may be used to critique the current trends in labour law development. Further to that, there will be an assessment of how the vulnerability critique, particularly in its modern formulation, can bolster some of the classical social justice theories of labour law and make them more relevant to the present day. The final section will present some critiques of the vulnerability approach.

Positive contribution of vulnerability theory

Vulnerability theory suggests that in order to challenge the current failure of our legal systems to achieve social justice, our focus must be turned to the reliance of

2 Law 53/2011 and Law 23/2012.
3 Law n. 92/2012 (*Legge Fornero*).

that law, and the economic and political systems within which that law is embedded, on the notion of the liberal subject. According to vulnerability theory, the reliance of our law and its institutions on the liberal subject is socially damaging and strips the law of its effectiveness. The liberal subject of our law and institutions is constructed as an independent autonomous rational being. The problem is that this presentation of the liberal subject is 'reductive' and 'fails to reflect the complicated nature of the human condition' (MA Fineman and Grear 2013, 17). Having this at the heart of our law feeds into and legitimises the domination of certain ideologies; namely, autonomy, self-sufficiency and the inevitability of economic progress (MA Fineman 2010, 263). These liberal institutions and ideologies obscure the realities of social practice and create real inequalities and division between individuals and groups.

In applying this to the employment context, it has been argued that the assumption of liberal law that the parties are 'separate, transacting and contracting individuals, equally capable of agreeing to terms of employment reflecting their respective best interests' is both misleading and divisive (MA Fineman 2018, 2). It is misleading because it suggests that employment relationships are 'private' matters, involving individuals free from social, legal and political constraint. In fact, the employment relationship is imbued with all the assumptions, beliefs, norms and values governing society as a whole. Law absorbs these norms and values and projects them onto the employment relationship and thereby acts to constitute as well as modify employer and employee identities. As a result, the employment relationship cannot be seen as a purely 'private' matter. It is constituted by dominant beliefs and assumptions which solidify in state regulation. It is argued that this liberal methodology is extremely damaging to individuals in employment relationships. The liberal assumption of (contractual) equality between parties to employment relationships which informs the regulation of work only serves to reinforce existing distributions of wealth, power and opportunity. The corollary is that liberal law has failed to respond adequately to issues of subordination and domination in employment relationships and has privileged employer needs over those of employees (ibid.).

It is suggested on the vulnerability approach that the liberal subject of law and politics should be replaced by the 'vulnerable subject' (MA Fineman 2010, 267). This rejects the notion that individuals are naturally autonomous, rational and self-sufficient beings. Rather, it suggests that the reality of the human condition is that vulnerability is universal, constant and inevitable. 'Vulnerability' is inevitable in a biological sense as a result of our corporality. It is also inevitable in a relational sense, given that we are all 'profoundly dependent on others for our physical and psychological well-being' (Herring 2016, 10). Vulnerability exists in an institutional sense too. That is, vulnerability is systemic as well as personal (MA Fineman 2008, 8, 11). This suggests that although we are all vulnerable, there are certain persons and groups who are particularly vulnerable and that vulnerability is created as well as ameliorated by societal institutions. The relationship between employees and employers provides one example of a site in and through which vulnerability is managed and created (JW Fineman 2013, 299).

It can be a site of vulnerability as a negative experience, a site of injury and harm. However, it can also be a site of vulnerability in the more positive sense, in which work provides the possibility for creativity, human connection and human flourishing.

This kind of analysis holds great potential for labour law as a subject. This analysis exposes a number of our current labour laws as unnecessarily limited and insufficiently dynamic. Take for example the Equality Act 2010. This equality law relies on static and historically defined characteristics such as race and sex which have created disadvantage in the labour market. Labour law has stepped in to ensure that employers do not treat employees less favourably because of a particular personal/social characteristic. The vulnerability approach suggests that the current approach to employment equality law will not achieve equality in practice because equality law does not extend to everyone. It only extends to those persons with certain identity characteristics identified in the law (MA Fineman 2018, 4–5). The problem is that privilege is not (solely) distributed along the identity lines suggested in equality law. Deprivation and social disadvantage cut across these lines such that equality law does not address the real problems experienced by labour or their employers. Moreover, equality law is individualistic and relies on empowered individuals to enforce it. It does not recognise the systemic vulnerabilities which affect employees which would prevent such enforcement.

It is further argued on the vulnerability approach that the current equality approach has eclipsed other approaches which might be more successful at achieving equality in practice. It therefore suggests that the structure of equality law needs to be rethought to address a wider range of vulnerabilities. More profoundly, it is suggested that the equality law model has come to dominate the whole of (labour) law. That is, the law is too static and unresponsive to the shifting nature of vulnerabilities to really be a force for achieving justice. The vulnerability approach suggests that both the law and the state should be more responsive to vulnerability (Fineman 2018, 273–274). It suggests a valid role for the state in addressing market inequality through protective measures, enhancing arguments for labour law based on this model. This provides new impetus for certain labour laws which have lost out in the marketisation of labour law. For example, unfair dismissal law (where it exists) has suffered significant deregulatory pressure in a number of jurisdictions over the last few years. It is viewed as overly protective and an unnecessary restraint on employee and employee autonomy. By contrast, the vulnerability approach has the potential to recognise the value in this kind of law, where it can be shown that vulnerability is experienced in the face of arbitrary decisions by employers (JW Fineman 2013, 292).

Vulnerability theory demands that more thought and consideration is given to how vulnerabilities affect labour market participants throughout their lifecycle. Workers are seen primarily through the lens of the risks and pressures of human existence, rather than labour market risks *per se*. For example, it has been argued that labour law has failed to adequately address the lifetime disadvantage suffered by women. Sergeant and Bisom-Rapp (2017, 141) identify that despite the fact that women make up nearly half of the workforce in the US, they continue to suffer multiple disadvantages during their working lives which result in significantly poorer outcomes for women in old age than men. The problem has been the lack of a joined-up approach to recognising those multiple disadvantages and responding to them in law. Policymaking has been disjointed and incremental in promoting gender equality as a result of a lack of an overarching narrative to monitor and adjust institutions to ensure persistent disadvantage is eliminated. The authors suggest that vulnerability theory provides such a narrative and instructs policymakers to further strengthen law and policy in light of working women's continued suboptimal experiences.

Indeed, vulnerability theory might be used to suggest that joined-up thinking needs to be applied not just to the measure of labour market disadvantage and the potential effect on the law but also the way in which different laws relate to each other. In vulnerability theory it is accepted that all workers are vulnerable. Such vulnerabilities (illness, incapacity, family commitments) will inevitably mean that workers drop out of the labour law system at some point in their lives. Indeed, all workers retire at some point. If this is the case then it makes sense that the law should be structured in such a way as to aid transitions not only between jobs but also between periods of work and non-work. In vulnerability theory, the aim of legislation is the building of resilience among parties to an employment relationship. This requires that its effectiveness should be judged in terms of its capacity for capability-building among labour market actors. The law should provide 'assets' which allow individuals to survive or recover from the harm or setbacks which inevitably occur over the life course (Fineman 2008, 14). In order to achieve this for all workers, the relationship between social security legislation and employment legislation needs to be reconsidered (see Jydebjerg 2017, 117).[4] The nature of social 'rights' also needs to be expanded to ensure that even those persons not working have sufficient resources and receive such care to allow them to return to work when personal/social circumstances allow (Supiot 2001, 221).

The question also arises whether vulnerability theory can be used to embrace and enhance the role of other institutions of value to labour. This is particularly important in the context of the move to view vulnerability as 'potentiality' in vulnerability theory. That is, a recognition of vulnerability as the shared human condition allows us to recognise the needs of others and to recognise that the achievement of justice for one is justice for all (Carse 2006, 48). This suggests that solidaristic institutions assume importance as channels for the potentiality of vulnerability under this new approach (Stone 2017, 54). Certainly the value of trade unions has been outlined on a number of occasions in the literature on vulnerability theory (Fineman 2004; Zietlow 2017). In practical terms, unions

---

4 For example, 'workfare' schemes designed to reintroduce individuals to the labour market often involve nonstandard work, which itself falls outside some or all labour law rules. The result is that changes in laws on social security which are presented as a way to lessen labour market marginalisation may serve only to heighten economic inequality.

can enhance working conditions by negotiating on behalf of workers, promote job protection when jobs are under threat, and provide support for workers in dealing with grievances with their employers both within and outside the court system. Collective bargaining agreements can also serve as a means to equalise pay scales and reduce gender- and race-based pay discrimination (Zietlow 2017, 60). Trade unions can thus be an important way in which worker vulnerability can be recognised for its potential be harnessed. This implies that vulnerability theory can not only be a means to enhance legal protection for workers but can also encourage support for institutions which can contribute to worker resilience over the longer term. This analysis is attractive for labour law which has long been concerned with both direct and 'auxiliary' means of ensuring empower-ment for workers (Davies and Freedland 1983, 45).[5]

It appears from the above section that the application of vulnerability theory to labour has a number of potentially very positive effects and might improve the social justice chances of workers. The next section considers other social justice theories in relation to labour law, in particular the theories espoused among clas-sical labour law scholars. The aim of this section is to consider the relationship between these theories and the vulnerability approach. It is hoped that bringing the insights of vulnerability theory to bear on these approaches might identify their weaknesses yet bolster their claims so that social justice can be a real pro-gressive alternative for labour law.

Vulnerability theory and theories of social justice in labour law

In some senses, the concept of 'vulnerability' reflects labour law's oldest tradi-tions and deepest concerns. The 'founding fathers' of British and German labour law, Hugo Sinzheimer (1927) and Otto Kahn-Freund (Davis and Freedland 1983, 69), both recognised a set of systematic vulnerabilities affecting workers. They were heavily influenced by Marx's ideas about the 'alienation' and 'subor-dination' of workers under a capitalist mode of production. They were concerned that under this system, human beings are reduced to goods that can be exploited for profit; they are essentially slaves to the power of capital. Furthermore, the capitalist system creates an inequality of bargaining power between employers and employees, based on the ownership of the means of production by employ-ers and the reliance of employees on their engagement in the capitalist system to meet their subsistence needs (ibid., 17).

This set of vulnerabilities under the capitalist system are only reinforced by the operation of liberal legal structures which assume contractual equality and auton-omy. In a similar way to the vulnerability approach, they recognised the damaging 'fictio juris' of the contract as the basis for the regulation of employment (ibid., 24).

---

5 Kahn-Freund outlines a difference between 'regulatory legislation', which lays down rules of employment, and 'auxiliary legislation', which sets the boundaries of trade union action.

That contract of employment was merely a legal guise to hide the realities of social domination embedded in relationships between employers and workers. Any regulation based on the contract of employment was bound to reinforce the interests of the dominant class and keep workers in a position of subordination. Kahn-Freund was particularly critical of the liberal notion of freedom of contract when applied to employment. For this labour law scholar, that freedom of contract was a pure myth: it 'usually represent[ed] only the freedom to restrict or give up one's freedom' (ibid.). Given the imbalance of power between employment parties, there was almost no possibility for employees to negotiate terms to their own advantage. Instead, employees had to accept the terms laid down by employers in order to ensure the fulfilment of their subsistence needs through employment. The result was that the legal system served to reinforce the inequalities and disadvantages naturally present in the relationships between employers and workers.

Both Kahn-Freund and Sinzheimer argued that top-down state regulation by itself will have little impact in improving the position of workers. For Sinzheimer, this state-based mode of regulation is too embedded in the privatised aims of liberal capital to have any real impact. Unless the state moves to recognise collective rather than purely private interests, it will always be subject to the whim and will of major capitalist players. What is required is a redesign of the constitutional system. He envisaged the creation of an economic constitution, under which collective interests (such as trade unions) work in conjunction with employers to design laws which function in the public interest (Dukes 2014, 18). He argued that it is only laws devised in this way which would have any legitimacy and have the flexibility and immediacy to be effective. In a similar fashion, Kahn-Freund was adamant that legal norms could only have any power when backed by social sanctions: the 'countervailing power of trade unions and other organised workers asserted through consultation and negotiation with the employer, and ultimately, if this fails, through withholding their labour' (Davies and Freedland 1983, 20). He was particularly scathing about the possibilities of the common law for the protection of workers. Kahn-Freund argued that the court system was too embedded in the liberal systems of 'balance' to provide any real redistributive mechanism which would benefit workers. The courts were only interested in the individual and the adjudication of individual disputes (ibid., 12). They were not interested in the public interest which might be served by a rebalance of employer–employee relationships in favour of the employee.

However, despite the rejection of the institutions of liberal law, Kahn-Freund and Sinzheimer appear to put forward a view of the liberal *subject* of law: workers as autonomous, independent and rational beings (Rodgers 2016, 11). For example, Sinzheimer (1976) developed a concept of 'dependent labour' to explain the position of workers operating under the capitalist system of production. He argued that the capitalist system distorted the central value of human activity in favour of the promotion of individual ends. The insertion of workers into the system meant that they were separated from their own labour, and work no longer performed a personal or social function for them. As their labour was externalised, workers themselves became wedded to the 'world of things', and they were unable to develop their own autonomous ends in and through their own work (Dukes 2014, 15). Sinzheimer (1976), relying on the work of Kant, argued that workers should be viewed as separate from the world of 'things'. They should be viewed as elements of 'dignity', adhering to the world of 'spiritual beings' who have their own autonomous ends. Sinzheimer saw labour law as part of a system which could defend humanity against the oppression of excessive capitalist control and allow workers to regain some control over their working life. That in turn would allow them to pursue their own purposes with the independence and rationality they naturally possess. Sinzheimer's views were echoed by Kahn-Freund who argued for the dignity of labour outside of the excessive constraints of the whims of the owners of capital (Davies and Freedland 1983, 69).

This narrative appears to reflect liberal legal conceptions of the self which vulnerability theory specifically tries to expose and criticise. It appears that under the classical narrative of labour law, the humanity of workers is associated with the liberal values of autonomy, independence and rationality. Dependence is viewed negatively; indeed, it is the dependence of workers under the capitalist system which disenfranchises them and makes them liable to exploitation and manipulation. Under this system, it is the law's role to protect the individual from unwanted intrusions and to allow those individuals freedom to pursue their own goals. The problem of course is that this presents a negative view of the subject of the law. That subject is viewed as autonomy's 'other', a negative situation of weakness and dependency which implies 'disability, lack of capacity, of competence or victimhood' (Diduck 2013, 97). The subject of the law is not seen in terms of totality of his or her human condition. This implies that a worker's inherent capacity for resilience is also not seen. The vulnerability narrative suggests that there needs to be a move away from this reductive view of humanity in order to better build strategies to support workers and encourage their flourishing.

The association of classical labour law scholars with the promotion of the liberal values of dignity and autonomy may explain in part why these theorisations have not represented a successful alternative to the liberal theoretical domination of labour law or the downgrading of labour law protection in practice. On the classical scheme, employment legislation may be introduced to negate the exploitative effects of the capitalist system which threatens the autonomy and dignity of workers. However, given that the capitalist relationship is essentially based on power, the stronger in the labour market will (already) be able to assert their autonomy and resist these exploitative effects. It is the weaker elements of the labour market who are in particular need of employment law protection (particularly where trade union organisation is absent). The problem with this, of course, is that employment law itself becomes marginalised and viewed in a negative way. Employment law becomes reserved for the precarious, the peripheral and the atypical, rather than the core of labour market participants (Collins 2001, 29).

The application of employment law becomes a sign of weakness rather than strength.

It may well be that the work of certain authors in the vulnerability theory tradition can be drawn upon to bolster the claims made by classical labour law theorists and identify their potentiality. A number of vulnerability theorists have suggested and argued that labelling concepts such as 'dignity' or 'autonomy' as liberal is simply part of the hegemony of that discourse. These concepts can be reconceived and reworked in order to achieve a more responsive approach to law and a wider recognition of human potentiality. A good starting point is the work of Martha Nussbaum (2006), who specifically rejects the Kantian notion of dignity, a notion which is specifically referred to in the classical labour law tradition (Sinzheimer 1976, 8). She suggests that this notion is based on a false separation of two realms of human existence: on the one hand, the realm of 'natural necessity' and on the other hand, the realm of rationality (Nussbaum 2006, 131). She argues that for Kant, dignity is associated squarely with rationality; it is that rationality which places humans apart from the world of 'things' and ensures that they are ends in themselves. By contrast, 'animality', the crude and base state of nature which informs our animal existence, is not an end in itself. Hence, this aspect of human nature is not part of dignity (ibid.). Nussbaum suggests that Kant's notion of dignity is 'deeply problematic' (ibid., 132). The Kantian split between the two realms of human existence underestimates the extent of human need in the political: the need to have and make associations is also fundamental to human existence. Furthermore, the Kantian notion denies that 'our dignity is just the dignity of a certain sort of animal' (ibid.). She argues that dignity for humans cannot exist without reference to our vulnerability and neediness because that would deny a fundamental part of what it means to be human.

What is particularly interesting about Nussbaum's approach for our purposes is that her notion of dignity and humanity is specifically linked to Marx. She uses Marx's ideas about the nature and conditions of 'truly human flourishing' to underpin her claims that dignity is relational and political rather than static and rarefied (ibid., 74). This allows her to consider the fullness of human need and the ways in which these needs are compromised 'in the context of the current globalisation of capitalism and profittaking' (ibid., 277). She suggests that these processes create conditions in which people are being used as means and in which their dignity is at risk (ibid.). By contrast, although Kahn-Freund and Sinzheimer accept Marx's analysis of the dangers of the capitalist system in terms of creating a threat to human dignity, they do not use this analysis to argue for the richness of human need. This is implicit in the value that these authors place on the role of trade unions in improving working conditions. However, they do not appear to see the relational as part of dignity, and so the potentiality of dignity as an empowering, political discourse is lost. Arguably, vulnerability theory presents a way in which these connections can be made and these different theoretical elements linked. This in turn could make these theories more important and relevant to the present day.

Vulnerability theorists have also claimed that the notion of autonomy should be reconsidered as a concept away from the individualistic notions of liberal theory. It has been argued that the view of autonomy as being able to make your own choices and control your own circumstances is far too reductive and 'cramped' (Anderson 2013, 137). It does not recognise either the social or contextual nature of autonomy. It does not recognise the relationships which form and moderate an individual's choices and ability to take advantage of them (ibid., 137). It is also incorrectly pitted against the notion of 'vulnerability'. The view that vulnerability impinges on autonomy by limiting choice is both false and damaging. It reinforces negative views about vulnerability and dependence and reinforces individualistic and reductive notions of autonomy. Rather, vulnerability and autonomy should be seen in fundamental connection. Vulnerability is part of our autonomy because it represents and encompasses elements of the human condition which are not only limiting but also enabling. Being vulnerable while exposes us to harm also endows us with certain capacities; ability to 'fall in love, to learn to take pleasure and find comfort in the presence of others' (Gilson 2011, 310). It is essential to relationship building, which in turn is essential to human flourishing (Herring 2016, 38).

In a similar way to the analysis in relation to dignity, revisiting autonomy as a concept could help to bolster the claims made by classical labour law theorists. Classical labour law theorists were convinced by the importance of the relational in arguing for the centrality of worker associations in achieving social justice for workers. However, the denial of the importance of association for the notion of dignity has arguably undermined its theoretical force. The danger is that if dignity can be viewed as separate from the relational then it is arguably best served by the light-touch methodology of liberal law. Incorporating the vulnerability analysis forces an alternative view. It forces the admission that the individualistic nature of the support offered by (labour) law is a threat to both dignity and autonomy in the modern labour environment. It is only when that law recognises the importance of the relational that it can ensure dignity and autonomy for workers.

Potential problems with vulnerability theory for the labour law project

The previous section described the very positive potential contribution of vulnerability theory to building on and bolstering the arguments made by the classical labour law scholars. By contrast, this section sounds a note of caution in the application of vulnerability theory to the labour law field. Two particular concerns are addressed. The first concern is the apparent contradiction in vulnerability theory which exists between claiming that all are vulnerable and claiming that certain persons are particularly vulnerable. The second concern is the application of the vulnerability analysis to employers and the assertion that employers have their own particular vulnerability which should be legislated through (employment) law.

Vulnerability of all and regulation of vulnerable groups

In vulnerability theory, there exists a potential tension between the recognition that all individuals are vulnerable and recognising the particular vulnerability of certain groups. It has been suggested for example that the claim that everyone is vulnerable made under the auspices of vulnerability theory is regressive as it fails to account for the fact that vulnerability is context specific, unequally distributed and affects some more than others. In turn, the legislative response to vulnerability is weakened on the 'everyone is vulnerable' approach as it undermines the use of vulnerability to highlight particular groups worthy of special protection by the state (Rogers, Mackenzie and Dodds 2012). At the same time, the 'everyone is vulnerable' approach has the potential to lead to excessive paternalistic responses in law. If everyone is vulnerable and unable to make their own decisions or look after themselves, then the state can legitimately step in to redress vulnerability in all areas of social life. The result is an erosion in the capacity of individuals and groups to achieve self-determination (critiques of the paternalistic nature of vulnerability theory are presented in Kohn 2012; Munro and Scoular 2012).

This is worrying from a labour law perspective because regulation targeted to particular groups has been a strong weapon in the fight to address systematic disadvantage. Indeed, there is evidence that this targeted regulation has had some success in modifying and addressing disadvantage for those groups. For example, equal pay law has had a significant impact on improving pay rates for women, but the gender pay gap still persists throughout the labour market.[6] Likewise, legislation targeting atypical work has allowed part-time workers to claim entitlements unfairly reserved for full-time colleagues (see *O'Brien v Ministry of Justice* [2013] ICR 499 under which it was decided that part-time judges were entitled to access to pension entitlements reserved for full-time staff)[7] and fixed-term workers to gain permanent contractual status after a succession of fixed-term contracts.[8] A recognition of particularly vulnerable groups or populations can be helpful as a means to achieve some of labour law's aims.

However, there have been a number of authors who have rejected the necessary contradiction between the 'everyone is vulnerable' approach and the recognition of specific vulnerability. Herring suggests that the recognition that everyone is vulnerable does not mean there is a recognition that everyone is 'equally

---

6 See ONS, 'Annual Survey of Hours and Earnings: 2017 Provisional and 2016 Revised Results' available at file:///C:/Users/Ian/Downloads/Annual%20Survey%20of%20Hours%20and%20Earnings%202017%20provisional%20and%202016%20revised%20results.pdf last accessed 12 February 2018. The survey reports that in April 2017, the gender pay gap based on median hourly earnings for full-time employees decreased to 9.1%, from 9.4% in 2016. This is the lowest since the survey began in 1997.

7 Regulation 5 (1) Part-Time Workers (Prevention of Less Favourable Treatment) Regulations 2000.

8 This is demanded by Regulation 8 of the Fixed-Term Employee (Prevention of Less Favourable Treatment) Regulations 2002.

vulnerable' (Herring 2016, 23). Rather what the vulnerability approach aims to do is to show that the inequality in position experienced between individuals and groups is not an individual failing but an institutional one (MA Fineman 2017, 147). The emphasis is on the question of access to different resources, with a 'deficit' indicating that there has been a failure to provide sufficient assets to ensure resilience. Indeed, it is argued that the particularity of some vulnerability only serves to strengthen arguments for state accountability and responsiveness. The call to action is strengthened by a belief in the ability of society to 'mediate, compensate and lessen our vulnerability through programmes, institutions and structures' (MA Fineman 2012, 80).

Vulnerability and corporate vulnerability

There is another feature of the particular application of vulnerability theory to labour law and relationships which requires further consideration. That is the suggestion that 'both employees and employers can and should be seen as vulnerable, only differently so' (JW Fineman 2013, 299). This suggestion derives from the recognition on vulnerability theory of both 'personal' and 'institutional' vulnerability. The recognition of institutional vulnerability allows personal vulnerability to be contextualised. Personal vulnerability must be seen in the context of the ability of social institutions to respond to individual needs. Furthermore, the recognition of institutional vulnerability forces the realisation that institutions are products of society and, hence, challenges their separation from the bounds of human existence (ibid., 300). As a corollary, social institutions are themselves vulnerable in the wake of market fluctuations, changing international policies, and institutional and political compromises or human prejudice (MA Fineman 2010, 12).

On the one hand, this personalisation of institutions and their categorisation as vulnerable serves useful functions for labour law. First, it enables the role of the employer and the employee to be viewed as socially constructed. The social construction of those relationships means that law is implicated in *creating* the inequalities and imbalances which exist rather than merely acting in response to a factual 'truth'. In particular, it is recognised that the casting of employees and employers as equals in law does not reflect the differences in their social position, and, hence, this casting often works to increase rather than reduce social disadvantage (JW Fineman 2013, 299). Second, the recognition of employer vulnerability implies an inevitable connection between employer and employee fortunes. Both employers and employees are bound up in the financial and economic system, and, hence, both are in need of a state response. Of course, the response to employer vulnerability will differ from that in relation to employee vulnerability because the vulnerabilities are qualitatively different. Employers suffer different risks and achieve different rewards. However, state action is empowering for employers just as it is for employees. Law is a major source of resilience, a privilege bestowed on companies in recognition of their particular position (JW Fineman 2017, 29). Vulnerability theory challenges the liberal abstractions which dominate the regulation of employment relationships and opens up the space for a greater state responsiveness to both employer and employee needs.

However, assigning vulnerability to companies may detract from moves to ensure a more positive notion of vulnerability as the creation of growth and connectivity between individuals. This is because corporate vulnerability allows vulnerability to be theorised apart from embodiment. This has the potential to undermine the claims under vulnerability theory that there is an intimate connection between embodiment and rationality, embodiment and autonomy, embodiment and dignity (see Grear 2010, 114–116). Companies can achieve vulnerability without *embodied* rationality, autonomy and dignity. Hence, the potential to read these concepts expansively, beyond the reductive liberal framework, is severely compromised. Companies do not have the corporeal features which imply openness to harm and, correspondingly, do not have those features which allow empathy and intimate connections to be forged. The version of vulnerability applied to companies thus appears to be a negative one. This is damaging to the vulnerability project as it suggests that vulnerability is something to be negated and avoided rather than embraced.

Furthermore, it is difficult to see how responses to corporate vulnerability would produce better outcomes for employees than the liberal system of law. Certainly, there is a recognition in vulnerability theory that the interests and needs of employers and employees may be different and may contradict each other. However, the solution is to *balance* the needs and interests of the parties to the relationship and 'resolve the contradiction in favour of one or the other' (JW Fineman 2017, 27). It has been suggested that the balancing mechanism should be weighted in favour of employees and this would ensure that the vulnerability approach achieves more favourable outcomes. The 'costs' of employer actions should be viewed more widely, and there should be a recognition of the need to redistribute these costs more fairly to achieve employee resilience. For example, it has been identified that the costs of termination of employment relationships are currently unfairly heaped on individuals and the state. There should be a more balanced approach, whereby the employer should be asked to bear some of the costs of the action of termination. It is suggested that this should be a balancing exercise in recognition of the vulnerability of both employees *and* employers: 'some parity is surely not too much to demand' (ibid., 31).

The problem is that the reality of this kind of balancing in the current politico-economic context implies that employer's needs win out over those of employees' (Garben 2017). Employer's needs are seen as more pressing, and under the economic efficiency paradigm which dominates the actions of modern neoliberal states, actions to support companies may also be seen as more efficient than actions to support employees (acting in favour of the employer means that employees will eventually reap the benefits as a result in a raising of living standards as a whole; Coyle 2013, 61, 72). The risks involved in the designation of employers as vulnerable appear to undermine the aims of the vulnerability project to make labour law more responsive to embodied vulnerability. If vulnerability theory is to be of use to employment law, then it is this *embodied* vulnerability which must be at its heart. Alternatively, the effect of this analysis implies that we reach the conclusion that law *itself* will always be a limited and blunt tool with which to tackle the inevitable inequality of employment relationships. It is only by boosting other social institutions that progress can be made. Hence, resources and support should be invested in thinking more creatively about the way in which the relational aspects of vulnerability can be exercised within the constraints employees find themselves. This suggests encouraging new relationships of solidarity and new forms of 'resilience' among workers (Stone 2017, 53).

Conclusion

The recognition of vulnerability is not a new phenomenon for labour law. Classical labour lawyers have long recognised the vulnerabilities to which employees are subject as a result of their insertion into the capitalist system. However, vulnerability theory appears to present an exciting and innovative narrative through which to build on and enhance this vulnerability recognition. Vulnerability theory suggests that vulnerability should be seen more expansively than systemic disadvantage brought about by capitalist processes. Vulnerability can be caused systemically, but it is also a biological fact and thus attaches to all individuals as a result of their humanity. It also should not only be seen in economic terms; vulnerability can be caused by legal and other institutional processes which fail to properly recognise and respond to different layers of disadvantage. Vulnerability on this thesis appears to be a levelling tool as it recognises that all persons/actors can be vulnerable and therefore acts to remove the stigmatisation of vulnerability attached to many modes of analysis (including classical labour law theory). In particular, it appears to offer an interesting challenge to the powerlessness of institutional actors in the face of dominant neoliberal ideology. It suggests that the state and the law (including labour law) should be co-opted to ensure resilience for all those in positions of disadvantage. This is empowering and progressive, in that it suggests more rather than less labour law, and opens up new avenues for enquiry. It gives space for a reconsideration of protective labour law, develops the scope of equality law and suggests new lines of solidarity for excluded groups.

That said, it is the contention of this chapter that there should be caution in the way that the notion of vulnerability is used and assigned under the vulnerability approach. In particular, there are potential dangers which arise from labelling corporations as 'vulnerable', even if the nature of that vulnerability is recognised as different from that experienced by workers. This is because the adoption of vulnerability theory and its application to the employment relationship must be centred on the recognition of *embodied* as well as *embedded* vulnerability. It is the recognition of the embodied nature of vulnerability which appears to hold the most potential for challenging the institutions of liberal law and for recognising vulnerability itself as a positive trait. It is this embodiment which exposes the relational nature of humanity and the need for liberal institutions to support human (relational) development more widely. It appears that it is in this commitment to supporting and engaging relational vulnerability that there is a more sustained possibility of achieving dignity and autonomy for workers.

Bibliography

Adams RJ, 'On the convergence of labour rights and human rights' (2001) 56 *Industrial Relations/Relations Industrielles* 199.

Alston P, (ed) *Labour Rights as Human Rights* (Oxford University Press 2005).

Anderson J, 'Autonomy and vulnerability entwined' in C Mackenzie, W Rogers and S Dodds (eds), *Vulnerability: New Essays in Ethics and Feminist Philosophy* (Ashgate 2013).

Bisom-Rapp S and Sargeant M, 'Acknowledging but transcending gender at work: applying the model of lifetime disadvantage and vulnerability theory to women's poverty in retirement' in MA Fineman and JW Fineman (eds), *Vulnerability and the Legal Organisation of Work* (Routledge 2017).

Boubil E, 'The ethics of vulnerability and the phenomenology of interdependency' (2018) 49(3) *Journal of the British Society for Phenomenology* 183.

Carse A, 'Vulnerability, agency and human flourishing' in C Taylor and R Dell'Oro (eds), *Health and Human Flourishing* (Georgetown University Press 2006).

Collins H, 'Regulating the employment relation for competitiveness' (2001) 30 *Industrial Law Journal* 17.

Collins H, 'Theories of rights as justifications for labour law' in B Langille and G Davidov (eds), *The Idea of Labour Law* (Oxford University Press 2011).

Coyle S, 'Vulnerability and the liberal order' in MA Fineman and A Grear (eds), *Vulnerability: Reflections on a New Ethical Foundation for Law and Politics* (Routledge 2013).

Davidov G, 'In Defence of (efficiently administered) just cause dismissal laws' (2007) 23(1) *The International Journal of Comparative Labour Law and Industrial Relations* 117.

Davies ACL, *Perspectives on Labour Law* (Oxford University Press 2009).

Davies P and Freedland M, *Kahn-Freund's Labour and the Law* (Stevens 1983).

Diduck A, 'Autonomy and vulnerability in family law: the missing link' in J Wallbank and J Herring (eds), *Vulnerabilities, Care and Family Law* (London Routledge 2013).

Dukes R, *The Labour Constitution: The Enduring Idea of Labour Law* (Oxford University Press 2014).

Ewing K and Hendy J, 'The Strasbourg Court treats trade unionists with contempt: Svenska Transportarbeareforbundet and Seko v Sweden' (2017) 46(3) *Industrial Law Journal* 435.

Fineman JW, 'The vulnerable subject at work: a new perspective on the employment-at-will debate' (2013) 43 *Southwestern Law Review* 275

Fineman JW, 'A vulnerability approach to private ordering of employment' in MA Fineman and JW Fineman (eds), *Vulnerability and the Legal Organisation of Work* (Routledge 2017)

Fineman JW 'Introducing vulnerability' in MA Fineman and JW Fineman (eds), *Vulnerability and the Legal Organisation of Work* (Routledge 2017)

Fineman MA, *The Autonomy Myth* (The New Press 2004).

Fineman MA, 'The vulnerable subject: anchoring equality in the human condition' (2008) 20(1) *Yale Journal of Law and Feminism* 1.

Fineman MA, 'The vulnerable subject and the responsive state' (2010) 60 *Emory Law Journal* 251

Fineman MA, '"Elderly" as vulnerable: rethinking the nature of individual and societal responsibility' (2012) 20 *Elder Law Journal* 101.

Fineman MA, 'Vulnerability and inevitable inequality' (2017) 4(3) *Oslo Law Journal* 133.

Fineman MA and Grear A, 'Introduction: an invitation to further exploration' in MA Fineman and A Grear (eds) *Vulnerability: Reflections on a New Ethical Foundation for Law and Politics* (Ashgate 2013).

Fudge J, 'The new discourse of labour rights: from social to fundamental rights?' (2007–2008) 29 *Comparative Labour Law and Policy Journal* 29.

Garben S, 'The Constitutional Imbalance between the 'Market' and the 'Social' in the European Union (2017) 13(1) *European Journal of Constitutional Law* 23.

Gearty C, 'Against judicial enforcement' in C Gearty and V Mantouvalou (eds), *Debating Social Rights* (Hart 2011).

Gilson E, 'Vulnerability, ignorance and oppression' (2011) 26(2) *Hypatia* 308.

Grear A, *Redirecting Human Rights* (Oxford University Press 2010).

Herring J, 'Defining vulnerability' in J Herring (ed), *Vulnerable Adults and the Law* (Oxford University Press 2016).

Jydebjerg CS, 'Vulnerability, workfare law and resilient social justice' in MA Fineman and JW Fineman (eds), *Vulnerability and the Legal Organisation of Work* (Routledge 2017).

Kilpatrick C and de Witte B (eds), 'Social rights in times of crisis in the Eurozone: the role of fundamental rights challenges EUI working paper series law 2014/05' (*European University Institute* 2014) <http://cadmus.eui.eu/bitstream/handle/1814/31247/LAW%20WP%202014%2005%20Social%20Rights%20final%202242014.pdf?sequence=1> (access 18th December 2017).

Kohn NA, 'Vulnerability theory and the role of government' (2012) 6 *Yale Journal of Law and Feminism* 1.

Mantouvalou V, 'Are labour rights human rights?' (2012) 3(2) *European Labour Law Journal* 151.

Munro V and Scoular J, 'Abusing vulnerability? Contemporary law and policy responses to sex work in the UK' (2012) 20 *Feminist Legal Studies* 189.

Nussbaum M, *Frontiers of Justice: Disability, Nationality, Species Membership* (Harvard University Press 2006).

Office for National Statistics, 'Annual Survey of Hours and Earnings: 2017 Provisional and Revised Results' (*Office for National Statistics*, 26 October 2017) <https://www.ons.gov.uk/employmentandlabourmarket/peopleinwork/earningsandworkinghours/bulletins/annualsurveyofhoursandearnings/2017provisionaland2016revisedresults> (access 12th February 2018).

Pizzoferrato A, 'The economic crisis and labour law reform in Italy' (2015) 31(2) *Comparative Labour Law and Industrial Relations* 187.

Rodgers L, *Labour Law, Vulnerability and the Regulation of Precarious Work* (Edward Elgar 2016).

Rogers W, Mackenzie C and Dodds S, 'Why bioethics needs a concept of vulnerability' (2012) 5 *International Journal of Feminist Approaches to Bioethics* 11.

Sinzheimer H, 'Grundzüge des Arbeitsrechts' (1927) in H Sinzheimer (ed), *Arbeitsrecht und Rechtssoziologie: Gesammelte Aufsätze und Reden (Band 1)* (Otto Brenner Stiftung 1976).

Stone KVW, 'Green shoots in the labour market: a cornucopia of social experiments' in MA Fineman and JW Fineman (eds), *Vulnerability and the Legal Organisation of Work* (Routledge 2017).

Supiot A, *Beyond Employment: Changes in Work and the Future of Labour Law in Europe* (Oxford University Press 2001).

Turner BS, *Vulnerability and Human Rights* (Penn State University Press 2006).

Zietlow RE, 'The constitutional right to organise' in MA Fineman and JW Fineman (eds), *Vulnerability and the Legal Organisation of Work* (Routledge 2017).

Response
Vulnerability and labour law: on the transition from theory to practice

Nicole Busby

In her thought-provoking chapter concerning vulnerability theory's application to labour law Lisa Rodgers is positive about its potential as an analytical tool for the purposes of identifying law's shortcomings yet cautious about its application within the policy context. In her analysis, she reminds us of the importance of retaining labour law's original democratic objective and warns against the dangers of overlooking the inherent inequality in the employer–worker relationship in our quest to find alternative solutions to contemporary regulatory dilemmas. In this response, which accords with Rodgers' analysis, I posit that such dissatisfaction arises not because what Fineman asserts in her theory is at odds with the current labour law landscape. In fact, vulnerability theory provides the appropriate tools with which to paint an accurate picture of the nature of the relations surrounding the exchange of labour for capital and, in this respect, has much more in common with traditional theories of labour law than might be immediately apparent. The difficulty with its transition from theory to practice arises because law's ability to respond to the many challenges associated with the regulation of work in the modern setting is blighted by certain features of the political environment within which it currently operates, in particular the shift from liberalism to neoliberalism.

In its failure to provide a solution to the systemic inequality that exists in the relationship between worker and employing organisation, vulnerability theory is in excellent company. As Rodgers points out, traditional theories of labour law such as those espoused by Hugo Sinzheimer and Otto Kahn Freund are similarly capable of accurately and precisely diagnosing the problems arising from the increased marketisation of labour yet are also insufficiently positioned to respond effectively in the contemporary context. This disconnect can be tacked to the shift from social to political liberalism that has been taking place in Western democracies over the past 30 years and which has set the labour law framework adrift from its economic and political counterparts. In the early days of the free market economy, legal and political systems were intended to be mutually beneficial and reinforcing. The current dominance of neoliberalism in mainstream political doctrine has led to deregulation in some areas, while in others it has disenabled specifically targeted legal interventions that are rooted in the sociocultural movements of an earlier era. In the UK, the movement away from collective bargaining, once seen as the necessary counter to an inherent imbalance of power within the employment relationship, has been led and facilitated by successive governments' reorientation of the legal framework on ideological grounds (Davies and Freedland 1983). In its place, conflict has been individualised and its resolution reframed as a contractual issue rather than a collective responsibility. Through the state's careful and targeted use of the rights discourse, the relationship between worker and employer has been recast as a private matter. The net result is the loss of labour law's democratic function by which labour inequality was traditionally viewed as a matter of public concern (Ewing 1995).

Fineman's (2008) rejection of autonomy as the definitive aspirational state, personified by the liberal subject, is reflected in labour law's paradigm of the standard (male) worker which serves to exclude or 'other' those who work under 'non-standard' arrangements either through the necessity of balancing paid work with caring commitments or because such conditions are unilaterally imposed on them by employing organisations. In either case, the worker's autonomy is severely restricted and subject to wider institutional control through the performance of social expectations and economic demands within the family and the labour market. As Rodgers notes, the marketisation of labour law has left its mark – the widening of the gulf between the richest and poorest in society reflected in divergent working and living conditions. However, on paper the law has adapted exponentially in order to respond to the individual needs of workers. Changes in social organisation are reflected in law's provision so that family formation no longer acts as a restriction on labour market participation but is formally accommodated through paid maternity leave and the right to return to legally protected flexible forms of work. Furthermore, women and men are entitled to equality of treatment and remuneration; discrimination on a number of grounds, including race, disability, age, sexuality, and religion or belief, is countered by targeted legislation intended to respond to the prohibited acts and behaviour of employers. Yet something is still going wrong in the connection between need and response as evidenced by the persistence of gendered and other inequalities within labour markets. The carefully targeted interventions are missing their targets, hence Fineman's (2008) dissatisfaction with the use of individual legal identities as the defining criteria for equality claims.

Rodgers (this volume, 140) rightly cites vulnerability theory's value as a levelling tool – its acknowledgement of vulnerability as the natural human condition sets it in diametric opposition to the myth of the autonomous liberal subject and enables us to embrace rather than to reject what lies at our core and makes us human. Fineman's central claim that we bear the effects of our vulnerability all of the time so that it is not our vulnerability that varies but rather our capacity to build resilience in order to bolster our ability to respond to it has a particular salience in the labour-for-wages exchange (Rodgers, this volume, 141). In identifying the many parallels between the observations of labour law's founding theorists Sinzheimer and Kahn-Freund and Fineman's thesis, Rodgers hits on an important point. In her consideration of Kahn-Freund's and Sinzheimer's affirmation and promotion of the 'liberal values of dignity and autonomy', she rightly posits the risk posed through reliance on such an approach as a foil to exploitation in the contemporary context (ibid., 134). In line with Fineman's rejection of autonomy, Rodgers' concern is that a reliance on the individual's ability to achieve autonomy within the employment relationship is largely thwarted by the subordinate nature of that relationship. The imbalance of power between worker and employer leaves the worker exposed to exploitation through the harshest excesses of the market order with law's ability to intervene undermined as reliance on its protection is perceived as a form of weakness.

If a contemporary reading is applied to the work of the earlier scholars it would appear that their overarching hypotheses are far more closely aligned with that of Fineman than might initially appear to be the case. In their apparently distinct references to 'autonomy through dignity' and 'vulnerability', Kahn Freund and Sinzheimer on the one hand, and Fineman on the other, are essentially talking about the same thing. Both refer to our common humanity and, using different nomenclature, articulate the quality or state at the core of our existence. The individual's 'spiritual' or internal life with its religious connotations typical of mid-nineteenth-century thought can be substituted with the secular and, thus fittingly contemporary, 'human condition' so that both apparently make the same assumption that it is our embodied state that distinguishes labour from other forms of exchange and which should guard against its commodification (which is based on a Marxist analysis of labour; see Marx 1976). 'Vulnerability' in the language of the foundational scholars is used to refer to the external state or situation in which the individual finds herself, somewhat akin to the modern equivalent of 'precariousness', hence the belief that 'vulnerability is created as well as ameliorated by societal institutions' (Rodgers, this volume, 129), to use Fineman's (2010) terminology, through the building of resilience which is defined as 'having the means to address and confront misfortune'. In her rejection of autonomy, Fineman (2018, 3) eschews its liberal conceptualisation as the idealised and most highly prized personal state positing vulnerability as the natural human condition, 'finite and fragile, as well as socially and materially dynamic'. This poses a direct challenge to the notion that human fulfilment is an individual rather than societal responsibility – a position which sits comfortably with labour law's public interest function espoused by the earlier labour law scholars.

In their dissatisfaction with law and legal process – in particular party-party litigation – as the sole means of responding to the inequalities inherent in the employment relationship, Sinzheimer's and Kahn-Freund's approaches are also attuned to the observations implicit in Fineman's theory. In constructing its responses to the inequality of the relationship between worker and employer, labour law's key foundation was collectivism – the organisation of labour and its operation through collective bargaining which produced the most effective response to the excesses of an earlier age and their exploitative effects. Over time, a range of forces – globalisation and the free movement of capital, enhanced marketisation and a combination of deregulation of the labour market and strict regulation of organised labour – served to move labour law's needle away from its attachment to collective bargaining and its public-facing democratic (redis-tributive) ethos and towards private individual dispute resolution. As well as contributing to the loss of labour law's democratic function, this approach can serve to isolate and alienate the individual worker who is often unable or disin-clined to seek recourse to law (Busby and McDermont 2015). The application of a vulnerability analysis would see the building of resilience as a necessary coun-ter which, for those who work in the most atomised and precarious enclaves of the contemporary labour market, would surely necessitate a return to collectiv-ism. This begs the question: does vulnerability theory amount to an alternative theory in the field of labour law, or is it rather a more contemporary means of identifying the same problems with the same diagnosis? If this is the case, one cannot help but conclude that labour law as it was originally conceived already had the tools – both diagnostic and remedial – to counter the threat of labour's commodification. Why then does a solution remain elusive?

In Fineman's estimation the answer lies in the requirement of a responsive state as the central means by which resilience can be attained. Here again, vul-nerability theory aligns closely with traditional expositions of labour law. In seeking a return to what earlier theorists largely took for granted, Fineman (2008, 19) asserts that it is the state's responsibility to ensure access to the in-stitutions that distribute resources. Implicit in this call for state engagement is a convincing pro-regulatory argument. The state envisioned is not coercive but responsive – 'an active State in non-authoritarian terms' – and plays a critical role in ameliorating the effects of marketisation. While not in itself a liberal theory due to its strong rejection of the established tenets of liberalism, vulner-ability does acknowledge the market as a centrifugal force in the provision of goods and services, asserting that state intervention is necessary to take account of the vulnerabilities of individuals and institutions and to respond through the bolstering of resilience. This is presented as 'an alternative basis for de-fining the role of government and a justification for expansive social welfare policies' (Kohn 2014, 3). However, the state that Fineman refers to is that of the US where her theory was developed. Although the UK model of labour regulation has moved closer towards the US model of a largely unregulated neoliberal regime, this was not always the case and certainly the earlier era on which Kahn-Freund's writings were based was very different. The regulation of labour in the US varies substantially from its UK counterpart due to the 'at will' doctrine by which an employer can terminate an employment contract with-out notice, for any reason, so long as doing so is not a violation of a protected class (JW Fineman 2013). Nevertheless, the responsive state can be seen as a declining influence on the UK's system of labour law and those of her fellow European states (Rodgers, this volume, 4).

In considering how vulnerability theory might transition into public policy, Sean Coyle (2014, 61) raises a number of reservations. Although receptive to Fineman's idea of the responsive state, Coyle sees more potential in the location of vulnerability and resilience within civil society. This is because the market and the state have become so intertwined that they are almost indistinguishable.

This is not a party political point (ibid., 70)[1] but is rather a logical consequence of the particular stage of liberalism reached: economic liberalisation brings with it social liberalisation which, in turn, leads to social destruction – 'the collapse of social organisation and the system of meanings that the market was originally meant to serve' (ibid., 63). This has the effect of commodifying all human behaviour, which becomes engulfed by the market, hence the turn towards economic efficiency theory cited by Rodgers (this volume, 127, 139). As liberalism reaches maturity and is subsumed by the economic and political partnering represented by neoliberalism, the market and state cannot be said to operate independently of each other leaving the state in no position to identify and implement public values. Its neutrality is severely contested. This is ably demonstrated by recent government policy aimed at restricting work-based rights through the use of extended qualifying periods and the imposition of barriers to justice such as the introduction of fees for claimants to the Employment Tribunal – a policy ultimately struck down by the Supreme Court as unlawful due to, inter alia, its disregard for 'the public interest' intrinsic in workers' rights (as per Lord Reid's judgment in *R (on the application of UNISON v Lord Chancellor* [2017] UKSC 51, [72]).

Although theoretically sound, vulnerability theory's pro-regulatory stance depends for its realisation on the enactment of law and policy which in turn relies on the state's ability to separate its law-making function from potentially conflicting political and economic goals. At its current stage of maturity, rather than the neutral mediator of disputes involving the exchange of labour and capital, the neoliberal state finds itself embedded in the market order disenabling both its willingness and ability to be 'responsive'. This casts the separation of law and politics as an ideal rather than a reality, scuppering any appropriate regulatory programme and thwarting the prospects for resilience-building. Thus, the potential for vulnerability theory to fail to prioritise the persistent disadvantage faced by labour due to its focus on corporate as well as worker vulnerability is compounded by the state's embeddedness in the market (Rodgers, this volume, 138–139). The theory's reliance on the state's ability to be a neutral actor in its prioritisation of demands makes real Rodgers' fear that 'vulnerability' and 'resilience' can be co-opted by broader economic objectives.

The application of Fineman's vulnerability theory to labour law provides us with a contemporary lens through which to view the field of study and usefully serves to update and modernise the terminology utilised by its foundational theorists. Its value is that it brings us back to the very origins of labour law and reminds us of the astute observation and intellectual robustness on which they were built. The shortcomings that it uncovers and the conclusions that it enables us to reach, however, are not new but are closely aligned with those of its foundational theorists such as Sinzheimer and Kahn-Freund. Furthermore,

---

1 Coyle's argument is that Socialists see vulnerability as something that is done to us, whereas Conservatives see it as something that we do to ourselves.

its apparent inability to transition from abstract theory to contemporary practice is shared with those more traditional theories. Responding to the commodification of labour has in fact become an ever-more-challenging task as the state's own marketisation has resulted in the strategic circumvention of the very conditions necessary to counter the vagaries of the market.

In the earlier era, the appropriate response was identified by Kahn-Freund as collectivism's 'countervailing force' necessary to provide a bulwark against the exploitative tendencies of the capitalist system. In Fineman's estimation, the building of resilience has the same effect – in fact could be achieved through the same means – and relies for its realisation on the necessary interventions of the responsive state. In order to respond to labour law's current inability to counter labour's commodification, the conditions that would galvanise state action are certainly needed to remove the current restrictions on collective forms of action, in order to improve and strengthen the structures which facilitate access to justice through the provision of effective rights and the public enforcement of remedies. Such action would enable labour law to recapture its democratic function and recognition as a public good. By shining a much-needed light on the critical role of the state in halting the commodification of labour, vulnerability theory provides a lifeline. Is vulnerability theory good for labour law? Undoubtedly.

Bibliography

Busby N and McDermont M, 'Access to justice in the employment tribunal: private disputes or public concerns?' in E Palmer, T Cornford, A Guinchard and Y Marique (eds), *Access to Justice: Beyond the Policies and Politics of Austerity* (Hart 2015).

Coyle S, 'Vulnerability and the liberal order' in in MA Fineman and A Grear (eds), *Vulnerability: Reflections on a New Ethical Foundation for Law and Politics* (Routledge 2014).

Davies P and Freedland M (eds), *Kahn-Freund's Labour and the Law* (3rd edn, Stevens and Sons 1983).

Ewing K, 'Democratic socialism and labour law' (1995) 2 *Industrial Law Journal* 24.

Fineman JW, 'The vulnerable subject at work: a new perspective on the employment at-will debate' (2013) 43 *Southwestern Law Review* 275.

Fineman JW, 'Introducing vulnerability' in MA Fineman and JW Fineman (eds), *Vulnerability and the Legal Organization of Work* (Routledge 2017).

Fineman MA, 'The vulnerable subject: anchoring equality in the human condition' (2008) 20(1) *Yale Journal of Law and Feminism* 5.

Fineman MA, 'The vulnerable subject and the responsive state' (2010) 60 *Emory Law Journal* 251.

Kohn NA, 'Vulnerability theory and the role of government' (2014) 6 *Yale Journal of Law and Feminism* 1.

Marx K, *Capital Volume One* (Penguin 1976).

Part 5
Human Rights Law

Embracing vulnerability

Notes towards human rights for a more-than-human world*

Anna Grear

Introduction

This chapter follows human corporeality into a more intimate engagement with materiality in order to explore embracing vulnerability as one way to reimagine human rights for a more-than-human world.

Human rights have a meta-ethical status in the juridical order but are currently profoundly challenged by rights-threatening developments: growing levels of populist authoritarianism; deepening forms of surveillance and control (including the increasing surveillance and control of public, quasi-public and private spaces); widespread corporate rights abuse (see Jochnick 1999, 65); extensive panoptic eco-governance; and – not least – by a whole range of crises threatening the future survival of multiple species, communities and ecosystems. Meanwhile, human rights continue to reveal familiar paradoxes and tensions. On one hand, human rights are celebrated as cardinal achievements of humanism – their post-war inauguration characterised by the Universal Declaration of Human Rights (UDHR)[1] as being an international humanitarian reaction to 'barbarous acts'[2] searing the conscience of humankind,[2] '[needing no] philosophical argument in addition to the experience of the Holocaust' (Morsink 1993a, 358). On the other hand, human rights are subjected to important critiques, the two most relevant of which for present purposes concern their attachment to an exclusory form of rationalist anthropocentrism (Gearty 2010), and (relatedly) their legitimating role in an international order consolidating oppressive levels of neocoloniality (Anghie 2005; Kapur 2006).

Human rights also confront a range of posthuman challenges, and the humanist subject undergirding human rights faces a deepening crisis of legitimacy (Baxi 2009). Braidotti (2013), addressing the crisis of humanism, identifies three strands of posthumanism. First, *reactionary posthumanism* – an intensified commitment to humanism: some neo-Kantian accounts of human rights might fit

* I would like to thank Daniel Bedford for his insightful editorial comments.
1 GA Res. 217(111) of 10 December 1948, UN Doc. A/810 at 71 (1948).
2 Ibid., Preamble.

this category – as does Nussbaum's non-Kantian 'humanistic cosmopolitan universalism' (ibid., 702). Second, *analytic posthumanism* emerging from contemporary science and technology studies – the implications of which undermine the centrality of the human and generate important dilemmas for human rights law and theory.[3] Finally, *critical posthumanism*, Braidotti's 'own variation', the goal of which is to 'move beyond analytic posthumanism and develop affirmative perspectives on the posthuman subject' (ibid., 822).

It is important to admit the depth of the contemporary challenges faced by traditional humanistic conceptions of human rights. Breakthroughs in biotechnology and cybernetics, and developments in artificial and robotic intelligence, challenge the idea that the human is neatly separable from the machine, and is uniquely capable of reasoning and higher-level calculative function. Meanwhile, increased understanding of the multiple forms of intelligence and vulnerability distributed across animal, bird and fish populations, and among trees and other living ecosystems, has generated impetus towards the award of rights to range of non-human beneficiaries (see, for example, Solum 1992; Cavalieri 2001; Teubner 2006; Stone 2010). Rights claims for animals, 'plants and even inanimate objects' respond to the fact that anthropocentrism is increasingly anachronistic – and that the current global order feeding off it produces extensive and multiple dangers for all forms of life – including the human (Pennock 1987, 19). Indeed, multiple crises emerging from the centrality of 'the human' and its transnational corporate avatar (Grear 2015) feed the pervasive vulnerability and deepening levels of violence linked with neoliberal globalisation (Kirby 2006) and to its 'global commodification of living organisms' (Braidotti 2013, 205).

This chapter, in response to such concerns and developments, seeks, in line with the affective nuances of critical posthumanism, to offer a reflection on human rights and vulnerability in an ultimately affirmative register. It does so by 'following' vulnerable corporeality towards New Materialist understandings of materiality and towards a human rights ontology embracing the decentring of the human and the refusal of its hierarchical ontological primacy. Human rights are reimagined here through an (in part, critical) 'embrace' of vulnerability theory to resituate human rights as a form of juridical attentiveness to human 'critters' (Haraway 2008) in a more-than-human world, contributing, it is hoped, to vulnerability theory in the process.

The chapter offers an unapologetically theoretical experiment – a setting off without final arrival. It opens by offering an account of the relationship between vulnerability and human rights (and examining the politics of vulnerability in human rights) before introducing 'the vulnerability thesis' and human rights, and reflecting briefly on the relationship between vulnerability and dignity.

---

3 See (2018) 43/1 *Science, Technology and Human Values*, Special Edition: 'New Technologies, Developments in the Biosciences and the New Frontiers of Human Rights' 016224391773614 (available at http://journals.sagepub.com/toc/sthd/43/1) (date of last access: 9 March 2018) (Guest editor: N Vaisman).

It then gestures towards an as-yet contingently traced, broadly New Materialist approach to vulnerability and human rights before offering some concluding thoughts and further research directions.

Vulnerability and human rights – opening critical notes

Human rights – for all their *putative* focus on the human – have never been entirely dedicated to the protection of human beings as corporeally vulnerable living beings: the universal subject of human rights has been criticised for its relative disembodiment and invulnerability (Otto 2005; Grear 2007), and human rights have been criticised for gaps between the 'human' and the 'citizen' through which human beings *as such* tend to fall (Arendt 1971, 299; see also Grear 2010 150–155). Meanwhile, conceptual and linguistic conflations between 'the human', the 'person' and the 'legal person' have been widely exploited by transnational corporations to such an extent that the UDHR paradigm has mutated into a neoliberal 'trade-related market-friendly' paradigm of human rights (Baxi 2002; Harding et al. 2008). This paradigm (Baxi 2002, 132)

> seeks to demote, even reverse, the notion that universal human rights are designed for the attainment of dignity and well-being of human beings and for advancing the security and well-being of socially, economically and civilizationally vulnerable peoples and communities. The emergent paradigm insists upon the promotion and protection of the collective human rights of global capital in ways that 'justify' corporate well-being and dignity even when it entails gross and flagrant violation of human rights of actually existing human beings and communities.

Perhaps such critiques and anxieties can be summed up by saying that human rights express ineradicable ideological tensions reflecting struggles for their meaning and for the meaning of the human, and that such struggle has reached an urgent contemporary intensity. Capitalist formations use human rights law to claim a form of legal humanity (Grear 2007; 2010), while advocates for marginalised humans, non-human animals and other forms of life imperilled by the corporate colonisation of lifeworlds fight back against the global production of precarity (Standing 2011; Nasstrom and Kalm 2015) and the 'neoliberalisation of nature' (McCarthy 2005, 11). Both sides in the struggle draw upon 'the logics, paralogics and languages of human rights' – logics and languages that have never lost their meta-ethical and political potency, despite being assailed by critiques and doubts (Baxi 2002, 132).

The struggle for human rights meanings is thus a key battleground. A particularly salient and influential critique concerns the dominance of the archetypal conceptual paradigm of the liberal (humanist, Eurocentric) subject of rights, which 'stands at the centre of the universe and asks the law to enforce his entitlements without great concern for ethical considerations and without empathy for the other' (Douzinas 2000, 238). It is this paradigmatic subject of human rights that is exposed as being – as Nino has argued – 'prior to any end, interest and desire' (Nino 1993, 110), whose most fundamental characteristic is the 'ability to choose' (Douzinas 2000, 235). The ontological separation assumed between the wilful Eurocentric subject-at-the-centre and the world as an objectified field has in turn resulted in 'the impoverishment of the subject' (ibid., 236). This is a process, according to Douzinas (ibid., 242), by which human rights have become susceptible to trivialisation and commodification and their 'endless extension . . . to match ever expanding desire threatens their protective role'.

Yet, despite their ideological weaknesses, human rights, for those deploying them in political struggles or claiming them as forms of protection against injustice, offer an unrivalled degree of semantic force. And, at the heart of such struggles and claim-making practices, the potential of human rights can readily be understood to have an intimate relationship with human vulnerability.

Indeed, at first glance it might seem that the relationship between vulnerability and human rights is somewhat self-evident. Human rights, according to their own dominant self-presentation in the UDHR and in related treaties,[4] emerged as a response to the pathogenic imposition of suffering, expressing an 'unprecedented international consensus on substantive norms with high moral voltage' (De Sousa Santos 2000, 260). At the heart of the UDHR lay the visceral experience, according to Morsink's (1993a; 1993b) analysis of the drafting process, of the Holocaust, and while the precise role of the Holocaust can be disputed, there is no doubting the public shock at 'the haunting and nightmarishly painful visibility of corpses: corpses piled high, in pallid, ravaged mounds at Auschwitz and other concentration camps – and the possibly even more unbearable images of the ghostly living bodies of the emaciated, skeletal survivors in their ragged camp uniforms' (Caven 2001). Something deeply *creaturely* was at work in the international response to such corporeal violation. And, in this respect, as in others, the UDHR follows the earlier French Declaration of the Rights of Man and the Citizen for which outraged political response to corporeal violation was also decisive (Hunt 2007).

Nevertheless, the visceral energies inspiring the genesis of both Declarations were selectively muted by influences at work in the *realpolitik* of rights institutionalisation (Stammers 1999). The UDHR, textually modelled on the earlier Declaration, installed an abstract subject of rights (only this time, a 'human' instead of a 'man') – a move repeating, in effect, the earlier Declaration's universalisation of a Eurocentric masculinist particular (Hunt 1996; Scott 1996; Marks 1998). Indeed, a pattern of elite property-centred retrenchment is visible throughout the history of human rights – a pattern for which the abstract human rights subject is ideologically pivotal (Ishay 2008).

4 See, especially, the International Covenant on Economic, Social and Cultural Rights (ICESCR): Opened for signature 16 December 1966, 993 UNTS 3 (entered into force 3 January 1976), and the International Covenant on Civil and Political Rights (ICCPR) Opened for signature 16 December 1966, 999 UNTS 171 (entered into force 23 March 1976).

The very purpose of according priority to the abstract subject is, of course, to submerge social conflicts and fractious politics (see Norrie 2014). As Keenan (1997, 3) puts it, 'ethics and politics ... are evaded when we call on the conceptual priority of the subject, agency or identity as the grounds of our action' (Swanson Goldberg and Schultheis Moore 2012, 3). It is highly significant that '[o]nce the slightest empirical or historical material is introduced into abstract human nature, once we move from the declarations onto the concrete embodied person, with gender, race, class and age, human nature with its equality and dignity retreats rapidly' (Douzinas 2000, 96). So too does corporeal vulnerability, because the abstract subject of human rights installs a particular form of relative *in*vulnerability into the subject of human rights.

The dignified, autonomous subject of human rights is a subject whose vulnerability consists primarily in the possibility of attacks upon its (predominantly Kantian) dignity and/or autonomy – or upon the preconditions/conditions for that autonomy (Anderson 2014). This autonomy is built, as numerous critics have noted, upon Eurocentric 'Reason', which operates a 'politics of disembodiment and embodiment' (Baxi 2010) operationalising what Kapur (2006; 2007, 541) calls the 'dark side' of human rights.

This variant of autonomy is also foundational to the 'philosophical speciesism' (Gearty 2010) of human rights and deeply complicit in the 'entanglements of oppression' (Nibert 2002; Dekha 2008) driving spiralling levels of multi-species vulnerability and industrial-scale violence against nonhuman living beings and systems (Nibert 2002; Kirby 2015).

The politics of disembodiment and embodiment is also a politics of vulnerability. The abstract (quasi-disembodied) human rights universal produces a set of 'others', disqualified from being its paradigmatic instances. Pride of archetypal place is reserved for the construct of the rational, white (European) male – the complete and self-evident exemplar of human universality (the most rational of subjects ['*the* subject']). This subject's less-than-fully-rational 'others' are constructed, meanwhile, as inherently and quintessentially vulnerable in ways that hinge precisely upon their assumed/asserted lack of rationality – glaring examples being 'women and children' (Otto 2005, 105–106) and 'savages' (Matua 2001).

These quintessentially vulnerable (less-than-fully-rational) human beings are constructed as needing the protection of the white-male saviour/rescuer/ protector/civiliser through the construction of an agency-denying victimology (Otto 2005). These others, paradoxically, are constructed as being especially inherently vulnerable precisely because they are deemed incapable of the *kind* of vulnerability fundamental to the human rights universal. Again, this is because the *kind* of vulnerability central to the human rights universal turns upon the possibility of injury to fully rational autonomy and/or the dignity founded upon it. And, in a further insult, paradigmatic human rights violations are thus also imagined primarily as violations of (white) male bodies (Beveridge and Mullally 1995). These, after all, are the smuggled bodies that alone bear the fully dignified rational autonomy not attributed to the 'others' of the human rights universal (Ahmed 1995, 56).

In short, the abstract universal human rights subject is simultaneously relatively invulnerable *and* uniquely vulnerable. It is relatively *in*vulnerable compared to the quintessentially vulnerable others of human rights, but uniquely vulnerable to the *kind* of injury most significant to the liberal subject of rights.

The body politics involved in this sleight of hand constructs 'others' to the abstract subject as marginal precisely because they are deemed to be closer to the 'animality' of the body and to the 'mess and irrationality' of 'nature'. It is only these others who need 'protection', or 'civilization' or 'saving' (Matua 2001; Otto 2005; Kapur 2006, 2007). Vulnerability functions, therefore, as an ideological mechanism intrinsic to the hierarchical production of marginalised human rights bearers and moves along a bipolar axis between the full rational agency of the human rights universal and the 'victimhood' of its quintessentially vulnerable others. In this respect, the universal is at odds with the impulses of universalisation driving the genesis of rights documents declaring the inclusion of previously excluded others: women, children, indigenous peoples and others have all fought for inclusion as specific rights-bearing subjects, as is well known. The very need for them to have done so, however, points to the pervasive exclusions haunting the abstract universal with its smuggled, uniquely rational and uniquely *in*vulnerable/uniquely vulnerable beneficiary.

Perhaps another way of getting at these complexities is to argue that vulnerability is not – and cannot be – monolithic – including for human rights. MacKenzie, Rogers and Dodds (2014, 3–4, 7) have recently offered an account of vulnerability that helps to respond to this point. Addressing the foundational question of what vulnerability *is* and addressing tensions between the two dominant answers to this question in the relevant literature, the authors distinguish between 'distinct but overlapping kinds of vulnerability'. In this context, they identify three *sources* of vulnerability useful for the argument to come: *Inherent vulnerability* refers to 'sources of vulnerability intrinsic to the human condition', which arise from human corporeality and vary in response to resilience. *Situational vulnerability* is 'context-specific' and arises in response to conditions that can be 'short term, intermittent or enduring' (ibid.). (Despite their analytical distinguishability, these two sources of vulnerability are not ultimately separate and vulnerability is always ultimately 'experienced in the body'; ibid., 8.)[5] *Pathogenic vulnerability* arises from a range of sociopolitical, social and interpersonal sources, and 'a key feature of pathogenic vulnerability is the way it undermines autonomy or exacerbates the sense of powerlessness engendered by vulnerability in general' (ibid., 9).

Notable in all these formulations is the centrality of human corporeality and the semiotic imbrication of vulnerability, powerlessness, need, dependency,

---

5　These two sources can both manifest as either of the two *states* of 'potential versus actual' vulnerability, *the dispositional* and *the occurrent*. The authors explain that women of child-bearing age are all dispositionally vulnerable to complications in childbirth, but whether or not that actualises as occurrent vulnerability turns on a host of situational and/or inherent factors.

suffering and harm. In both these respects, the formulations closely chime with two leading accounts of 'the vulnerability thesis'.

The vulnerability thesis and human rights

I turn first to the 'vulnerability thesis' developed as a critical heuristic by feminist legal theorist, Martha Fineman (2010). I begin here because Fineman's thesis is highly influential and was explicitly first developed as 'a stealthily disguised human rights discourse' aimed at her 'audience' in the US (ibid., 255). Central to Fineman's thesis is a sustained attack on the relatively invulnerable 'autonomous subject' of the liberal order: Fineman (2008, 2) argues that the trope of 'the vulnerable subject' is 'far more representative of actual lived experience and the human condition and should be placed at the center of our political and theoretical endeavours'.

The language that MacKenzie, Rogers and Dodds (2014, 7) use to describe inherent vulnerability, which addresses 'sources of vulnerability intrinsic to the human condition' that arise from human corporeality and vary in response to resilience, applies directly to Fineman's thesis. For Fineman (2010, 269), vulnerability is 'common and enduring', 'universal and particular':

> We have different forms of embodiment and also are differently situated within webs of economic and institutional relationships. As a result, our vulnerabilities range in magnitude and potential at the individual level. Vulnerability, therefore, is both universal and particular; it is experienced uniquely by each of us.

Fineman's emphasis on inherent vulnerability does not mean that she ignores situational and pathogenic vulnerability: Fineman (2008, 8) would be especially suspicious of some situational accounts of vulnerability – arguing, for example, that vulnerability has been unfairly characterised as being the particular condition of identified social groups and has been pejoratively deployed to construct unacceptable forms of victimhood, dependency and even pathology (see also Fineman 2003, 33–35). Fineman (2010, 255) presents her vulnerable subject as an explicitly post-identity conception focusing upon 'exploring the nature of the human part, rather than the rights part, of the human rights trope'.

Fineman is not, however, a human rights theorist and nor does she claim or set out to be. Despite that, her argument that universal variably experienced vulnerability should replace the relatively invulnerable autonomy of the traditional liberal subject chimes well with attacks on the deceptive universality of the autonomous, dignified subject of human rights declarations, as does her wariness concerning pejorative deployments of vulnerability to pathologise certain groups and identities. Fineman's work is not free, though, from important ambiguities from a human rights perspective.

Her positioning of institutions as vulnerable (Wall 2008), her notion of the 'responsive state' (Coyle 2013) and her deployment of the market-soaked language of 'assets' in the production of resilience (Wall 2008, 54) are all reasons why scholars have had cause to question her approach, but the most relevant ambiguity for present purposes concerns Fineman's ontology. Fineman (2008, 15) argues that

> [o]ne promising theoretical potential of making vulnerability central in an analysis of equality is that attention to the situation of the vulnerable individual allows us to redirect our focus onto the societal institutions that are created in response to individual vulnerability. This institutional focus has the effect of supplementing attention to the individual subject by placing him/her in social context.

Fineman's language is revealing: societal institutions are *'created in response to* individual vulnerability' – and 'this institutional focus *supplements attention to the individual subject* by *placing* him/her *in* social *context'*. The individual here appears to be in some sense, pre-social, requiring insertion into 'social context', and Wall (2008, 54) has argued (for different but related reasons) that 'the assertion that placing the individual in its institutional context socialises the individual is far from satisfactory,' because it appears to refract sociality through institutionalisation.

This sociality, I suggest, is also too limited in its embrace of the corporeality of the vulnerable human subject and its implications: it is the fundamentally natal eco-sociality intrinsic to human corporeality that is so promising for an ontology of vulnerability and human rights responsive to the entangled materio-sociality of the human and nonhuman. It is this natal, materially entangled eco-sociality, moreover, that offers a more empirically faithful – and politically radical – account of the world (see Tsing 2015).

Some of these potential limitations merely reflect that fact that Fineman's concern is not primarily with human rights but with the lack of substantive equality in the US. Fineman (2010, 255) explicitly leaves behind her disguised human rights discourse relatively early on in her work to focus more broadly upon 'vulnerability and the human condition'. Her observations concerning the lack of a US human rights discourse, US exceptionalism in relation to core international human rights instruments and its judicial resistance to human rights as a 'foreign fads', were never intended to offer an extended engagement with human rights or with their ontology (ibid., 254–255). For that, we turn to the work of Bryan Turner.

In *Vulnerability and Human Rights*, Turner (2006, 2) provides a sustained sociological account of the vulnerability thesis and human rights, identifying human 'embodied vulnerability' as the ontological foundation of human rights universalism. In this section of my reflection, I will examine Turner's argument, drawing on my earlier discussion of it in *Redirecting Human Rights: Challenging Corporate Legal Humanity* (Grear 2010).

Turner's conception of vulnerability, like Fineman's and the other accounts surveyed by MacKenzie, Rogers and Dodds, focuses on vulnerability's intimate relationship with the capacity of the human being to suffer. Turner (2006, 127) argues that 'suffering is inevitable and misery is universal' and that 'we suffer because we are vulnerable, and we need, above all else, institutions that will give us some degree of security.' Human rights are 'rights enjoyed by individuals by virtue of being human – and as a consequence of their shared vulnerability' and can 'be defined as universal principles, because human beings share a common ontology that is grounded in a shared vulnerability' (ibid., 3, 6).

Turner draws upon an argument made by Michael Ignatieff (2001, 95), in which Ignatieff suggests that human rights need to be understood as the basis for a shared deliberation concerning how humans should treat one another but states that 'the ground we share may actually be quite limited: not much more than the basic intuition that what is pain and humiliation for you is bound to be pain and humiliation for me. But this is already something.' Turner (2006, 9) argues, extending Ignatieff's claim, that it is our 'capacity for suffering that creates a significant basis for universalism':

> While humans may not share a common culture, they are bound together by the risks and perturbations that arise from their vulnerability. Because we have a common ontological condition as vulnerable, intelligent beings, human happiness is diverse, but misery is common and uniform. This need for ontological security provides a strong moral argument against cultural relativism and offers an endorsement of rights claims for protection from suffering and indignity. While liberal theory is largely about the political dimension of human rights, ontological insecurity indicates a cluster of salient social and economic rights... fundamentally connected with human embodiment.

For Turner, it is the commonality emerging from the uniformity of misery and the need for ontological security that provides 'a strong moral argument' for universalism. Anticipating the obvious counterargument that suffering is not uniform, Turner (ibid., 35) concedes that while suffering may be variable, pain is not: 'Whereas bankruptcy, for example could involve some degree of variable psychological suffering, a toothache is a toothache.' Turner ultimately founds the ontology of human rights universalism, then, on the 'common and uniform' misery of physical pain. But pain, as Morris (1991, 1) has shown, is 'decisively shaped or modified by individual human minds and [by] specific human cultures'. It is 'historically, culturally and psychosocially constructed – [and] is "always more than a matter of nerves and neurotransmitters"' (ibid., 2). Pain, we might say, is *culturally relative*. Morris (ibid., 14, 19) demonstrates that '[w]e learn how to feel pain and what it means' and that '[w]hen we fall into pain, we also fall into a net of already constructed meanings.' If this is the case, then physical pain cannot be deployed to defeat cultural relativism in the way that Turner proposes. Indeed, the more we understand pain, 'the more we learn anatomically and neurologically about it, the more we learn that it is the very hard wiring of our bodies, that there is no "pain centre", there is no place in which the "objective" pain ends and the "subjective" suffering begins' (Wall 2008, 61). Turner did not, in any case, need to rely on pain in this way to ground vulnerability as the ontological foundation of human rights. Variable experience does not defeat a universalism drawing upon human corporeal vulnerability (Grear 2010, 134).

From the point of view of a critical human rights approach, there are further issues with Turner's thesis. First, his understanding of vulnerability leads him to suggest that 'ontological insecurity' implies a particular cluster of social and economic rights. He then anticipates the claim that 'the vulnerability thesis can be further criticized because it is very relevant to some human rights, but not to others' (Turner 2006, 36). This concession forces him to link democracy and the right to health in order to construct vulnerability as an indirect foundation for civil and political rights. However, it is not necessary to take such an indirect route when civil and political rights presuppose both corporeality and vulnerability (Grear 2010, 158–160). Second, Turner's account appears to assume that human rights are benign – an assumption ignoring the role of human rights in the construction of pathogenic forms of vulnerability and overlooking the distinction between politics *for* human rights and politics *of* human rights (Baxi 2002). Third, Wall (2008, 66–67, 55) has criticised Turner for constructing vulnerability as a condition that human rights seek to turn away from, producing an account of human rights that neutralises the *political* energy of vulnerability as suffering and enabling a discourse whereby human rights respond to (certain) subjective, visible harms while continuing to legitimate invisibilised structural violence.

Finally, for Turner (2006, 26), it is 'risk and uncertainty' that give rise to 'sympathy, empathy and trust' and drive humans to build forms of social organisation aimed at mitigating precarity. However, as I argued in *Redirecting Human Rights* (Grear 2010, 133), it is possible to imagine society as something more than 'a pact of the insecure and suffering-prone, huddling together in the face of a dark, frightening world of risk and conflict' and to respond to vulnerability as 'a core component of an alternative view of human relations – as far more than our capacity to suffer/feel pain, and as far more than a synonym for suffering'.

It is necessary to think beyond the threatened human and the frightening world and to *embrace* vulnerability as an aspect of ordinary natal sociality (Butler 2009) and of mundane corporeal entanglements that include nonhumans (although it is an anticipation of New Materialist approaches, see Tsing 2012). It is possible – and necessary – in short, to think towards questions of posthuman subjectivity, vulnerability and human rights in an affirmative register.

Vulnerability and dignity

It is important briefly to consider the relationship between vulnerability and dignity. Dignity is famously posited as being the foundation of human rights in much mainstream human rights theory, and, as Neal's (2012) analysis (to be discussed here) suggests, mainstream accounts of dignity construct dignity in terms of producing an ambivalent relationship with vulnerability. I choose Neal's work because Neal bases her analysis of dignity on vulnerability – and deploys Fineman's vulnerability thesis. Neal's (ibid., 180) survey of existing dignity scholarship and her reflections on dignity and vulnerability deliberately leave aside, it should be noted, the question of the dignity of 'non-human entities' (to be considered briefly below).

Neal (ibid., 177–185) argues that dignity is semantically unstable and potentially philosophically redundant. She also argues that it is necessary to move beyond the Kantian conception of autonomous dignity, attacking the Kantian conception for its central reliance upon rationality and suggesting that a shift towards 'an account [of dignity] based on the interconnectedness between dignity and vulnerability' would neutralise some of the most common critiques of dignity itself.

'Human dignity' should, Neal (ibid., 180) argues, be understood as an 'organizing idea'. An 'organizing idea', Neal explains, is something like Wittgenstein's notion of the 'family resemblance'. Understood in this way, dignity is a 'moral response to vulnerability', and spacious enough to ground all the various concepts and conceptions of dignity, not on a monolithic core, but within a clustered relationality. And it is here, at the level of the organising idea, that Neal (ibid., 181) locates her analysis of the imbrication between dignity and the 'phenomenon of human vulnerability': human dignity, she argues, is 'a particular sort of ethical response to universal human vulnerability – distinctive among ethical values in that it values us because of, rather than in spite of, or regardless of, our universal vulnerability' (ibid., 177).

In addressing vulnerability, Neal adopts Fineman's approach but supplements Fineman's focus upon what Neal calls 'negative' vulnerability (the capacity for suffering) with my 'positive' (Neal's terminology, not mine) account of vulnerability, offered in *Redirecting Human Rights*. Neal (ibid., 187) describes my position in the following terms:

> Crucially, [Grear] writes, vulnerability is 'a key incident of human embodiment', and the openness of our bodies exists not only in the negative sense of dependence and penetrability – sources of pain and suffering – but also in a positive 'affectability', an openness to all that is welcome and embraceable and dynamic about our interconnectedness with, and our ability to interface with, other beings and our wider environment. In Grear's words: 'The openness – the etheological nature – of the living body, once fully appreciated, might provide the foundation for a vulnerability thesis that allows us to embrace vulnerability as a dynamic interrelational concept highly suggestive of richer human bonds not only with human beings, but of humans with the world itself'.

Neal (ibid., 189) insists that vulnerability (understood in this more-than-negative sense) is what makes ethics *possible* – that 'in the absence of vulnerability, there would (could) be no ethics.' Vulnerability, on this account, is foundational to any human life worth imagining – an anchor for that which is valued and worthy of compassionate consideration. It is not merely a susceptibility.

For Neal, the all-embracing power of the connection between vulnerability and ethics opens out the distinctiveness of dignity by establishing its 'unique' connection with vulnerability. This unique connection is not, however, to be found in the Kantian conception of dignity. Like Harris (1997), upon whose work on dignity and vulnerability she draws (with reservations), Neal (2012, 184) eschews the Kantian view of what dignity is and argues that Kantian dignity as a universal foundation for human rights is problematic. She points out that 'there is ... a significant difference between observing that my abilities to reason and to act autonomously are critical to my moral agency, and making the more controversial claim that unless I possess the capacities for reason and autonomous action... I cannot matter morally, or cannot matter morally as much as someone else who does possess these capacities' (ibid.).

Neal's argument has obvious resonance with the critiques of human rights, noted above, concerning the oppressive use of 'Reason' in the construction of the universal's 'others'. Kantian dignity purports to ground a human universal, yet in both theory and in practice, the human rights universal thus grounded is parochial, a deceptive placeholder guarding a privileged space for the quasi-disembodied Eurocentric rational human subject, which is as property-centred and exclusory as its broader ideological foundation in the liberal legal and political order as a whole (Nedelsky 1990; Halewood 1996).

Although Neal explicitly avoids the question of nonhuman dignity, her fundamental argument about the ontology of dignity is compatible, I suggest, with the dignity of nonhumans. If dignity is a particular sort of ethical responsiveness to vulnerability, there is no reason not to respond to the universal vulnerability of nonhumans once anthropocentric assumptions are put to one side. Indeed, as more is understood about the intelligences, agencies and socialities of nonhumans, the more challenging it becomes to accept the idea that humans have a sole – or even a unique – claim to any given characteristics founding ethical regard (see Haraway 2008; 2016; Tsing 2012).[6] And, even if one were successfully able to argue that humans uniquely possess particular characteristics, deepening understanding of nonhuman intelligence and agency makes it increasingly implausible – notwithstanding such an argument – that humans should be granted the *a priori* centrality assumed by traditional dignity accounts. In short, once humanistic assumptions are rejected, it becomes possible to see the universal vulnerability of nonhumans as a basis for nonhuman dignity. Universal vulnerability understood as an intrinsically socio-material, corporeal openness, moreover, could provide a strong bridge into a theory of nonhuman dignity without

---

6 Study of the nonhuman world – indeed – increasingly reveals the implausibility of human uniqueness and priority. Humans emerge from contemporary biology as entangled partners in a world full of livelier partners than Kantian and Cartesian suppositions allow for.

negating the ethical significance of potential differences in the experiences and sources of human and nonhuman vulnerability at work in any given situation.

Towards a new materialist account of vulnerability and human rights

If the vulnerability thesis is to be ontologically consistent with the implications of the corporeality at its heart, then vulnerability must necessarily be conceived of as a more-than-human entanglement, for the human body is an 'intrinsically open, sensing, feeling, desiring, libidinal, expressive circuit with the world' (Grear 2010, 132) – inescapably entangled in porous, lively materialities of the same 'order of touch' as itself (Merleau-Ponty 1968, 134). Such an ontology offers the possibility, I suggest, of an affirmative prefigurative politics of human rights responsive to multiple human–nonhuman entanglements – opening the possibility, in the process, of human rights-based objections to the denial of such important relationalities.

Indeed, in the light of the multiple contemporary crises marking the posthuman epoch, an understanding of materiality itself as vulnerable is now a prerequisite for human rights realisation – and while this point may be relatively obvious in the case of 'environmental human rights' (see Alaimo 2010),[7] it nonetheless applies to *all* human rights, as an implication of the porous, transcorporeal (ibid.) nature of the human embodiment foundational to all human rights (see Grear 2010, 156–161). Human rights theory and practice must evolve, therefore, by putting to one side the patterns of injustice visible in the politics of disembodiment and by embracing the ontic fact of human co-enfoldment in a living, vulnerable mesh (addressing an analogous argument in relation to political analysis and progressive politics; see Braidotti 2013). Taking up Fineman's (2008, 2) admonition to position 'the human condition ... at the center of our political and theoretical endeavours' therefore means embracing the human being as but one vulnerable partner in a vulnerable entanglement – paying close attention to the differential patterns of vulnerability – inherent, situational and/or pathogenically generated – of multiple human and nonhuman partners (Grear 2011). It is precisely in relation to this expansion of focus and concern that New Materialist thought is so promising.

New Materialism draws on Spinoza, Merleau-Ponty, and Deleuze and Guattari, combining such theoretical influences with developments in cutting-edge science that make the human exceptionalism and bounded individualism that have for so long underpinned humanism and human rights '...[s]eriously unthinkable: not available to think with' (Haraway 2016, 30). What happens, we might therefore ask, to theories of *vulnerability* when an affirmative prefigurative politics for the posthuman situation can no longer do its job with 'bounded

---

7 Environmental human rights are a particularly promising site for the acknowledgement that all forms of corporeality exist in a transcorporeal planetary flow.

individuals plus contexts', or bodies plus environments, with the subject and its objects (ibid.)? What happens when such constructs can no longer offer even an empirically sustainable way of seeing *what's/who's here*?

New Materialism challenges 'received concepts of agency, action, and freedom sometimes to the breaking point' and aims to 'sketch a style of political analysis that can better account for the contributions of nonhuman actants' (Bennett 2010, 108–109). Such an account exceeds the foundational Cartesian and Kantian assumptions dominating mainstream human rights discourse and doctrine and expresses 'an alternative to the object as a way of encountering the nonhuman world' (ibid., 231). The ethical aim of such approaches is to cultivate 'the ability to discern nonhuman vitality, to become perceptually open to it' (ibid., 553–554), and this cultivation of discernment should explicitly include, I suggest, the fundamental affectability of materiality – in short, its vulnerability. If '[t]he locus of agency' is 'always a human-nonhuman working group' (ibid., 236–237), so too is the locus of vulnerability.

For New Materialist accounts, 'agency' becomes *affect* – and the capacity to affect or to be affected is typical of all matter (Deleuze 1988, 101; Fox and Alldred 2015, 401). The affectability of matter is key to an adequately materialist understanding of vulnerability.[8] Analytical attention to 'assemblages' (including 'the body') as processes of production that emerge 'in a kind of chaotic network of habitual and non-habitual connections, always in flux, always reassembling in different ways' (Potts 2004, 19; Fox and Alldred 2015) suggests the need for vulnerability analyses to range back and forth, tracing 'shifting states and capacities, which in turn produce further shifting states and capacities in a non-linear, rhizomatic way that spreads out in all directions sometimes in patterned ways, sometimes unpredictably' (Grear 2011, 23). Deploying this method of analysis, the affects of macro-structural projects (such as the international economy) can be drawn together with 'micro-powers of governmentality' and with 'a whole constellation of actants; biological urges; movements of herds or flocks; transits of toxins, viruses, nutrients, water, air; the physical infrastructure of a power supply and so much more' (Grear 2018–2019). Such a field of attention might yield a more complete engagement with the complexities of vulnerability as it emerges in multiply constructed ways and is promisingly multilayered (Fox and Alldred 2015, 402).

Because 'agency' is distributed as affect, the human subject (vulnerable or otherwise) is no longer an automatically prioritised ontological, epistemological or axiological *pivot*. Dissipating the subject–object divide that has underpinned human rights and so much vulnerability theory does not imply, however, the dissolution of all boundaries into an undifferentiated flux (Haynes 2014, 135). Barad (2007), for example, argues that subject–object distinctions become

---

8 It should be noted that various other accounts of vulnerability emphasise affectability and its implications – and affectability, in this sense, provides a rich convergence point between New Materialism and such accounts. I am grateful to Daniel Bedford for raising this point.

contingent – constructed for a particular purpose from a particular perspective. Human beings will obviously continue to distinguish things from persons, but it is vital to acknowledge that 'the sort of world we live in makes it constantly possible for these two sets of kinds to exchange properties' (Bennett 2010, 451–453). Perhaps it is here, in this onto-epistemic move, that human dignity might find some theoretical space. Human exceptionalism might be unsustainable, but human distinguishability as particular but contingently understood and positioned diffractions of relationality remains meaningful and ethically important, while human rights and vulnerability analyses can both become, along with other modes of navigating the world, more responsive to the implications of the connectedness between bodies of *all kinds*. This expanded epistemic embrace can enable 'wiser interventions' into the ecology of embodied entanglements at stake in any given question of injustice. The ethics implied by this distribute significance, value and vulnerabilities to 'bodies *as such*', and generate, as Bennett puts it, 'a great sense of the extent to which all bodies are kin in the sense of inextricably enmeshed in a dense network of relations' (ibid., 353–355, 508–511).

This then is an ethics of attentiveness to multiple modes of co-situatedness. As Haraway (2016, 31) argues, it matters *'who we are bound up with and in what ways'* – and this 'who' is made up of kin of all kinds, human and nonhuman. Human beings are thus a 'specifically endowed (but not special) . . . species' (ibid., 185). And as a specifically endowed species, human beings can still form the focus of a human rights ethic – only now, nonhuman actants also take their place, in full view, no longer *invisibilised* by anthropocentric epistemological closures. Human beings can be understood as vulnerable and materially entangled, but not uniquely so. Human rights analysis will retain, though, the task of remaining especially sensitive to the affectability of humans in any given situation.

Human rights thus become a specific way of asking 'who we are bound up with and in what ways', alert to the idiosyncratic ways in which humans collectivise. Even for human rights analyses, however, nonhuman actants are, as Bryant (2011, 23–24) puts it, 'pertinent', not least 'to why collectives involving humans take the form they do':

> the 'nonhuman . . . in the form of technologies, weather patterns, resources, diseases, animals, natural disasters, the presence or absence of roads, the availability of water, animals, microbes, the presence or absence of electricity and high speed internet connections, modes of transportation, and so on . . . and many more besides play a crucial role in bringing humans together in particular ways'.

Returning to Bennett's (2010, 510–511) invitation to perceive and to respond to the 'extent to which all bodies are kin in the sense of inextricably enmeshed in a dense network of relations', it is enriching to turn to Haraway (2016), who encourages human beings to 'make kin' of all kinds.

Active kin-*making* necessitates an active kind of world-making. Haraway (ibid., 42) proposes that humans should take up 'tentacular thinking' and 'tentacular worlding', which is an

> ecology of practices, [a commitment] to the mundane articulating of assemblages through situated work and play in the muddle of messy living and dying. Actual players, articulating with varied allies of all ontological sorts (molecules, colleagues and much more) must compose and sustain what is and will be.

The 'seriously tangled affair' (ibid.) of such world-making necessarily concerns the vulnerability of messy living and dying – with all its rich imperatives for close ethical attentiveness. Thus, while vulnerability as suffering ignites radical human rights politics, vulnerability as affectability points unambiguously towards multiple forms of interconnection and co-flourishing between humans and other multispecies partners and allies in a way that might inspire 'new [human rights] practices of imagination, resistance, revolt, repair and mourning, and of living and dying well' (ibid.). Vulnerability means taking up Haraway's (ibid., 55) call to stay willingly immersed in all the messy incompletion of resistive living: 'We are at stake to each other... The order is reknitted: human beings are with and of the earth, and the biotic and abiotic powers of this earth are the main story' – *not* human centrality. The biotic and abiotic *vulnerabilities* of this earth are *also* the main story. As Bryant (2011, 24) argues, 'in an age where we are faced with the looming threat of monumental climate change, it is irresponsible to draw our distinctions in such a way as to exclude nonhuman actors.' This urgently needed new approach to 'the main story' of humans as 'with and of the earth' contains in its tissues, I suggest, threads for a reimagined human rights.

Threads in new materialist human rights making

What then are some potential threads in New Materialist human rights making? And what implications does a broader view of vulnerability have for existing theoretical engagements with human rights and vulnerability?

First, understanding vulnerability as a form of affectability intrinsic to materiality opens up to view multiple ethological and corporeal dynamics of connection drawing vulnerability theory towards an enriching embrace of human–nonhuman socialities exceeding the socialities imagined by Fineman and Turner. It could also enable human rights and vulnerability theory to be freshly responsive to materiality's rich hints concerning the dynamics of ecstasy, well-being and flourishing, open to the 'other-seeking' nature of bodies as they reach towards other bodies of all kinds – *not* merely to huddle together against precarity. Relatedly, a New Materialist political ecology of human rights would be *intrinsically* open to the more-than-human world – an openness supporting epistemic justice for indigenous cultures and bringing human rights into line with the cutting-edge science now dismantling their humanist foundations.

Second, New Materialist ethics call for deep attention to the action of bodies upon bodies – *of all kinds*. Such ethics calls for 'a praxis-oriented, spatially specific, material approach that considers every problem in its singularity' (Philippopoulos-Mihalopoulos 2011, 21). Here, New Materialist analysis converges human rights as a 'politics of singularity' – as a practice of 'right-*ing*' amidst the humus of material entanglement (Wall 2008, 74 emphasis added). This approach would resist a 'rushed search for short term solutions that misunderstand . . . complexity' (Philippopoulos-Mihalopoulos 2011, 22). Human rights thinking and practice will need to step beyond the neat discursive containers set up by humanism, to move forward into the complex realities of the haunting ambiguities of the posthuman situation: climate change, biotechnologies (GMOs, bioengineering, new medical technologies, genetic recombination, shared genetic materiality etc.), instantaneous algorithm-driven global capital flows, rapidly evolving artificial and robotic intelligence, the saturation of contemporary life in digitalisation and virtual technologies and so on make the re-imagination of human rights entanglements in world-making increasingly urgent. Familiar linear legal assumptions concerning causation, responsibility and agency are simply not up to the enormity or complexity of the challenge. Such re-imagination is now both an intellectual and practical necessity (Coole and Frost 2010, 2).

Third, since science reveals matter to be 'materialization [,] a complex, pluralistic, relatively open process', it is necessary to locate all human knowing 'as thoroughly immersed within materiality's productive contingencies' (ibid., 7). Human theory and practice – including human rights approaches drawing upon vulnerability – now need to face up to the fact that the centre ('the subject') has gone and needs to be replaced by a contingent, purposive placeholder. Legal epistemologies, accordingly, need to embrace a profound degree of onto-epistemic humility (see Code 2000).

Fourth, the decentring of the human means that Fineman's vulnerable subject must also explicitly be understood as a contingent identification. Fineman's ontology is only partly reformulated by later applications of her theory to animals as 'vulnerable subjects' (Satz 2013)[9] and to 'ecological vulnerability' (Harris 2014).[10] There is more consistent theoretical work to be done if decentring the

---

9 Satz's new paradigm for the legal regulation of human use of domestic animals, which combines equal protection and capability theory approaches to generate a non-discrimination approach giving rise to presumption against the use of animals who have the capacity to suffer, does not fully explore and extend the underlying ontology of Fineman's approach.

10 Harris's extension of Fineman's theory to embrace 'ecological vulnerability' is problematically uncritical of 'recent policy and theoretical efforts to develop assessment systems for quantifying ecosystem processes' (at 116) and 'ecosystem services' and the 'services' provided by microbiota. Harris does not advert to significant contradictions between the foundational assumptions of such 'services' (and of the broader panoptic, neoliberal eco-governmentality operative in the quantification of ecosystem processes) and her embrace of New Materialist ontology. In addition, given her (potentially strawman) argument concerning the need for a strong subordination critique to supplement Fineman's vulnerability analysis, addressing the oppressive impacts of the

human is to do its most powerful ethical work. Decentring the human does not mean that we can no longer speak meaningfully of the vulnerable human being for human rights – but the dynamics between bodies *as such* now matters more explicitly as a central part of understanding the onto-political question of *'who we are bound up with and in what ways'* (Haraway 2016, 31). Human rights can – in this light – be imagined as special forms of attentiveness to the situation of human 'critters' understood as entangled kin in a world inevitably marked by multiple forms of vulnerability.

Concluding thoughts and further research directions

Human rights look very different when humans are seen as partners in 'world-making entanglements' 'in which diverse bodies and meanings coshape one another' (Haraway 2008, 4). Human rights emerge as a particular form of juridical attention and become part of expressing a wider call for sensitive engagement with the patterns and dynamics through which bodies (human, institutional or otherwise) can be called 'to account for the ways in which they affect other bodies of all kinds' (Barad 2007, 1891). Situational and pathogenic vulnerability reminds us to be constantly vigilant concerning the politics of unevenness. Critique remains essential. New Materialist accounts do not necessarily detract from this responsibility, for they insist that there is a deep ethical responsibility for 'the fact that our practices matter' (ibid.).

One particularly important future-facing research question concerns the role that such an account of human rights might play in offering renewed attentiveness to the marginalisations and exclusions *still marking human rights themselves.* Other future reflection could address what such theoretical shifts might mean in practical terms for courts, human rights institutions and human rights activists.

While this chapter offers an unashamedly theoretical reflection, hints already exist in relation to future-facing legal praxis. The use of animal movements to derive rules governing property rights and relations in the upland highlands of the UK, for example, hints at the way in which normativities emerge from a human–nonhuman working group (Peracinni 2012; Philippopoulos-Mihalopoulos 2012). The deployment of legal personification/rights for nonhuman entities and living systems promises new ways of thinking about legal subjectivity and repositioning human–nonhuman relationalities in the practice of legal judgment crafting – ideas anticipated by projects such as the 'wild law' judgment project (Rogers and Maloney 2017). Meanwhile, the creation of greater epistemic space and respect for the worldviews of indigenous peoples hints at the promise of exploring a 'pluriverse' of ontologies (Escobar 2015)[11] compatible with New Materialist science. The potential deployment of algorithms as digital partners in the mapping of affective flows affecting human rights, handled with immense care and critical

---

ontological commitments of environmental law and its broadly anthropocentric understanding of environmental vulnerability, is an important omission.

11 The 'pluriverse' is explicitly *contra* the 'One World' of neoliberalism and its Eurocentric ontology.

awareness in order to avoid simply replicating forms of techno-capitalist governmentality (see Luke 1995), might be worth exploring. The materio-semiotic teachings of forests and plants, water, animals, minerals and multiple other non-human actants could also fruitfully be explored by courts deliberating on human rights issues (Philippopoulos-Mihalopoulos and Brooks 2017, xii).

Such possibilities could play a role in developing law's threaded contribution to the necessary 'reknitting' of the world. The ongoing power of human rights as a politics and ethics of singularity arguably now depends upon such a reorientation and on embracing vulnerability as the material affectability of the more-than-human entanglements we call the world.

One thing is certain – reimagining human rights and vulnerability for the posthuman situation and the multiple crises facing humans and nonhumans alike demands a thoroughgoing, fearless and imaginative 'critical-creative engagement with deeply embedded, yet often uncontested assumptions about human subjectivity and agency [that] (often silently) inform the instituted social imaginary ... and tacitly constrain ... thinking' (Code 2015, 46). Given all that is now at stake, nothing less will do.

Bibliography

Ahmed S, 'Deconstruction and law's other: towards a feminist theory of embodied legal rights' (1995) 4 *Social and Legal Studies* 55.

Alaimo S, *Bodily Natures: Science, Environment and the Material Self* (Indiana University Press 2010).

Anderson J, 'Autonomy and vulnerability entwined' in C MacKenzie, R Rogers and S Dodds (eds), *Vulnerability: New Essays in Ethics and Feminist Philosophy* (Oxford University Press 2014).

Anghie A, *Imperialism, Sovereignty and the Making of International Law* (Cambridge University Press 2005).

Arendt H, *The Origins of Totalitarianism* (Harcourt 1971).

Barad K, *Meeting the Universe Halfway: Quantum Physics and the Entanglement of Matter and Meaning* (Duke University Press 2007) (Kindle Version).

Baxi U, *The Future of Human Rights* (Oxford University Press 2002).

Baxi U, *Human Rights in a Posthuman World* (Oxford University Press 2009).

Baxi U, 'Foreword', in A Grear, *Redirecting Human Rights: Facing the Challenge of Corporate Legal Humanity* (Palgrave MacMillan 2010).

Bennett J, *Vibrant Matter: A Political Ecology of Things* (Duke University Press 2010) (Kindle Edition).

Beveridge F and Mullally S, 'International human rights and body politics' in J Bridgeman and S Millns (eds), *Law and Body Politics: Regulating the Female Body* (Dartmouth Publishing 1995).

Braidotti R, *The Posthuman* (Polity Press 2013) (Kindle Edition).

Bryant L, *The Democracy of Objects* (New Humanities Press 2011).

Butler J, *Frames of War: When is Life Grievable?* (Verso 2009).

Cavalieri P, *The Animal Question: Why Nonhuman Animals Deserve Human Rights* (Oxford University Press 2001).

Caven H, 'Horror in our time: images of the concentration camps in the British Media 1945' (2001) 21 *Historical Journal of Film, Radio and Television* 205.

Code L, *Ecological Thinking: The Politics of Epistemic Location* (Oxford University Press 2000).

Code L, 'Ecological subjectivities, responsibilities, and agency' in A Grear and L Kotze (eds), *Research Handbook on Human Rights and the Environment* (Elgar 2015).

Coole D and Frost S (eds), *New Materialisms: Ontology, Agency and Politics* (Duke University Press 2010).

Coyle S, 'Vulnerability and the liberal order' in MA Fineman and A Grear (eds), *Vulnerability: Reflections on a New Ethical Foundation for Law and Politics* (Ashgate 2013).

De Sousa Santos B, *Towards a New Legal Common Sense: Law, Globalization and Emancipation* (Butterworths 2000).

Dekha M, 'Intersectionality and post-humanist visions of equality' (2008) 23 *Wisconsin Journal of Law, Gender and Society* 249.

Deleuze G, *Spinoza: Practical Philosophy* (City Lights 1988).

Douzinas C, *The End of Human Rights* (Hart 2000).

Escobar A, 'Commons in the pluriverse' in D Bollier and S Helfrich (eds), *Patterns of Commoning* (The Commons Strategies Group, 2015) 348.

Fineman MA, *The Autonomy Myth: A Theory of Dependency* (The New Press 2003).

Fineman MA, 'The vulnerable subject: anchoring equality in the human condition' (2008) 20 *Yale Journal of Law and Feminism* 1.

Fineman MA, 'The vulnerable subject and the responsive state' (2010) 60 *Emory Law Journal* 251.

Fox NJ and Alldred P, 'New materialist social inquiry: designs, methods and the research-assemblage' (2015) 18/4 *International Journal of Social Research Methodology* 399.

Gearty C, 'Do human rights help or hinder environmental protection?' (2010) 1(1) *Journal of Human Rights and the Environment* 7.

Grear A, 'Challenging corporate humanity: legal disembodiment, embodiment and human rights' (2007) 7 *Human Rights Law Review* 511.

Grear A, *Redirecting Human Rights: Facing the Challenge of Corporate Legal Humanity* (Palgrave MacMillan 2010).

Grear A, 'The vulnerable living order: human rights and the environment in a critical and philosophical perspective' (2011) 2(1) *Journal of Human Rights and the Environment* 23.

Grear A, 'Deconstructing *Anthropos*: a critical legal reflection on "anthropocentric" law and anthropocene "humanity"' (2015) 26(3) *Law and Critique* 225.

Grear A, 'Resisting anthropocene neoliberalism: towards new materialist commoning?' in D Bollier and A Grear (eds,) *The Great Awakening* (forthcoming, 2018–2019): file on copy with author.

Halewood P, 'Law's bodies: disembodiment and the structure of liberal property rights' (1996) 81 *Iowa Law Review* 1331.

Haraway D, *When Species Meet* (University of Minnesota Press 2008).

Haraway DJ, *Staying with the Trouble: Making Kin in the Chthulucene* (Duke University Press 2016).

Harding C, Kohl U, and Salmon N, *Human Rights in the Market Place: The Exploitation of Rights Protection by Economic Actors* (Ashgate 2008).

Harris A, 'Vulnerability and power in the age of the anthropocene' (2014) 6(2) *Washington and Lee Journal of Energy, Climate and the Environment* 98.

Harris G, *Dignity and Vulnerability: Strength and Quality of Character* (University of California Press 1997).

Haynes P, 'Creative becoming and the patiency of matter' (2014) 19(1) *Angelaki: Journal of the Theoretical Humanities* 129.

Hunt L, *The French Revolution and Human Rights: A Brief Documentary History* (St Martins Press 1996).

Hunt L, *Inventing Human Rights: A History* (WW Norton 2007).

Ignatieff M, *Human Rights as Politics and Idolatry* (Princeton University Press 2001).

Ishay M, *The History of Human Rights: From Ancient Times to the Globalization Era* (2nd edn, University of California Press 2008).

Jochnick C, 'Confronting the impunity of non-state actors: new fields for the promotion of human rights' (1999) 21 *Human Rights Quarterly* 56.

Kapur R, 'Human rights in the 21st century: take a walk on the dark side' (2006) 28 *Sydney Law Review* 665.

Kapur R, 'The citizen and the migrant: postcolonial anxieties, law, and the politics of exclusion/inclusion' (2007) 8 *Theoretical Inquiries* 537.

Keenan T, *Fables of Responsibility: Aberrations and Predicaments in Ethics and Politics* (Stanford University Press 1997).

Kirby P, *Vulnerability and Violence: The Impact of Globalisation* (Pluto Press 2006).

Luke TW, 'On environmentality: geo-power and eco-knowledge in the discourses of contemporary environmentalism' (1995) 31 *Cultural Critique (The Politics of Systems and Environments, Part II)* 57.

MacKenzie C, Rogers R and Dodds S, *Vulnerability: New Essays in Ethics and Feminist Philosophy* (Oxford University Press 2014).

Marks SP, 'From the "single confused page" to the "decalogue for six billion persons": the roots of the universal declaration of human rights in the French Revolution' (1998) 20 *Human Rights Quarterly* 459.

Matua M, 'Savages, victims and saviours: the metaphor of human rights' (2001) 42(1) *Harvard International Law Journal* 201.

McCarthy J, 'Commons as counterhegemonic projects' (2005) 16(1) *Capitalism Nature Socialism* 9.

Merleau-Ponty M, *The Visible and the Invisible* (Northwestern University Press 1968).

Morris DB, *The Culture of Pain* (University of California Press 1991).

Morsink J, 'Hitler's organic state and articles 1 and 2' (1993) 15 *Human Rights Quarterly* 359.

Morsink J, 'World War Two and the declaration' (1993) 15 *Human Rights Quarterly* 357.

Nasstrom S and Kalm S, 'A democratic critique of precarity' (2015) 5(4) *Global Discourse* 556.

Neal M, '"Not Gods but animals": human dignity and vulnerable subjecthood' (2012) 33 *Liverpool Law Review* 177.

Nedelsky J, 'Law, boundaries and the bounded self' (1990) 30 *Representations* 162.

Nibert D, *Animal Rights, Human Rights: Entanglements of Oppression and Liberation* (Rowman and Littlefield 2002).

Nino C, *The Ethics of Human Rights* (Clarendon 1993).

Norrie A, *Crime, Reason and History: A Critical Introduction to Criminal Law* (Cambridge University Press 2014).

Otto D, 'Disconcerting "masculinities": reinventing the gendered subject(s) of international human rights law' in D Buss and A Manji (eds), *International Law: Modern Feminist Approaches* (Hart 2005).

Pennock JR, 'Rights, natural rights and human rights – a general view,' in JR Pennock and J Chapman (eds), *Human Rights: NOMOS XXIII* (New York University Press 1987).

Philippopoulos-Mihalopoulos A, '"... the sound of a breaking string": critical environmental law and ontological vulnerability' (2011) 2(1) *Journal of Human Rights and the Environment* 5.

Philippopoulos-Mihalopoulos A, 'The Trivenuto transhumance: law, land, movement' (2012) 3 *Politica and Societa* 447.

Philippoulos-Mihalopoulos A and Brooks V, *Research Methods in Environmental Law* (Elgar 2017).

Pieraccini M, 'Property pluralism and the partial reflexivity of conservation law: The case of upland commons in England and Wales' (2012) 3(2) *Journal of Human Rights and the Environment* 273.

Potts A, 'Deleuze on Viagra (or, what can a Viagra-body do?)' (2004) 10 *Body and Society* 17.

Rogers N and Maloney M (eds), *Law as if Earth Really Mattered: The Wild Law Judgment Project* (Routledge/Glasshouse 2017).

Satz A, 'Animals as vulnerable subjects: beyond interest-convergence, hierarchy and property', in MA Fineman and A Grear (eds), *Vulnerability: Reflections on a New Ethical Foundation for Law and Politics* (Ashgate 2013).

Scott J, *Only Paradoxes to Offer: French Feminists and the Rights of Man* (Harvard University Press 1996).

Solum LB, 'Legal personhood for artificial intelligences' (1992) 70 *North Carolina Law Review* 1231.

Stammers N, 'Social movements and the social construction of human rights' (1999) 21 *Human Rights Quarterly* 980.

Standing G, *The Precariat: A New Dangerous Class* (Bloomsbury 2011).

Stone CD, *Should Trees Have Standing? Law, Morality and the Environment* (Oxford University Press 2010).

Swanson Goldberg E and Schultheis Moore A, *Theoretical Perspectives on Human Rights and Literature* (Routledge 2012).

Teubner G, 'Rights of non-humans? Electronic agents and animals as new actors in politics and law' (2006) 33 *Journal of Law and Society* 497.

Tsing A, 'Unruly edges: mushrooms as companion species' (2012) 1 *Environmental Humanities* 141.

Tsing A, *The Mushroom at the End of the World: On the Possibility of Life in Capitalist Ruins* (Princeton University Press 2015).

Turner B, *Vulnerability and Human Rights* (Pennsylvania University Press 2006).

Vaisman, N (ed), 'Science, technology and human values special edition: new technologies' (2018) 43(1) *Developments in the Biosciences and the New Frontiers of Human Rights* 3.

Wall IR, 'On pain and the sense of human rights' (2008) 29 *Australian Feminist Law Review* 53.

Response

On some problems with rights

Fiona de Londras[1]

Introduction

Human rights law doesn't work. Or at least, it doesn't work if we think that (inasmuch as any *law* can) human rights law ought to enable and support human flourishing in meaningful ways in order to make life better for all. In other words, it doesn't work in ways that ensure not only that the negative limits of state power are clear (e.g. that the state may not arbitrarily detain someone) but also that states can be compelled to act in ways that address significantly the material privations of everyday life so that, at a minimum, everyone has enough to eat, adequate shelter and healthcare, and access to education. Moreover, it has thus far, by and large, failed to address the misery – planned and unplanned – of everyday life in a world beleaguered by continuing inequality, conflict and distributional biases (Marks 2011).

There are different ways of looking at why it is that human rights law does not work, especially given the existence of legally enforceable rights – often bolstered by specialised enforcement mechanisms, including human rights courts – intended to address precisely those questions of material deprivation. For some commentators, the problem is that human rights law is a radically neoliberal enterprise. As such, it is structured and enforced in ways that fail properly to see states as having meaningful positive obligations (as opposed to merely being capable of restraint through the application of law) and, indeed, enable states to use rights to further individualise the human, bolster biopolitical capitalism (see Douzinas 2007) and underpin military intervention (see Orford 2003). If this is so, then human rights law does not have a meaningfully redistributional character and, instead, works to maintain, and perhaps even to justify (global and local) societal stratification, lending only a bare minimum of protection to individuals against state brutality and very little against the brutality of a systemically unequal world. In this reading, human rights law fails to address racialised, sexist, classist and exclusionary patterns of the distribution of goods within states (see Anghie 1996). For others, the problem is that human rights law, like the rest of international laws, is fundamentally predicated on colonialist

1 I am especially grateful to Daniel Bedford for his comments and conversations on this commentary.

structures and discourse that not only enable but also rely on processes of division and othering (see Conklin 1998; Mutua 2002; Ibhawoh 2007; Ozoki 2014), now sometimes cloaked in languages of humanitarianism but nevertheless legitimating 'exploitation, domination, invasion and governance' (Orford 2003, 189). As such, it cannot effectively address either the historical or the (connected) contemporary inequality of resource, resilience and power between Global North and Global South. And for still more, many scholars are of the view, including Grear (2007), that human rights law is improperly constructed because of its anthropocentric foundations, its insistence on the particularity of the human and its failure to see the connections and interdependencies of human and nonhuman life (and, increasingly, of human and nonhuman life with nonhuman artefacts that interact therewith). In this critique, human rights law is predicated on (disembodied) reason masquerading as dignity, and both human and nonhuman 'critters' (to use Grear's term) remain underserved because of their normative disconnection from their bodies, from the world around them and from each other.

In her contribution to this collection, echoing themes in much of her earlier work (see Grear 2013), Anna Grear argues that we ought to 'follow' vulnerability into New Materialisms and, in so doing, to move away from anthropocentrism and towards a new way of thinking about human rights. For Grear, the failure within human rights law and discourse to think seriously about the connections and interdependencies between human and nonhuman forms of life and other materials is a significant shortfall. It both exposes the shortcomings that come from construction of the liberal (male, white, nondisabled and disembodied) human as the central referent for human rights law with the attendant primary focus on negatively constructed approaches to rights and the failure to seriously deal with important inter- and trans-generational questions of justice. However, in her argument, Grear argues not for the turn towards a discourse other than human rights – such as vulnerability, for example – but for the rejuvenation of human rights (and human rights law) through the construction of what she has elsewhere called 'a new juridical ontology' of rights (Grear 2018). For Grear, it is this fundamental reorientation of rights, rather than an embrace of vulnerability reasoning and thinking *apart from rights discourse*, that offers a way out of the inadequacies she identifies within the human rights milieu as it currently stands.

In this short commentary, I reflect on whether the move advocated by Grear would address substantially the shortcomings in human rights law understood in the way I have already outlined, whether to do so requires a move away from human rights law and towards a new paradigm, and, if so, whether the turn towards vulnerability as advocated by Fineman might offer an alternative solution to the shortcomings of rights.

Grear's critique and new materialisms turn

Grear's contribution to this collection builds on her earlier work on the connections between human rights and vulnerability to argue, in sum, that human rights ought to be reimagined so that, rather than seeing human beings as exceptional or special (either on the basis of reason or of dignity), it would regard (and cause us – states and non-state actors – to regard) all beings with special ethical attention, recognising and valuing our interconnectedness and interdependence. In doing so, it seems to me that Grear makes a number of critically important moves. First, she returns us to the conventionally under-stood origins of modern human rights law in the wake of the Second World War and Holocaust. The emergence then of human rights, she argues, was a recognition and response to the suffering of the vulnerable human body. In other words, human rights law was a reaction, a response and a measure of protection against embodied vulnerabilities and the brutalisation of those bod-ies through state-sponsored cruelty. However, as human rights law developed, these corporeal beginnings were replaced with a focus on dignity, understood as reason (and thus as disembodied) and exemplified by the liberal, rational subject. The implication is that the idea of human rights and the radical reach of human rights law understood in its earlier guise was limited by such a move (just as, as Fineman has showed in much of her work, happened in domestic constitutional systems as well; Fineman and Dougherty [2005]). Of course, such arguments have been made by others as well; for example, Joseph Slaugh-ter (2018) offers a particularly compelling picture of the 'hijacking' of human rights in the 1960s and 1970s as their radical potential began to be harnessed by anti-imperialism movements, including the Non-Aligned Movement. Some might argue that even in the wake of the Holocaust human rights was not as embodied or engaged with the vulnerable human subject as Grear suggests. However, taking at face value this claim, there can be little argument with the idea that human rights law has been tamed and disciplined over time, including through the development of hyper-pragmatic modes of interpretation and en-forcement (such as the doctrine of proportionality), even as legally enforceable rights *per se* have proliferated.

For Grear, one consequence of this turn in the ontological underpinnings of human rights law is the neglect of nonhuman beings and systems within and by human rights law, so that (rational, liberal, individual) human subjects are treated as if they were separate from the nonhuman world in which we are embedded; therefore, human rights law's attentiveness to the conditions of life is insufficient properly to account for and rearrange those conditions. However, that need not be the case. Grear argues that it is possible to reconceptualise dignity as an ontological principle of rights in order to depart from the liberal individualism of the rational human subject and instead to capture within the embrace of human rights law nonhuman vulnerabilities, thus (I take it) return-ing more faithfully to human rights law's originating concern with vulnerabil-ity. In doing so, she does not argue, necessarily, for the complete decentring of the human but rather for an approach to human vulnerability that recognises and takes account of the connections between human and nonhuman life in order to ensure that, within human rights law, bodies would be held account-able for their impacts on other bodies. Human rights law would continue to function, then, but the harms it would recognise, the actors it would hold accountable and the scope of the rights it would protect would be recalibrated to take account of, and respond to, the lived realities of humans as critters in a more-than-human world.

New materialisms: rights retrieved?

As is clear from my reading of Grear offered above, she remains throughout this piece committed to the retrievability of rights, that is, to the possibility that – appropriately reoriented – rights can still address the material challenges of life on earth. However, what her approach advocates, it seems to me, is primarily the broadening-out of the category and concept of rights-holder and perhaps the understanding of the kinds of harms to which human rights law ought to attend, but not necessarily a reconsideration of the obligations that are attached to rights. In this respect, I do not mean to suggest that enjoying and being about to enforce rights is contingent on rights-holders fulfilling certain obligations; to do so is to skirt perilously close to a 'forfeitability' approach to rights that calls into question their resilience and normative universality in deeply problematic ways. Rather, I want to focus on the shape and nature of the obligations that accompany rights and to ask whether, even if the category of rights-holder is expanding to move away from anthropocentric fixation on the human or the way we conceptualise rights-holder is expanding to recognise differently the nature of being human in the world, the fundamental problems of human rights as I sketched them in the opening of this commentary might remain.

For me, at least, the critical challenge with human rights law as a mode of making life better on earth is that, notwithstanding rights having become 'a fact of the world' (Rorty 1993, 134) and the fulcrum of politico-legal attempts to advance flourishing (recognised as requiring and including the flourishing of the natural world as well as of human beings), the shape and nature of the *legal* obligations (and, relatedly, remedies [on which see Shelton 2015]) that attach to these rights is seriously inadequate. In a general sense, states are obliged to *respect, protect* and *fulfil* rights, but what this means in practice is often severely limited. Furthermore, because human rights law is addressed to states, addressing non-state harm through human rights law generally requires the imposition of oblique obligations on states to regulate certain forms of non-state behaviours, rather than imposing directly legally enforceable human rights obligations on non-state actors.

I want to flesh out this critique of rights-related obligations a little more fully at this point. First, in a general sense, there remains a significant emphasis on negative obligations in human rights law. In other words, on the proposition that for an individual actor to hold a right means that the state (or another entity acting on behalf of the state) must refrain from interfering with that actor in prescribed ways. The right acts to create what might be described as a zone of non-interference around the rights-holder, infringement of which is either not permitted (in the rare cases of absolute rights) or must be justified by reference to a legal test (such as proportionality, for example). Within that zone of non-interference, the rights-bearer acts not only uninhibited but also unassisted by the state; they are, if you want, the most typical illustration of the rational, disembodied, liberal subject imaginable – precisely the subject that Grear rightly note is the paradigm legal subject notwithstanding its almost complete abstraction from the reality of embodied, embedded and situated beings. Increasingly, there is a recognition in human rights law that the obligations on the state are not merely negative; there are often also positive obligations, many of which are procedural. For example, in respect of many rights the state will be obliged positively to investigate where it appears that a violation of rights (i.e. of the negative obligation) has taken place. In some cases, the state will also be treated as having a preventative positive obligation, for example, to take reasonable steps to prevent foreseeable harms by making violatory actions unlawful or by acting to protect individuals when circumstances suggest they are at particular risk of being subject to a violation (on positive obligations, see Mavronicola 2017). However, within that zone of non-interference there is little even about positive obligations that tends to make life more liveable in a quotidian, everyday sense. Of course, the third element of the implementation triad – the obligation to *fulfil* rights – suggests that states ought to take steps to secure what Kunnemann calls rights-holders' 'existential status' (Kunnemann 1995, 326), but in a manner that is merely subsidiary. In other words, 'The obligation of the State is only to provide the remainder (i.e. to fulfil what is still lacking) after individuals have tried their best to secure their existential status' (ibid., 328).

One might imagine that socioeconomic rights, protected by the International Covenant on Economic, Social and Cultural Rights, would intervene here to make better the everyday conditions of life, that is, to ensure that even this 'subsidiary' obligation might be treated as substantial. After all, these rights very often depart from an emphasis on the negative obligation mould and, instead, appear to focus on obliging states to take actions that improve material conditions of life relating to, for example, food, water, shelter, and healthcare. However, under the ICESCR states are obliged progressively to realise these rights, taking into account the available resources and so on. Although 'progressive realisation' principle has largely been misinterpreted and misapplied, the reality is that many states simply do not comply with their obligations under the Covenant, instead making resource allocation decisions that exacerbate privation, including by exacerbating climate change and environmental degradation. In times of austerity, this is not only treated as if it were permitted under international human rights law (see especially Warwick 2016, 2019) but more or less required by the funding programmes and conditions imposed by actors such as the IMF often with devastating human impact (Saloman 2015).

For me, a question that remains unanswered when one considers Grear's advocated move from vulnerability towards New Materialisms and to a renewed ontology of rights is whether such a shift in fact addresses these critical questions of obligation – questions that shape much state action – or whether in fact the shift would leave this more or less unresolved, so that what we might recognise as a rights-related harm would be expanded, and the category of rights-holder likely pluralised, but the nature of state action compelled by a rights-based analysis would not change. Grear is surely correct when she writes elsewhere that 'The twenty-first-century world remains an emphatically uneven one. The intransigent injustices of attenuated anthropocentrism in the traditional foundations of human rights still mark the material order of newly visible relationalities revealed by new materialist insights' (Grear 2017, 141). But, if – as I do – we see the problem with rights not only as their exclusion or elision of nonhuman life (and the suppression of many forms of human life due to their radically unequal foundations) but rather as lying also in their insufficiency in actually making meaningful and appropriate change in state behaviour in order to *make life better*, then what would a turn to New Materialisms actually resolve? If the answer to that question does not penetrate the entrenched difficulties with the very limited ways in which human rights *laws* actually improve everyday life due to the limited nature of the obligations they impose on states, then one wonders whether and why the expansion of the category of rights-holder – even if predicated on revisiting of notions of dignity – *effectively* addresses the practical and political limitations of rights in practical and practicable ways.

Vulnerability as an alternative way forward

What, then, of vulnerability? For Grear, the way in which prominent theorists of vulnerability have conceptualised it is also inadequate. In respect of Fineman in particular (on whom I focus here), Grear expresses concern that her notion of the vulnerable subject is too focused on the human, that the notion of resilience is problematically focused on resources and assets, and that this in turn continues to centre the human and instrumentalises nonhuman aspects of the world as sources of resilience. Grear is also critical of the way that Fineman, like other prominent theorists, reduce vulnerability to the capacity for suffering/feel pain (see Grear this volume, 160–161) This is, I would argue, too narrow a reading of Fineman's thesis, especially as it has developed over the past decade of workshops, articles and edited books. For Fineman, vulnerability is, clearly, generative; it 'presents opportunities for innovation and growth, creativity, and fulfilment' (Fineman 2012, 96). As well as insisting on the generative nature of vulnerability for humans and on the need to recognise vulnerability as *the* universal human condition (Fineman 2008; 2011), Fineman has increasingly explored the stretchability of the concept, recognising nonhuman entities as potentially vulnerable.[2] Fineman is also, I would argue, far more engaged with the connectedness of human beings than Grear suggests. This has, of course, always been true of Fineman's work – the notion of the liberal autonomous individual has long been identified in her work as a conceit divorced from the realities of life and favoured

---

2 See, for example, the Vulnerability and the Human Condition Initiative workshops held on animals (May 2017), the environment (April 2017 and April 2016), professionalism (October 2017) and 'the firm' (October 2015) among others. The workshops archive is available at http://web. gs.emory.edu/vulnerability/workshops/past/index.html.

by states because it minimises their responsibilities or what a certain form of statehood presents as a legitimate claim on its resources (including its law- and policy-making resources; Fineman 2005).

Through her work on vulnerability Fineman makes claims that, it seems to me, are not dissimilar to those to which Grear seems committed. She argues that all people are vulnerable, that all people are embodied and that all people are embedded (including in environmental and nonhuman contexts). For Fineman, variations in experienced vulnerabilities arise from variations in resilience, and resilience is a multifaceted 'thing' encompassing everything from basic goods, to family, to legal protection, to environmental and food security, to education and so on, which Fineman organises into five categories of resource: physical, human, social, ecological or environmental, and existential (Fineman 2008). Seen in this way, prevailing inequality is perpetuated by how states do – or do not – act to (re)distribute resilience-enhancing resources and assets, that is, by state action (Fineman 2011).[3] The logical conclusion then is that states are *obliged* to make appropriate redistributional decisions in order to address vulnerability and, when vulnerability is seen (as Fineman insists) as both embodied and embedded, these decisions should (and I think will) include decisions that take proper account of the connections and dependencies between and of both human and nonhuman entities.

Taken in this way, then, it seems to me that vulnerability does considerable work to address shortcomings in human rights law. Although not framed in this way (or, indeed, developed for this purpose[4]), it provides a different ontological basis for thinking about the nature and scope of state obligation (namely, vulnerability) that might be applied within and alongside human rights law argumentation to reshape our understanding of what rights demand of states. It escapes a legal framework of rights that designs into it notions of progressivism and permitted limitation and, instead, asks states to think differently about their obligations and about resource allocation. It broadens out the concept of resource that can be allocated by states to take into account not only economic resource but also support (including through regulation or recognition) of different forms of resilience-enhancing entities (including institutions like corporations, or churches, or tax subsidies, or early years childcare). It does not decentre the human; the core of the vulnerability thesis is the proposition that vulnerability is *the* universal human condition. But neither does Grear's approach decentre the human; rather, it argues for a re-conceptualisation and re-embedding of the human within rights-based

---

3 As Fineman writes, 'the choice is *not* one between an active state on one hand versus an inactive state on the other. Rather, the choice is whether or not the state is going to act to fulfill a well-defined responsibility to implement a comprehensive and just equality regime that ensures access and opportunity for all consistent with a realistic conception of the human subject': 'The Vulnerable Subject and the Responsive State', (2011) 60 *Emory Law Journal* 251.

4 See Fineman, ibid, on how as her theory of vulnerability has developed it has gone beyond seeking to provide an alternative vocabulary to address human rights violations in the United States and instead become a distinct but political project of its own.

analysis. A vulnerability analysis is predicated on quite the same proposition. There is, perhaps, more that unites the approaches than divides them.

Concluding remarks

The core difference, it seems to me, between the approach advocated by Grear and Fineman's approach to vulnerability is in their adherence to human rights law as a mode of reasoning. For Grear, human rights law is retrievable, still usable, capable of salvage; her mission is in rehabilitation and reorientation but not in its abandonment. On my reading, Fineman is also not interested in the abandonment of human rights law per se but rather in addressing the fact, alluded to at the start of this chapter, that human rights law is not enough.

If, as Susan Marks (2013, 231) writes, 'becoming the victim of a violation is ... a state of affairs that depends crucially on vulnerabilities that are systematically produced and reproduced,' and if 'the suffering of victims ... [has something to do with] the historical legacies and the current realities of exploitation domination and dispossession'[5] then there is, it seems to me, something to be said for thinking about human rights law and the protections it offers as a source of resilience but not, in itself, as enough to make life better.

Bibliography

Anghie A, 'Francisco de Vitoria and the Colonial Origins of international law' (1996) 5 *Social and Legal Studies* 321.

Conklin AL, 'Colonialism and human rights: a contradiction in terms? The case of France and West Africa' (1998) 103 *The American Historical Review* 419.

Douzinas C, *Human Rights and Empire: The Political Philosophy of Cosmopolitanism* (Taylor and Francis 2007).

Fineman MA, *The Autonomy Myth: A Theory of Dependency* (The New Press 2005).

Fineman MA and Dougherty T (eds), *Feminism Confront Homo Economicus: Gender, Law and Society* (Cornell University Press 2005).

Fineman MA, 'The vulnerable subject: anchoring equality in the human condition' (2008) 20 *Yale Journal of Law and Feminism* 1.

Fineman MA, 'The vulnerable subject and the responsive state' (2011) 60 *Emory Law Journal* 251.

Fineman MA, '"Elderly" as vulnerable: rethinking the nature of individual and societal responsibility' (2012) 20(2) *The Elder Law Journal* 71, 96.

Grear A, 'Challenging corporate "humanity": legal disembodiment, embodiment and human rights' (2007) 7 *Human Rights Law Review* 511.

Grear A, 'Vulnerability, advanced global capitalism and co-symptomatic injustice: locating the vulnerable subject' in Martha Albertson Fineman and Anna Grear (eds), *Vulnerability: Reflections on a New Ethical Foundation for Law and Politics* (Routledge 2013).

Grear A, 'Human rights and new horizons? Thoughts towards a new juridical ontology' (2018) 43(1) *Science, Technology, and Human Values* 129.

---

5 Susan Marks, 'Four Human Rights Myths' in David Kinley, Wojciech Sadurski and Kevin Walton (eds), *Human Rights: Old Problems, New Possibilities* (2013; Edward Elgar).

Ibhawoh B, *Imperialism and Human Rights: Colonial Discourses of Rights and Liberties in African History* (Statue University of New York Press 2007).

Marks S, 'Human rights and root causes' (2011) 74(1) *Modern Law Review* 57.

Marks S, 'Four human rights myths' in D Kinley, W Sadurski and K Walton (eds), *Human Rights: Old Problems, New Possibilities* (Edward Elgar 2013).

Mutua M, *Human Rights: A Political and Cultural Critique* (University of Pennsylvania Press 2002).

Orford A, *Reading Humanitarian Intervention: Human Rights and the Use of Force in International Law* (Cambridge University Press 2003).

Ozoki V, 'The imperialism of rights: tracing the politics and history of human rights' (2014) 4 *American International Journal of Contemporary Research* 1.

Rorty R, 'Human rights, rationality and sentimentality' in Stephen Shute and Susan Hurley (eds), *On Human Rights: The Oxford Amnesty Lectures 1993* (Basic Books 1993).

Salomon M, 'Of austerity, human rights, and international institutions' (2015) 21 *European Law Journal* 521.

Shelton D, *Remedies in International Human Rights Law*, (3rd edn, Oxford University Press 2015).

Slaughter J, 'Hijacking human rights: neoliberalism, the new historiography, and the end of the third world' (2018) 40 *Human Rights Quarterly* 735.

Warwick B, 'Socio-economic rights during economic crises: a changed approach to non-retrogression' (2016) 65(1) *International and Comparative Law Quarterly* 249.

Warwick B, 'Unwinding retrogression: conflicting concepts and patchy practice' (2019) 19(3) *Human Rights Law Review* 467.

Index

Note: Page numbers followed by "n" denote endnotes.